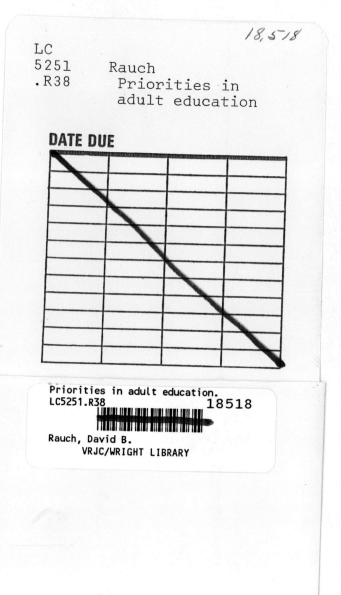

Priorities in Adult Education

PRIORITIES
in Adult Education

D A V I D   B.   R A U C H

A Publication of

the Adult Education Association

of the U.S.A.

THE MACMILLAN COMPANY / New York

COLLIER-MACMILLAN LIMITED / Canada

The Macmillan Company
866 Third Avenue, New York, New York 10022

Collier–Macmillan Canada Ltd., Toronto, Ontario

Library of Congress Catalog Card Number: 72–77273

printing number

1   2   3   4   5   6   7   8   9   10

Contents

People do no automatically flock to a new adult education program. No matter how good or exciting the project can be, it still has to be sold—those for whom it is intended must be motivated to participate. Planning is not complete without *The Public Relations Factor in Planning Successful Adult Education Ventures.* There is a great deal more to public relations than putting a notice of the activity in the local paper.

Preface

How to Use This Book

Most people responsible for planning educational programs and projects for adults have come into their jobs, paid or as volunteers, through the back door. While there are professional graduate courses in adult and continuing education at a few universities, the field is new enough and unusual enough (and part time enough) so that a large number of programs are more hit and miss than professionally planned.

A very small number of people in the United States have full-time positions in the field of adult and continuing education. The largest number of the people in "the field" do not even identify themselves as adult educators. They are program chairmen for PTAs, League of Women Voters chapters, or other community organizations. They are staff members of economic opportunity projects, social workers, or high school principals. They are volunteer leaders of Boy or Girl Scout groups, Council of Jewish Women sections, the Junior League, or the local Chamber of Commerce. Or they are education chairmen of medical and dental societies, local bar associations, a hospital medical staff, or a church or synagogue.

No one really knows how many adults participate in some kind of continuing education program each year, because it is hard to formally identify everything that provides a learning opportunity for an adult. But we do know that the need for well planned educational opportunities for adults is increasing rapidly, and that already are more adults participating in continuing education programs than the combined total of all children and young people in schools and colleges!

The Adult Education Association of the United States of America is called by professionals in the field the "umbrella" organization for everyone involved in or thinking about education for adults. The eight people who agreed to share their professional knowledge and skills with you by writing chapters for this book were selected because of their respected reputations, their vast store of knowledge, and their great amount of direct experience in planning and carrying out some of the most successful and creative adult education projects in the country.

Not everything they share with you will apply directly to your own individual situation. You can judge best what will be most useful to you by going over the chapter headings and reading carefully those chapters that seem to relate to your own needs. But do not put down the book without scanning the remaining chapters. Good ideas come from a variety of sources. And many times a bit of philosophy or a miraculous insight will pop up in a context that did not look as if it had direct meaning for you.

While the aim of the book is to give you direct and practical help —guidelines, checklists, and formats that will be useful in starting or improving your own projects—one cannot help but feel that the chapters are also interlarded with some important philosophical concepts that should be part of your overall approach to planning educational programs for the adults of your community, your organization, or your firm or institution.

Some important concepts in approaching your work as an adult educator are these:

1. Adults *can* learn, whatever their age or state of maturity.
2. The traditional "classroom" or "lecture" approach is not necessarily the best educational device for adults, who of necessity can devote only a small amount of their total time to a learning situation.
3. Adults bring to the learning situation a lot of living and experience in a wide variety of fields. This must be given consideration in planning the learning experience. They do not come to the experience empty-handed.
4. Adults coming into a learning situation may know more about some parts of the subject than the leaders or resource people. Sometimes they know more about the entire subject than the leaders or resource people. This holds true for "well educated" adult participants as well as "undereducated" adult participants. Almost everyone has had to learn a great deal, in school or out of school, just to exist in the present world.
5. The day has gone by when one group of people can plan an educational program for another group of people. While one group—your group—may have the facilities, the funds, or the resources; the other group—those whom you expect to participate in your program—must be brought actively into the planning process, not just by token representation but by massive involvement.

6. Our society in the United States is much more segmented than we used to believe. It is segmented into age groupings, racial and ethnic patterns, geographical differences, economic status groups, and probably a hundred more different ways. The Melting Pot was a theory that did not work. We are a diverse country. And, while we each know something about other groups, what we know is frequently superficial. Therefore, if we are planning for the educational needs of a community or part of a community, we cannot be satisfied with what *we* think other people need.

7. The best place to begin in planning is the project that is most likely to succeed. If you find a major problem in your community is ecology but people you talk to want to learn typing, you had better sharpen your teeth on the typing. Adults are going to do what they want to do, not what you think they ought to do.

8. Publicity, by itself, does not bring people to a meeting or a program or project. But you cannot run a program or a conference or a seminar without a good public relations plan. People cannot come if they do not know about it.

9. Boards and committees are a necessary paraphernalia of most kinds of community activity—including adult education. Whether or not they are successful is more often a function of the skills of the leadership than the nature of the people serving. Properly used, they can be a valuable asset to the project or program.

10. The difference between a "volunteer" and a "professional" is primarily that one works without financial compensation and the other gets paid. The one who is paid may have greater overall responsibility, but not necessarily. The problem of working with a volunteer is almost identical with working with a paid staff. Volunteers may come late, not show up on certain days, or do a sloppy job. But paid staff, too, may come late, take excessive days off, or perform less than adequately. The ability to work well with volunteers is really the same ability required to work well with paid staff—and the techniques that yield results are the same too. Community adult education or any kind of adult and continuing education is a "people project," and the most important asset is to be able to work with a very wide variety of people.

While the aim of all of the contributors to this book is to help you to succeed in planning and carrying out educational projects for the adults you or your organization or institution feel an obligation to serve, even with what we hope is wise guidance you may fail. Every good PTA program chairman has a last-minute fear and anxiety that no one will show up for the meeting. And once in a while it happens —no one or hardly anyone shows up for a meeting that has taken weeks and months to plan. I was once involved in a project designed to develop a better understanding of the nature of family life in suburbia. Our keynote speaker was a well-known anthropologist. We felt we oriented him well, suggesting to him concerns of our community and carefully instructing his dinner host to serve wine rather than liquor and to give him a last-minute indoctrination. But, in spite of our careful preparation, the keynote address had nothing to do with family life in suburbia but was on the importance of breast feeding, which was apparently this anthropologist's topic of the year.

When you fail in adult education, you quietly lick your wounds, quickly try to figure out what went wrong, and try again in a new or different way—with a different format, with different kinds of planning, changing whatever you perceive as your mistakes.

Fifteen years ago a committee with which I was working, nudged on by our local League of Women Voters, felt there was a need for more people to understand how local government functioned so they could become better citizens and participate more wisely in political activities.

The first project was a workshop conducted by a knowledgeable League of Women Voters resource person. Not one person came! The second project was a series, bringing local governmental officials to tell about their work and their problems. No one came. The third attempt was a one-night community forum scheduled for an elementary school auditorium under the title "Where is Great Neck Going?" asking if we were becoming too urbanized, were we in danger of losing our parks, were our schools becoming prohibitively expensive. To be meaningful, the topic had to include the mechanism and format of local government. A local clergyman was asked to be moderator, and knowledgeable local citizens were invited to be panelists. The auditorium seated three hundred and twenty-five. We had five hundred people attending and many others went home when they could not find parking space near the school. Even after all these years we are not sure what made the difference, but every three or four years we schedule something using the same title, "Where is Great Neck Going?", and we have never failed to find people who are seeking the answer.

David B. Rauch
Director, The Adult Program
Great Neck Public Schools

CHAPTER ONE

New Priorities for Adult Education

DAVID B. RAUCH

Dr. David B. Rauch has been, since 1952, Director of The Adult Program, Great Neck Public Schools, a program begun in 1901. He has taught courses in philosophy, practice, and administration of adult education at Hofstra and New York University and at Teachers College, Columbia University.

ADULT EDUCATION, despite its importance, has never been the major cultural factor in the United States that it is in England, the Scandinavian countries, and Russia. The problem in our country has been the lack of identification of "adult education" as a specific field, a dearth of major educational opportunities for adults, and an almost complete absence of institutions with a major commitment to educating adults. There are very few organizations or institutions that identify adult education as their major responsibility.

One large part of adult education is taking place in industry—occupational training, in-service training, occupational upgrading, management and executive training. Another part takes place in labor unions—apprentice training, preparing union officers and foremen for leadership roles, training for better jobs. Colleges and universities provide for adults in extension divisions, public school systems in units that are usually just called "adult education." Most armed forces training involves adults even though, for understandable reasons, it lacks the self-motivation and voluntary aspect common to most education for adults.

Churches of all faiths and synagogues carry on an adult education function, and Ys, community centers, and community recreation programs almost always include adults in what they understand as their community responsibility. Every branch of the Junior Leagues trains its members and most women's and men's clubs believe educational meetings a major reason for their existence. Professional organizations have annual national conferences and conventions, realizing the necessity for updating the knowledge and skills of their profession. And the big national health organizations rank community education second only to research among their major goals. Museums and galleries, public libraries, political parties, the United States Department of Agriculture, local service clubs such as Rotary, Kiwanis, and Lions, Chambers of Commerce—most of the meetings that middle America finds occupy a major part of its free time—are educational in nature and planned for members of the adult community.

Adult education is everywhere and yet, in a sense, it is nowhere because it is no one's specific responsibility. Some cities and small communities have magnificent opportunities for the education of adults: The New School for Social Research in Manhattan, the Emily Griffith Opportunity School in Denver, the New Hampshire Crafts League, the Santa Barbara Community College in California. And yet other cities and communities have nothing except occasional Great Books discussion groups or Thursday Club book reviews. Educational television has, for the first time, brought outstanding cultural stimulation to large segments of our population who had nothing. But television unfortunately lacks the opportunity to discuss with others or to talk back to the knowledge merchants.

The big development of what we now call adult education came after World War II, starting in 1945. Previous to that time it was generally conceded that adults, once they were past adolescence, had very little learning capacity. The "bell-shaped learning curve" that was drawn on the blackboards of educational psychology classes seemed to show that for most people there was little ability to learn new material once one became a legal adult at age twenty-one.

When World War II veterans returned to high schools and college campuses, there was great fear on the part of educational administrators and faculty members. These adults, many now married, would not be able to learn and would drag the classes down. But the results were not that at all. Lo and behold, the older veterans did even better academically than their younger colleagues. They could study and they could learn—in many cases better because they were older and more mature and had lived longer and experienced more things than those who had never had time off for living.

Now we know that adults, whatever their age, can learn anything. As they get past middle age, they may take a little longer, but they can learn. And the methodology may have to be different because, as adults, they are bringing a great deal of personal knowledge and experience to the learning situation.

We have found that adults (and probably children) learn best when they are participants in the learning situation, not just silent student recipients. And adults may well know more about some parts of the subject matter than the person leading their educational program. (At times they may even know more about the total subject matter than the one who has been selected to teach them.) To accommodate this, in the forties and fifties we developed group discussion techniques, group dynamics, and audio-visual learning aids. We redefined the position of the "teacher" when working with adults, and even recognized that a teacherless or leaderless group could be a legitimate adult education venture.

At this very moment we are trying to include the concept that learning, for adults, does not involve only subject matter or content. It also involves emotions. And we are working with sensitivity training, T-groups, brainstorming, confrontation groups, creative problem solving, Esalen, attributive listening, and synectics—each a special way of adding an emotional component to the content of education for adults.

But the most important push of the present moment is the push to provide adult education opportunities for the people who have been left out, the people we forgot existed. The most valuable experience that adult education in the past had with "the poor" was the early and famous program to teach the English language to non-English-speaking immigrants to our country. But this experience did not provide us with many of the skills we need to work with today's poor. Immigrants who spoke another tongue were highly motivated to "make it" in America; this was why they came here. And they knew that to get any kind of a job they would have to learn English. The "poor" that we awoke to when John F. Kennedy became president were people who had been here all the time, most of them for many generations; some, such as the native American Indian, were here long before the Pilgrims and long before Christopher Columbus or Leif Ericson.

As we realized that we had not noticed or given serious thought to our native poor, we became aware of the complicated mechanisms our society developed to keep them "in their place" and away from the mainstream of life in the United States. Blacks have lived under a difficult and cruel system of U.S. apartheid that kept them out of our schools, out of our neighborhoods, out of our theatres, away from our churches, out of our jobs and mostly out of our sight and out of our minds. Indians were carefully hidden away on reservations. Mexican-Americans and our own native Spanish-speaking people in the Southwest had completely segregated institutions much like the blacks. And poor whites from the mining areas and the agricultural states were kept from being absorbed into the mainstream by extreme economic dependence that reduced their mobility and their opportunities to almost zero.

Our native "poor" do not need Americanization classes. They were for the most part Americans before most of the rest of the population. Maybe, we thought, they needed to learn to read and write, and we established adult literacy or adult basic education classes for them. While some attended—and these programs are still providing us with a beginning contact so we can at least communicate with some of our native poor—our adult literacy program in this country, even with small amounts of federal money giving us the opportunity to go into areas we have never been in before, has not yet been the smashing success we had anticipated. The government monies have turned out to be on-again-off-again from one year to the next, and have been a pittance in terms of the total adult education that has to be provided for our poor.

While a few of the poverty adult education projects have been remarkable and successful, most have been minor and many have been washed away. This has forced us to look again at our country, our people, and ourselves. It has forced us to look at what we know about educating adults and what we do not know about educating adults. As we know more about recipient groups and as we know more about ourselves, hopefully, we will be able to do a better job in all our efforts to educate adults—rich and poor, well educated, poorly educated, and uneducated. If we really found out after World War II that adults can learn, then poor adults can learn as well. But we have to look into our own prejudices, the prejudices of our institutions, and the blocks developed over generations that have permitted parts of our population to forge ahead while keeping other parts from making any headway at all. Literacy is important. But, by itself, literacy may be only a small part of the answer.

The challenge of the seventies, to reach and provide meaningful skills and knowledge and relevant services to our entire population, has become an important concern for everyone involved in community education for adults. There is no simple solution. But the massive attack, just beginning to form, permits us to make some tentative conclusions based upon successful ventures and some general guidelines based upon unsuccessful ventures.

Working with the People We Forgot

My own first contact with "minority" people occurred when I was a college student. Except that I was a member of a minority myself! I was born and grew up in Minneapolis, Minnesota, which in the 1930s was identified by Carey McWilliams as the most anti-Semitic community in the United States. And I was Jewish.

My family lived in a very "WASP" part of town, but that word for White Anglo Saxon Protestant had not yet been invented. There was one Roman Catholic family on our block but none of us had very clear notions of what Roman Catholic meant. The main reason we knew the family was Roman Catholic was that an aunt used to come and visit in the summer and she was a Mother Superior—she wore a traditional nun's habit and we found her exotic and a little confusing because we knew so little about the religion.

Two families on the block were Christian Scientists, but all we knew was that they did not use physicians. There was a rumor that the Christian Science family that lived across the street from us had called a reader to minister to a sick mother and all of the mother's toes fell off because of the lack of medical attention. I doubt that it really happened. Everyone on the block was aware that my family was Jewish, but it did not cause me any serious difficulty. I always knew that I was Jewish and, therefore, was "different." I had been called a "Christ killer" when I was five or six years old, but I was not sure who Christ was. And I felt that being Jewish was why my parents did not socialize with the other parents on the block. I assumed, but it may not have been true, that the other kids' parents all knew each other well but when my parents had a party they never invited anyone on our block. In Minneapolis, the small Jewish community felt they all knew each other, and few people then stepped "over the line" into the non-Jewish world.

We not only had no black people in our neighborhood, there were no blacks in any of my schools. The black population of Minneapolis was small and very segregated. I learned, when I was in college, that we really did have one black family—on the street in back of us. My brother happened to see on his teacher's desk the school registration card of a boy who was a good friend of his. Under the designation "race" he saw the word "Negro." No one in the family looked at all black. I knew the boy's sister very slightly; she had been a year ahead of me in high school. And I had noticed at the University of Minnesota, that the sister hung around with many Negro students. But I had attributed this to her being some kind of a "Negrophile." The fact that the family identified itself as Negro gave us a strange, but not antagonistic feeling. Here they were living with all the rest of us, and no one knew the difference or cared. But no one knew that they were Negro. The school must have kept their records confidential.

While I was attending the University of Minnesota I worked summers for a "rich" uncle who was in the real estate business in Chicago. Most of the property that my uncle managed or owned was black, and I was fascinated with Chicago's black communities.

One of the women from whom I had to collect the monthly rent was active in the National Council of Negro Women. I used to chat with her, telling her that my mother was an active clubwoman too. The tenant was a woman, maybe in her fifties, with whitish hair, and I enjoyed the fact that I could talk with her "just like anyone else." One month I went to collect rent which she thought she had already paid. Maybe she was right, or maybe I was right. But she lashed out at me, shaking her fists and using swear words that were frightening to me—coming from a nice "old" lady. I was shattered. Crossing the racial barriers, which I thought I had done with such aplomb, just did not work. This was in the late 1930s, before the days of narcotics and "crime in the streets." I thought of myself as being just a good-hearted college boy. But she probably thought of me as representing the white Jewish slumlord, living off the meager earnings of poor blacks, refusing to make repairs except in an emergency, and squeezing an extra month's rent out here and there.

During World War II I got to know a few blacks. At Fort Sam Houston in San Antonio, Texas, I heard that a fellow officer whom I had known at a previous post was at the same camp, and I looked him up. He was Lieutenant Davis; I do not remember his first name. I think he was a son or grandson of the one black general the army had at that time. We met outside his quarters, only to find we had no possible place to go, either on the base or in San Antonio, because everything on and off the base was completely segregated. So we just sat outside and talked.

Thus, with very little knowledge or understanding, I became an adult confused about blacks, coloreds, Negroes—trying to be friendly when I had the opportunity but seldom having the opportunity, and feeling a general sense of guilt for what "we" had done to the blacks, "we" being fellow Americans even though one set of my grandparents came from Russia and the other set from Romania. I was the kind of "liberal" that members of militant ethnic groups feel they can do without. When it was still possible to do so, I used to wander around the places where black people lived. But what I found interesting was probably being a voyeur, seeing how people were trying to live, work, and play surrounded by a hostile environment. No blacks did or could live near me. When I got to know black people socially, I found myself talking with them about "The Negro Problem," and I always wondered why I could not just relate to them as human beings. Discussing the Negro problem, I suppose, kept me as the superior one, the sympathetic white person. But it also kept them inferior, the sinned against, and I think it was this disturbing possibility that worried me.

Who Did We Forget?

It is only recently in the United States that we have come to realize that large numbers of our people are living in what has been either an invisible state or so completely segregated that we could ignore them. Black people are only one group. In the upper Midwest and the West large numbers of American Indians have found their way off their reservations where we knew they belonged and where it was easy to segregate them. On the West Coast are Mexican-Americans, Chicanos, but also Spanish-Americans, who were there when their land became part of the United States. Puerto Ricans are a little different because they are recent immigrants to the mainland. And so are other Latin Americans. Chinese who live in Chinatowns we always felt were quaint; we did not worry about them because we were told in sociology classes that they had no crime or juvenile delinquency. But in recent times poor Chinese have also been demonstrating for part of the action and greater control of the institutions and schools that serve them. Recently we have Filipinos amongst us. There are also the miners in West Virginia and Kentucky and the migrant workers. The people whom we forgot are emerging in all parts of the country, mostly people who have always been here but who have been left out of the mainstream of our society, in most cases people we pretended did not exist.

A black woman I know was telling me about her trip to Indianapolis. "The hotel was very strange," she said, explaining that, as you got off the elevator on your floor, there was a desk with an elderly woman sitting there, and this was where you left and picked up your key and mail.

"They used to run a lot of hotels that way," I said, "including hotels like the Biltmore in New York. It's really not that strange."

"Don't forget," my friend explained, "*we* haven't been going to hotels very long, so I really don't know how that many hotels function." My friend is a graduate social worker who grew up in Pittsburgh. But it jolted me to realize, even though I knew, that black people have only been staying in "our" hotels for the past fifteen years or so.

When I was in my teens Marian Anderson came in concert to Minneapolis and insisted that she must stay at a downtown hotel. The Radisson Hotel permitted her to stay there, provided that she did not linger in the lobby and took only the service elevator. And she accepted! It was written up in the Minneapolis *Journal* at the time because it was such a breakthrough, in this northern city. This was Minneapolis, not Jackson, Mississippi, and it was no more than thirty years ago. Any nonwhite person who is forty or older grew up with this, and younger people know of it from their parents.

When we were taught about the Melting Pot Theory in school, we all believed in it as if it was a religion. We were told that the great United States took all of the people with different backgrounds and made them one people—Americans. In the United States everyone could melt together and make it. And we believed it, even though we could see all of these other people who were not melting and were not making it and could not make it because law and custom would not permit them to do it.

I grew up believing that American Indians liked reservations, that the law in the state of Minnesota not permitting them to be sold liquor "was because they would go crazy if they had a drink," and that they were not interested in education because they were slovenly people. When I visited my sister in Albuquerque, New Mexico, I was told similar things about the local Spanish-speaking people. And in California they said that the Chicanos—who were then called Mexicans, not even Mexican-Americans—could speak English perfectly well but did not want to. For two months during World War II, I worked at an induction station in Roanoke, Virginia, and many of the inductees were coal miners. Many men, only eighteen or nineteen, looked as if they were in their mid-forties. These were white people, but this was what the mines and poverty had done to them.

We may feel tired of the war on poverty by now. But it is a war that has not yet had a significant victory. There have been some gains but we still have people with little or no education, people who can not possibly make it because they have nothing to make it with. And, while blacks can now stay at the Radisson Hotel in Minneapolis, things are still not very good for the nine out of ten blacks who can not afford to stay at the Radisson Hotel because they are too poor. Or the Indians, the Spanish-Americans, the Mexican-Americans, the hillbillies, the miners, and all the other groups in our country who are so poor that they cannot even get to a tributary of the mainstream of American life.

A few years ago I had the privilege of being part of a team evaluating something called STAR, a basic literacy program for adults in the state of Mississippi. The director of one of the branches was driving me around his area outside of Biloxi. On a country road we came upon a white woman walking with two dead rabbits and a shotgun in her hand. The director told me that she was one of the participants in their program, and agreed to see if she would talk with us.

She refused to invite us into her house, a tumbledown shack, because "things were not fixed up," but reluctantly let us sit on the steps in front and talk with her. Earlier, the professional director had explained the importance of hunting as a source of food to poor people. The large yard in front of the woman's house was barren, with an old car wreck close by.

I asked the woman if she liked school and she replied, like in the movies, "Yup." I asked why she wanted to go to school, and she said so she could learn. Seeing the dead rabbits on her lap that were going to provide her with meat, I asked whether she grew any vegetables, and she said, "Nope."

"Why not?"

" 'Cause once I did and the chickens and animals ate 'em all up."

"Too bad."

"Yup."

"Anything you could do?"

"Yup. I thought about gettin' some money to buy some wire and put up a fence. Then the animals couldn't get in, I figgered. It takes a lot of money, but I figgered I could do that and maybe I will if we can get money."

This is what adult education is all about. She may never learn to read well, but she is learning something by going to school. And even if nothing else changes in her life but she learns that a fence will keep out the animals and permit her to grow some vegetables, it will have been well worth the cost of her education. If she ever got the fence up, who knows where she could go with her education?

What Worked for One Ethnic Group May Not Work for Another

Those who have been responsible for planning programs for forgotten groups of people have learned that it takes more than just good will to reach segmented sections of the "poor" community. There have been a lot of successes but many more failures. Well intentioned "liberals" like me have had to face up to the fact that my "mainstream" idea of what "these people" need often has little relevance to either the needs or the way of life of the poor who have been left out.

One of my grandfathers started life in the United States as a peddler. And he was the "worst" kind of peddler. With a horse and buggy, he bought up dead animals from farms outside of Minneapolis and sold them to rendering plants to make soap and fertilizer. He later founded the Minneapolis Hide and Tallow Company, which may still be going, and when he retired sold out to his partner, a Mr. Eklund. But this has no relevance to the woman near Biloxi with the two rabbits she had shot, or to the miners in Roanoke or the lettuce workers in California or the Sioux Indian hospital orderly in Duluth. Or to the ghetto black in St. Louis. The chances of the rabbit woman forming the Biloxi Hide and Tallow Company are absolutely zero, unfortunately. She is probably thirty-five years old and in a sense is just beginning to invent the wheel. The rabbit woman and most of the people we forgot are third- or fourth-generation poor or descended from slaves, in the case of blacks, for whom the wonderful opportunities of our country have generally not been available and they have had to learn to live as best they could.

A charming black woman in her forties came into my office in the Great Neck Public Schools and asked if she could talk with me privately. She had heard that we had classes where adults could learn to read and write.

She had grown up in the rural South, she told me. There were schools, but there were a lot of children in her family. During the time that there was farm work to do she was needed to pitch in. And when there was no farm work to do, you needed shoes to go to school. Her father, she explained, would not let her go to school without shoes. It would be undignified and degrading. And shoes were a rarity—usually a gift every second Christmas. So she had gone to school a month or two every year, but not enough to ever learn to read or write "or figure," and she was excited when I told her that we would teach her.

"You should really call this the Second Chance School instead of The Adult Program," she exlaimed. "No matter what happened when you were a child, here's a second chance for you and for everyone," she said with great joy. She is already a mature person and learning while she is working as a domestic in someone's home. It may be too late for her but maybe her son can start a hide and tallow company, or whatever the equivalent is today. But her son will still be black and there are still not many black-owned businesses, even in these enlightened times.

If literacy—reading and writing—alone could do it, we could probably lick the problem. We know pretty well how to teach adults to read and write. But teaching an adult black woman domestic of forty years of age to read and write is probably not going to alter her economic and job picture very much, if at all, and she knows this. And while this second-chance woman was anxious to learn, most people at forty doubt very much that they can learn and do not know enough about the middle-class community to realize that there are places where they can learn. Or if they do know, they feel it is not for them.

Making First Contacts with "Those People"

How do you go about organizing an adult education program for "those people"?

We do not yet have a good word or phrase to describe a target group within our community of poor or alternate culture or undereducated or problem-ridden people. One phrase that carries violent objection is "those people" (or "you people," often used in face-to-face relationships). It strips away their dignity and assumes they are basically different. They are "people," or "our people," whether we like it or not. I use the term "target group" when everyone knows what the group is. A phrase that sets them apart not only has a high negative charge but actually corrupts our own thinking in trying to plan.

If we are organizing a class in German or Great Books or Steno-type we do not designate the potential participants as "those people" or any other designation, except the people who want to learn German or Stenotype or to study the Great Books. So we probably do not need to devise a term for our forgotten target group. But we *do* have to undertake special planning to get special groups of people into an educational program for adults.

The only possible way of planning for a special group of people is to plan *with* the potential participants. The day has long since passed when any group of adults will permit someone else to plan for them. And to plan with recipient people does not mean adding a poor or black person to the board of directors. The board of directors should have people on it from as many segments of the community as possible, including the recipient community. But the poor or black person on the board of directors is just one person, and is not likely to be poor and really undereducated. Even if he is a possible participant in the program, he is just one person. To plan with a group or segment of the community, you must have a fair number of people and, preferably, meet with them on their home ground.

If it is at all possible, arrange things in such a way that a potential group will make requests of you or your organization, asking for help in a project rather than you or your group going out to sell an already developed idea to a group of strangers. This is not easy to do but it is possible.

I once read in the local paper about a group of wheelchair adults who had formed an organization in our community, a chapter of the National Paraplegia Foundation. I wrote them a letter saying I would like to meet with them to see whether they were interested in any kind of adult education program.

After a couple of weeks, when I had not heard anything, I telephoned the person named in the article—his name was Dick Match —and mentioned my letter. In reply to his asking why I wanted to meet with them, I said that I was responsible for educational programs for adults and his organization was composed of adults and maybe there was something we could do together.

I had seen people on the streets in wheelchairs but I had never known any wheelchair people. When I went to the meeting and observed the participants, I quickly decided that I should remain seated, that it would be ostentatious of me to stand when I talked because they would never be able to stand. I had no idea what I could offer the membership or what they would want and, naïve as I was, I had no idea whether we had locations that were accessible by wheelchair. Even one raised step makes a place out of bounds if you are propelling your own wheelchair.

This was the beginning of many years of projects for handicapped adults. One of the opportunities we planned was a series of dog training courses in which wheelchair people brought their pets and learned to handle them better, even though they could not chase them on foot. And we ran "psychology" courses, how to live in a wheelchair. The longest lasting was Swimming for the Handicapped. The surprising thing to me was that the members were overjoyed to think that anyone in the community cared about them. And our community was so overjoyed to be easing the life of wheelchair people that we even had Board of Education members as swimming pool volunteers.

I suppose the very last thing I would have guessed that wheelchair adults wanted was dog training. And yet I am still very foolishly self-assured when I project that poor people should flock to courses that provide them with basic literacy skills.

One successful program we ran for poor people was the Big Red School Bus Program, in cooperation with one of our PTAs. In a middle-class community parents frequently take their youngsters to museums and galleries and zoos and other stimulating places on a Saturday or Sunday. Poor people may not have the time or the energy or the imagination.

Carefully, the PTA planned a series of Saturday morning trips for kindergarten, first-, second-, and third-grade parents. One parent could bring one child. Two parents were "in charge" of each trip. The Big Red School Bus left the schoolyard at 10:00 A.M. and returned at 1:00 P.M. There was a small charge. The PTA subsidized the program, so "target group" parents were invited by others whether they paid the entire fee, part of it, or paid nothing at all. The trips were to nearby places, with the hope that parents might make the trip on their own some Saturday with a minimum of expense. The first series went to a public park to see a puppet show, to an archeological grounds to dig for arrowheads, to a parade at the U.S. Merchant Marine Academy, and to the airport to watch the planes. There was a program on the school playground for other children who would be left at home so parents did not have to worry. The Big Red School Bus was "sold out" each series, with half the spaces reserved for people who did not have the four dollar fee. No one thought up the program in advance; it evolved after a number of meetings. No one questioned the reading level of the parents. The Big Red School Bus was their project, conceived and executed by parents.

Robert J. Havighurst of the University of Chicago completed a National Study of Indian Education for the United States Department of Education in 1971. Decision-making about Indian education and the implementation of these decisions should be increasingly in the hands of the Indians, the study concluded. "It appears to us that the basic problem of Indian education cannot be solved unless definite steps are immediately taken in this direction," said Havighurst. Curriculums compatible with Indian needs must be planned to retain identity, pride, and self-respect. Bilingual programs, Indian history, and culture and career development are needed, the study points out.

The study cost $515,000. But you do not need another study to confirm the main points, which have been found over and over in working with the people we forgot. Decision-making and the implementation of these decisions must be in the hands of the "target group." The role of the sponsoring group or agency or institution is to be the catalyst without preconceived ideas, to help provide resources for whatever the identified group feels it needs.

Dealing with Group Sensitivities and Prejudices

Be prepared for misunderstandings, communication gaps, "no shows" at meetings, language and word barriers, hostility, and general confusion. Meetings, the method most familiar to mainstream people to conduct business, are frequently unfamilar to other cultures within our community. Their formality, minutes, Robert's Rules of Order, committees and subcommittees, motions, and amendments are all easy to handle for sophisticated people, but may seem like just so many hindrances to getting something done to impatient recipient groups.

Before the word "black" came into common usage, my community planned a series of what we called "heritage evenings," to celebrate and involve what we identified as "pocket groups" living amongst us. We had an Irish-American evening and a Lithuanian-American evening, complete with costumes, dancing, talks, music—the works. Each was planned with local ethnic clubs. They were very successful. So we decided to try an American Negro Heritage evening and when we approached the local NAACP (National Association for the Advancement of Colored People) to serve as co-sponsor they were pleased. So we set up our usual joint committee, five of "them," five of "us." We had two black people as our delegates and they had one white as theirs, so the "them" and "us" was not completely a racial designation.

In the middle of the planning I got a bad tongue-lashing from a black lawyer on the other side because I had captioned a newspaper picture of our superintendent of schools with the attorney as "Dr. John L. Miller," our superintendent, and the lawyer's name without an "Esq." following his name. The "Esq." is, the lawyer nagged me, the proper identification for a lawyer. It was, he felt, a deliberate slap, using the "Dr." to show that the superintendent had an advanced degree but not using anything to show that the lawyer also had an advanced degree. I pleaded that I had never seen the "Esq." designation in a newspaper following a lawyer's name, although I remembered the designation did appear after his name on the NAACP stationery. If the designation was common in the black press, and not in the general press, I suppose I was as guilty for not being familiar with the other side as was the lawyer for not knowing that the designation is not used in the general press.

I felt very bad to have become hung up on such an innocent matter and sought advice from a friend who was with the United Nations. She said she was not aware of the "Esq.," but she did know that in India people frequently use the designation "Ph.D. failed" after their name, a custom that must have meaning in India but would be anathema in the United States. If I had had the good sense to let the NAACP handle the publicity, the incident could never have occurred. Or maybe the best procedure would have been to let both groups see all printed material before it went out.

Peoples who have been living in a somewhat invisible state for a long period of time have found ways of adjusting and living in whatever ghetto atmosphere has developed. They have a way of life, a "culture" and a language that is familiar to them. And they have soft spots—words and manners that set them off emotionally. Even when we feel we are familiar with their culture, we are probably only familiar with that part of the culture they have been willing to share with us. Their way of doing things is not necessarily better or worse than our way of doing things. If we want to work with another group, we must work with them on *their* ground and according to *their* rules as much as possible. They can learn from us. And we may be able to learn from them.

I was once on a bus going to Taos, New Mexico. An American Indian young man in army uniform was sitting next to me. He told me that he had been overseas and was being discharged.

"How does it seem," I asked, "having seen so much of the world to come back to New Mexico and an Indian community."

"Wonderful," he responded. "I hope I can stay here and never have to leave again. I'm very homesick and will be satisfied if I can just be home again." As a sightseer, the Taos communities looked very exotic but uncomfortable—for me. But for this Taos Indian, they were home.

Careful Dignity Helps People Improve Their Self-Image

Be sure, in all of your contacts, that you treat the recipient group with complete dignity. And be honest with them. In "our" majority culture, people are called by their first name through junior high and sometimes through senior high school. One of the dramatic changes between high school and college has been, in most places, the change from using first names to "Miss" or "Mr." or "Mrs." If you are dealing with adults, these are the proper designations—with last names, of course.

Because you know your own group, the tendency is to call members of your group by first names. Therefore, you may feel you are acting no differently when you call members of the "other" group by first names.

But first names, to "left-out" adults, were always a way of keeping people down. At meetings or educational programs, if you make sure that everyone has a designation and a last name you will not be crossing over any sensitivity lines. Do not ask a group of adults which they would prefer. Even if some of them ask for first names, your acceding to this may step on the toes of others. If someone calls you by your first name, you may, of course, do the same—in private conversation. But in any formal or group situation, no.

In the same way, avoid *any* group designations, no matter how well you feel you are accepted. It is true that a group can refer to themselves as "spicks" or "po' white trash," but this does not mean that an outsider can get away with it. The terminology that "pocket groups" use for themselves is very tricky, and you will do best by not trying your hand at it. The only correct way to refer to people of the Jewish religion is by using the word "Jewish." To call someone "a Jew" is offensive to most, and to use the term "Jewess" is as funny as calling someone a "Protestantess." It shows complete ignorance.

If you use the term "black" you are not apt to upset anyone, even people who avow that they have no objection to "Negro" or "colored."

But, once you are working on a project, it is wisest not to use any designation unless it is essential. If you find you are forever using group designations, you might ask yourself why—just as one may wonder why one cannot carry on a normal conversation with an American Indian without discussing the "Indian problem." Try to catch one word that people seem to use for themselves, and when you must use a designation use that one. If an American Indian group prefers to use the term "native American," use that term. Lately, the designation "Third World people" has become popular among intellectuals and militants to describe non-Caucasians. If your group uses it for themselves, then you may use it. "Street people" is another new term for an urban group we used to call "hippies" or "beats."

You May Have to Bend a Great Deal

Sometimes it is just as well to let people make their own mistakes. And sometimes their "mistakes" turn out to be successes. The success of an adult education project is not easy to predict, even when all those planning are on very firm ground. We have all been to PTA or church meetings where we felt sure we would get two hundred people but only twenty-five show up. I remember a PTA meeting when, with great care, the planners had invited as a main speaker the director of the Child Study Association of America. To try to ensure a crowd, they planned a short concert of the elementary school orchestra to precede the important lecture. When the meeting chairman got up after the musical interlude to introduce the speaker, three quarters of the parents in attendance also got up—to take their children home. The director of the Child Study Association of America, excited by an auditorium of two hundred parents when he arrived, talked to an audience of fifty, mostly the executive board and the people who were to serve the coffee when the meeting was over.

Part of the "education" in planning community adult education activities takes place in the planning. Whatever the process that develops with recipient groups, everyone is learning as the planning progresses. If the resulting project itself succeeds less well than anticipated, or even if it falls flat on its face, you will have gained something from the planning process and will be that much farther ahead for the next project.

A medical society decides to plan a course in health and first aid for people who live in a low-income housing project. A Junior League chapter offers to organize a group of low-income working mothers to help them establish a cooperative day care center. A League of

Women Voters chapter is willing to conduct a leadership training program on political involvement for residents of a poverty pocket. Or a Chamber of Commerce feels it can sponsor a course to train unemployed males to become draftsmen and designers. All laudable projects with those who "have" reaching out to help those who "have less"—what we call today "outreach" projects.

But as meetings are held with potential customers for these projects, it may turn out that the recipient groups are suspicious of the motives behind the offer and feel that other things have greater priority. They may also resent the fact that those proposed to conduct the adult education projects are the wrong people, that the project must be conducted by someone selected by the recipient group if it is to be effective.

The medical society may be told that what people in the low-income project need is an operating clinic in the housing unit. The Junior League may find resentment that Junior League mothers who stay home to take care of their children think that poor mothers should work and leave their children to strangers. The League of Women Voters may be told that the political system does not work anyway, so why learn about it? And the Chamber of Commerce may be asked to hire more "Third World" people in top executive positions and not try to train them for low-level, nonpromotional jobs.

Instead of giving up in despair, each sponsoring group has learned lesson number one, and the people who met with the sponsoring group have also made a beginning contact. At this point both groups must explore what is feasible and possible and likely to make a contribution. The original project idea may not have been a good one. Or it may be good, but not of primary interest or need, as the recipients see it. Or perhaps it needs some radical changes but still has the essence of a feasible project within it. Or sometimes, after a good deal of exploration, the group will come back to the original project but have bent it to suit the needs as they see them. The final project planned for the community may prove successful or may attract no one. It is not likely to be more of a disaster than a PTA meeting with no one in the audience. And the PTA will not stop planning additional meetings because one did not succeed. With the same kind of resiliency and determination to make a contribution, progress may be possible in the future.

Getting Down to the Nitty-Gritty

Once you and your group have established contact with another group in the community, you are ready for the sometimes laborious job of planning a specific project. You may find that the target group with which you are working has an exaggerated sense of your power or financial situation. They look upon you as the "haves," the beautiful people they see on television and in the movies, living it up by skiing in the summer in Chile and skin diving in the winter at Cozumel off the coast of Yucatan. So you will have to level with them. This is what you bring to the situation; this is what they bring to the situation. You have resource people, contacts with the media and certain parts of the community power structure, access to certain institutions. They have a knowledge of the recipient group; understanding of their problems and hangups and where they look for help and advice and their own resource people and access to certain institutions that have a credibility with those for whom you are planning. They also have a sense of possible timing for the project and contacts that will help in recruiting.

The important thing at the beginning is to get something started—almost no matter what it is—so you can build upon success if at all possible.

Professor Wilbur Hallenbeck, retired from Teachers College of Columbia University where he was a prominent adult educator, used to tell about the development of a literacy project under United Nations auspices in Mexico. The UN literacy experts went to a small, "backward" agricultural area and arranged to meet with a group of farmers to discuss the important adult education project they were prepared to bring the community. But the farmers showed no interest at all in learning to read and write. The only interest the UN people could evince was finding a better seed so they could improve their corn crop. So the flexible adult educators started a program to improve the seed and improve farming practices.

The second year, the farmers explained that the corn they were growing was a better grade but periods of drouth kept them from growing as much as they would like. So the second year's adult education project was on irrigation.

The third year, with higher yield and better quality, the farmers had more corn than they used to grow and wanted to know how they could sell their excess crops. "To market your corn," the UN adult educators explained quietly, you have to learn to read and write and figure, because you will have to deal with people from outside the community who could take advantage of you. And thus started the adult literacy project, two years after the original plan was conceived, but it started at a point when the need for reading and writing was apparent to the recipient group.

The lesson to learn is that you deal with people where they are and hope to bring them, step by step, to some new place. The original idea may come in time or it may never come. But as long as people are progressing and learning, and as long as they are becoming aware that education can bring change, everyone is winning.

The STAR adult literacy project in the state of Mississippi, mentioned earlier, was designed to give the poor whites, blacks, and native American Indians some of the tools to better themselves economically. And many people were able to get jobs or upgrade their jobs as the result of acquiring or improving reading and writing skills. But when I talked with a group of adult participants and asked them if anything had changed from what they were learning, few people responded in vocational terms.

"I am able to help my children with their homework," a young handyman told me. "When they bring books home from school, I can read their books with them and sometimes help them with their arithmetic. They know I am going to school and they are going to school. Going to school is something we are all doing."

"When I go to the store, they can't gyp me any more," an older woman reported. "If they tell me the package of flour is thirty-five cents and I look at the package and see a 2 and a 9 on the package I know that it means the price is 29. They will never be able to gyp me any more."

"Sometimes we get surplus foods like powdered milk," a man in torn blue overalls said. "We used to feed it to the hogs because we didn't know what else to do with it. Now my wife and I look at the package and it usually says how we can use it for ourselves and our children. We are both going to school, and together we can usually figure out how to fix things like powdered milk. So we drink it at home instead of giving it to the animals."

The people in the STAR project were using their adult education wisely, if not exactly in the way the sponsors had hoped.

One of the problems in most projects for segmented parts of the community is who is going to be in charge—who is going to conduct the learning group. No matter how well trained and skilled one may be, many times it is very hard for a member of a "majority" to completely understand and work with a member of the "minority." Good will and an excitement about the project are only two of the requisites. An ability to communicate, understand, use familiar terminology, and relate to the life style of the adult participants is equally important.

A black community leader at a meeting I attended perhaps oversimplified but dramatized the problem. "The teacher wanted to know if we had two cantaloupes and she had two cantaloupes, how many cantaloupes would there be. No one answered and the teacher thought we were just dumb. But she didn't know that most of the people didn't know what a cantaloupe was, and they were so busy trying to figure out what she meant by a cantaloupe that they didn't even realize she had asked them how much two and two was. Now if she had said that she had two hogs and we had two hogs and how many hogs were there, we could have figured it out right away."

If the recipient group does not have someone with the basic knowledge—but be sure they really do not—the best approach is to have two leaders, one with the greater subject knowledge and the other with the greater "people" knowledge. Or set up a screening committee so that everyone can meet with possible candidates and select the one they feel can best handle the group.

Team teaching is relatively new on the total education scene. It makes great sense when dealing with "left out" groups, providing that at least one member of the team is from the group trying to be reached. And both members of the team must be acceptable to the recipient group.

Sponsors sometimes make the mistake of assuring that anyone identifiable as a member of a recipient group is automatically acceptable to adult members of such a group. This is no more true than the reverse would be. Majority adults are very concerned about their group or class leader or teacher. If the choice is a poor one, they will not continue in the program. Just selecting a black to work with black people or a Mexican-American to work with Mexican-American people has not solved the problem completely. You must find a person who has credibility with the group and experience has shown that the person selected by a group itself is not always the identifiable member of that culture. A poor black may resent a middle-class black because he feels they have little in common. Or he may accept a middle-class black over a middle-class white because he feels at least they have one thing in common. So the important thing is to have the recipients in on the selection of the person or people with whom they will be working.

The guideline, then, is to work your way through the hurdles and get started someplace. Speed is not as essential as progress. It is better to start next month with more things going in favor of the project than to start this month with a lot of hurdles still in the way or agreements not yet reached. With a choice of projects, start with the one most likely to succeed, not with the one that seems most important. And the project most likely to succeed is probably the project in which you detect most enthusiasm from the recipient group. It may seem, at the beginning, to be least in line with your commitment or the commitment of your organization or institution. But explain to sponsors that it is very likely that, to accomplish their long-range goals, they have to make a beginning in a different way than they originally envisioned.

Adults who are not used to seeking solutions in group educational atmosphere have to have a successful experience before they are likely to trust the educational process. And this may be the most important point to begin. Start small but plan big. Be satisfied with little but have hopes for much. By the time your first project is off the ground, you should have clearly in mind a second and third project, so you do not lose whatever impetus you build up at the beginning. The biggest hurdle is to get people to try themselves out in an educational atmosphere and give them the feeling of success, that something is happening as a result of their efforts. But be ready immediately with step two so you can retain the excitement and motivation of the first group and hopefully add additional people.

At the beginning you will have to concentrate on recruiting people. But as you go along your best recruiters will be satisfied customers, even though you may still need to retain special recruiters. Provide opportunities for those attending to bring in a friend or members of their family to show them what is happening. Some of the friends will hopefully end up as participants.

Try to have a beginning and an end to your adult education project. Sometimes planners, in their enthusiasm, would like the project to go on for ever, or rationalize by saying they will keep it going as long as people want to attend. But few adults can plan to spend, say, every Tuesday night for an indeterminate period of time. Too many projects wither away to nothing because the planners have not included a beginning and an end point in the learning experience.

In a well planned, self-motivated adult education project, it is difficult to know how long it takes to learn something. How long does it take an illiterate adult to learn to read and write? How long does it take an adult to learn typing or drafting or switchboard operation? How long, for that matter, does it take to learn to draw or speak French or make ceramics?

In an adult math class I heard the complaint from the participants that the faculty member was going too fast, and that when he asked whether they understood something they were so far behind him that they said nothing, because they were still way back at the beginning. When I talked with the man in charge, he said that he had to go that fast to get through the book in the fifteen weeks allotted to the class. But he selected the book and was under no obligation at all to get through it. All that was expected was that at the end of fifteen weeks the participants had learned as much math as they could learn in fifteen weeks. If it was necessary and people were interested in learning more than fifteen weeks' worth of math, there was no reason why we could not plan a second or even a third and fourth series.

It is better to plan a short unit—maybe five or eight or ten weeks if there are weekly meetings—with ample opportunity to continue in a more advanced learning situation if necessary. But it is wise, particularly in early projects, to permit people to enter as late as possible if they will not hold the others back. Some way of absorbing new people once the project has begun will permit you to build within your population group. It takes time for adults to hear about a program, and time for them to get up nerve enough and arrange their lives so they can participate. Even colleges working with open enrollment programs have found that the important thing is to provide an opportunity for adults to learn; that the idea of how much one is supposed to learn in one semester is not as sacrosanct as we once believed.

What Does Adult Education Lead To?

When Columbia University celebrated its two-hundredth anniversary, they chose as their bicentennial motto "Man's Right to Knowledge and the Free Use Thereof." To me, the motto means that we have an obligation to provide as much education as people want and can take, at all points in their lives, and to everyone in our country. But what they do with their education is up to them.

The rabbit lady mentioned earlier may learn that if you put up a fence around a plot of ground you can keep animals out and plant vegetables for home use. A medical aide may learn how to handle patients in the emergency room in a hospital, and as a result move up the ladder from being an orderly. A Grandma Moses may learn to paint, or someone else may learn to put thoughts and ideas down on paper.

But people may also learn that the institutions that try to serve them are not providing for their real needs, and they may organize to change the institutions or to establish new ones that will serve them better. They may question the wisdom of elected political officials or demonstrate at a hospital that they feel is not giving their group a fair shake.

It is really not that "a little education is a dangerous thing." A little education is one step better than no education. More education is better. But the role of education is to give people tools for doing things and tools for further exploration and further thinking. Ordinarily, we cannot guarantee what the yield will be from education. Occasionally, someone cannot get a job unless he has a high school equivalency diploma or a college diploma. But in those cases what he primarily needs is the slip of paper. For some high school graduates and college graduates are exemplary citizens and some end up as criminals or as vagrants.

Education, and particularly adult education, can offer a person only learning. What he does with that learning is partially in his own hands and partially in the hands of society.

This point of view is important because, while everyone in a community is in favor of providing educational opportunities for that part of the community which has had few opportunities in life, some members begin to question the expenditure and the program. For instance, welfare mothers who have participated in educational programs sponsored by the Junior League or the Council of Jewish Women begin to appear at meetings of the city council or Board of Supervisors and, as the result of special training in public speaking, perhaps, make themselves heard on issues that are important to them.

Education, including adult education, is glorious and dangerous. But it can be no other way. Books and movies and radio and television and newspapers are in the same boat. Most people use what they learn carefully. Once exposed to a little good education, adults should develop an inquiring mind. They will ask searing questions and seek better answers. And if this is disturbing or dangerous, it should be no more so than sending a boy to Harvard or a girl to Radcliffe. This, I am sure, is what Columbia University meant by "Man's Right to Knowledge and the Free Use Thereof."

CHAPTER TWO

The Needs of People and the Needs of Their Communities

ERNEST E. McMAHON

Dr. Ernest E. McMahon is Dean Emeritus of the University Extension Division and Professor Emeritus of Adult Education at Rutgers, The State University of New Jersey.

T H E   N E E D S   O F   P E O P L E as individuals and their collective needs as members of communities are not always identical. The total educational needs required to solve or reduce a major community problem are different from the individual educational needs of the people who comprise the community. Meeting the total individual needs of the residents of a community in basic education, in self-identification, or in employment will not automatically solve the community problems of mass transportation, air pollution, and housing. Related as the two may be, their solutions—and their identification—require different approaches. We are here concerned primarily with the identification of community needs, with full realization that individuals comprise the community.

Let us trace briefly the historical development of adult education as an activity concerned with individual needs and the more recent evolution of its concern with group or community needs. Questions will be raised about the meaning of need and its determination. Certain obstacles which may hinder the adult educator in his or her efforts to meet identified needs will be discussed, and selected practical ways to determine community needs will be presented. The purpose is to help you, who suddenly find yourself an adult educator, to be more effective in serving the community in its total needs.

Often the assumption is made that community needs are obvious or may be determined and solved easily. In some cases they may be, but in most situations the obvious needs are only the part of the iceberg which shows above the water.

Community is defined as the specific population which an adult educator or his organization or institution seeks to reach with respect to a particular problem or set of problems. The community may be the people in a single apartment house or on a city block. It may be members of a trade union local, the employees of a company, the members of a county professional society, a religious congregation, the residents in a voting district; in other words, the adult educator must deal with varied groups of people who have common educational problems related to the particular and specific groups to which they belong.

It is true that community often means all or part of a municipality or a small region which encompasses several municipalities, and available literature about community needs is based on such a geographical concept. However, the ways of identifying need apply to any group which an adult educator serves. His task is to adjust the use of the method to the characteristics of the group with which he is planning the educational program.

The common problems may be technical, such as how the county medical society helps its members keep abreast of new professional and scientific developments or how a trade union local informs its members of available rehabilitation resources for handicapped dependents. Within the group there may be individuals who need basic education or information about personal finance. Such needs are real and they may be shared by other members of the group but, taken together, they do not comprise the group problem and require different approaches on the part of the educator.

Individual and Community

Historically, the focus of adult education was on the individual and his needs. It is only in recent years that attention has turned to community needs as such. Part of the shift came from within the field of adult education itself with the rise of "community development" as a recognized specialty of many agencies. But demands for "participatory democracy" on the part of militant groups have forced public schools, colleges and universities, governmental institutions, and many voluntary organizations to take a new look at their organization and structure, to re-evaluate what they are and are not doing, and to realize that there is a community out there, made up of individuals to be sure, but with community problems that are more than and different from the totality of the problems of each individual. Much of the material on the determination of community needs for educational purposes was written and produced by social workers, sociologists, political scientists, urban planners, and a variety of persons who probably did not and do not consider themselves adult educators. Yet, in the business of helping people to understand and to come to grips with community needs, everyone who provides information and understanding is in a sense an adult educator. Their adult education roles may be secondary to their primary roles as social workers or planners, but their adult education roles are nonetheless real.

The challenge of adjusting to the demands of a secondary role is the challenge to the man who functions part time as an adult educator for his company, union or church; for the woman concerned with the educational program of the League of Women Voters or the PTA. Inherent in the challenge is the changing nature of adult education today—an activity which is moving to add the dimension of community to educational planning but not to overlook the needs of the individual—and recognition of the significant educational role of many community agencies and organizations of which the professional educational establishment is only one.

THE INDIVIDUAL

The evolution in adult education may be traced briefly. In the early nineteenth century the emphasis was remedial, designed to help those with little or no formal schooling learn the simple fundamentals of reading, writing, and arithmetic. It is interesting to note that Adult Basic Education, aimed at the same objectives, is still a major emphasis within adult education despite the many years that "free public schooling" has been available.

Another early emphasis was the provision of cultural opportunities for the individual, such as those offered through summer schools, lectures, and correspondence by Chautauqua and through the local programs of lyceums. Weekend residential institutes in Great Britain and Europe dealt with economic, political, and social issues. The first efforts of general university extension in the United States were directed to the general educational needs of the people rather than to the business and professional type of instruction which later became prevalent in extension work.

The early work of the U.S. Department of Agriculture Cooperative Extension was to upgrade the skills of the individual farmer as contrasted with the growing emphasis on community activity. Indeed, the first major thrust of Cooperative Extension was to help the individual cotton farmer cope with the ravages of the boll weevil while at the same time the government home economics agent gave homemaking assistance to the farmer's wife.

Americanization classes in public schools enabled the individual immigrant to gain United States citizenship. Schools and colleges began to offer courses which would upgrade the individual for job placement and hopefully for job advancement.

Whether the goal of the adult education was to remedy deficiencies or fill vacuums in previous formal education, to help the individual gain a broader personal or social outlook, to enable him to qualify for a better job, or to make him a better citizen, the focus was on the individual.

As a result of the emphasis on the person rather than on the group, the study of how to identify and determine needs for the purposes of adult education was related essentially to the individual. But this was yesterday's focus. Today the emphasis is on community needs. The failure to add the community dimension is a major reason why the relevance of the adult education programs of many associations and organizations is challenged despite a long history of concern with needs. Unfortunately, the programs have not changed as rapidly as twentieth-century society has changed nor have they always been responsive to pressures within that society.

Harry Miller, long a student of adult education, pointed out in an analysis of participation in adult education activities that "personal needs do not operate in a vacuum; they are shaped, conditioned, and channeled by the *social structures and forces* of the human society in which each individual is born. Each of us is driven by survival needs, but the survival behavior of a primitive hunting tribesman is far different from that of the organization man in western industrial society." [1]

THE COMMUNITY

The solution of problems by the piecemeal method of individual achievement no longer suffices. The educational programs to help communities attack the problems of housing, transportation, narcotics, air pollution, crime in the street, and solid waste disposal require a total solution in which adult education on a community basis has a significant role. In this time of social crisis and community tension, adult education has not led the way to elimination of the problems. Its traditional focus on the needs of the individual has proven inadequate.

In writing about procedures in developing adult education programs, Paul Bergevin and his colleagues emphasized the identification of a *common* need or interest as the first step in a six-step procedure for community planning.[2] The stress on *common* need or interest points out the importance of need identification on the community level if adult education is to be effective.

The essence of the community quality of adult education was well set forth by Horace Kallen in an address to a meeting of evening college deans and directors:

What makes a community is communication, and communication is between people—between speakers and listeners. Speakers and listeners together form institutions, which are associations of inviduals who have developed a technique of mutuality in communication, transforming communication into communion. This communion turns them from an aggregate of separate persons into a team, or a community.[3]

The path to improvement is not one of abandoning the individual or of substituting community needs for individual needs. Unfortunately, the needs of the individual will remain and must be met. The adult educator must go beyond the "aggregate of separate persons" and help provide for the common needs and interests. Just as the individual needs help through education, the community must have help in building the bridges between its economic and social needs and the educational needs of the residents who must solve the economic and social problems.

Roadblocks and Hurdles

There are many obstacles that get in the way of the professional and lay adult educator trying to work on community needs. Some of the obstacles are built in or permanent and must be lived with; others can be changed. The important thing is to recognize the obstacles, understand their nature, and be willing to remove them.

THE MEANING OF NEED

One of the first obstacles is confusion over the meaning of *need*. When adult educators talk about meeting needs, they mean many things—and few of them agree on any single meaning. Nevertheless, each one must understand the differences in the context of his consistuency and must have a clear understanding of his *own* concept of need. The educator's own philosophy of education and of social process is a key element in his efforts to determine community needs. If he believes that all adults should pay the cost of any education they receive or that present-day welfare payments are excessive, he will not reach the same determination of community needs as will the director of education for the local antipoverty agency. Thus the individual's perspective will influence his ultimate conslusions about needs.

Sponsorship. Another element which influences the definition of need is the agency itself which sponsors the educational program. The objectives and purposes of the sponsoring institution or agency will have an influence on the final determination of need, and so will the capabilities of the sponsor. If the sponsoring organization is committed to hold down taxes, it is not likely to recognize community educational needs which will inevitably cause taxes to rise if the needs are met. In terms of capabilities, if a particular need requires a massive educational program and extensive research which will run into the thousands of dollars, an agency with a budget of only a few hundred dollars will have to tailor its educational approach to the problem involved. The agency may deliberately fail to recognize the existence of the need, or it may identify only a segment of the need.

Client impact. Just as the sponsoring agency may influence the determination of need, the interests and motivations of the prospective participants may affect the program. It is well and good to develop an education program for a housing project, but if the residents of the project fail to participate, the need will then have to be redefined in terms or extent acceptable to those residents.

Need or desire. The differences in personal philosophy and in the objectives of sponsoring organizations come to light in disagreement over the idea of the relationship between need and desire. Whatever that idea may be, it becomes the basis for the adult educator's efforts to design educational programs to meet economic or other needs; it becomes the basis for his notion about who really determines need; and it becomes the basis for his attitude toward the felt and unfelt needs of his adult constituency.

Bernard James and Harold Montross studied the relationship between needs and program development, and they pointed out the danger of confusing "need" with "want." Their experience with a community group indicated that the initial statement of what the group wanted educationally was far different from what was required to satisfy the needs that were finally determined. The experience led them to write, "How easily an adult educational program can misinterpret "needs' if it takes surface phenomena of group behavior at face value—if, for instance, a program is designed merely on the basis of 'want' statements." [4]

In a later article, James continued his exploration of need as a basis for determination of educational purpose. He examined three meanings of the word. First, he defined need in a technical way as the equivalent of a drive, such as the need for food and shelter. His second meaning was the routine, everyday usage of the word in expressing a desire: for example, a certain club "needing" a speaker. His third definition involved value judgments. "For example," he wrote, "a guidance expert may tell a student that he 'needs' more mathematics to prepare for engineering. The student 'ought' to have such training." [5]

The prescriptive dangers inherent in the third definition are obvious. Possibly one reason that so little attention has been paid by adult educators to the methods of determining community needs is that so many people in any community have made value judgments about the community's needs and the ways in which those needs can be met. Such predetermination closes the door to sincere, probing efforts to find out what the real needs are.

To the person who defines needs only in terms of basic survival, there are few that *must* be met. If the definition is that elemental, there is no reason for any educational program; such needs are met by food, clothing, and shelter. To another person, who believes that self-fulfillment is as important as sheer physical survival, there are many needs to be met. It is within the framework of sheer surival in contrast with self-fulfillment that the adult educator must forge his own concept of the relationship between need and desire.

If the adult educator will accept Maslow's hierarchy of values as a scale of motivation for the satisfaction of the individual, need and desire become virtually synonymous (in the sense of wish-fulfillment) as one moves from level to level in the hierarchy: from the satisfaction of physiological needs for survival to a sense of safety, to being loved, to enjoying the esteem of others, and finally to self-actualization.[6]

Acceptance of the notion of self-fulfillment, of the fundamental need of each individual to attain identity as a person, frees the educator of adults to become innovative in initiating new programs—whether in response to community requests or as a result of his own search to discover needs. He is then able to concede that a need is being met if the participation in the adult education activity helps the individual to achieve a goal, and he will no longer be hemmed in by the kinds of precedents which rigidify so many adult education programs.

Whether enrollment of an illiterate adult in an Adult Basic Education class is comparable in social gain to the enrollment of the new owner of a small boat in a course in Small Boat Handling is a value judgment by the adult educator which bears no relationship to either student's feeling of need or of self-fulfillment. If the community has both illiterates and small boat owners, the adult educator's task may be to provide educational opportunities for both.

Felt needs and their satisfaction. In trying to discover the meaning of need, it is necessary to review what is meant by another of the clichés of adult education, the statement that "we respond to the felt needs of people." The rationale of the statement is that the residents or members of a community *feel* specific educational needs or personal needs which can be satisfied by education and that adult educators respond to those feelings by providing the courses, discussion groups, and meetings which enable the individuals to satisfy the needs.

What usually happens is that the adult school, or the League of Woman Voters, or the Historical Society offers one or more courses and a number of people show up to enroll. Obviously, those persons feel such enrollment is a desirable investment of time and money. The adult educator, or education chairman of the sponsoring agency, may have arbitrarily chosen the course offering, advertised it in the local paper or by mail, and waited for enrollees. Yet, regardless of subject matter, the fact of enrollment is taken to indicate the existence of a felt need to which the adult educator has presumably responded by offering the course. His anticipation or divination of the need—be it bridge, slimnastics, politics, or local history—has proved to be right. Yet no attempt was made to discover other needs, and the extent of need is measured by enrollments. Possibly, the cliché should be revised from "we respond to the felt needs of people" to "people respond to our guesses."

In any event, the fundamental question is how valid the felt need theory is and what its role may be in relationship to the meeting of community needs. Feeling implies a desire to do something about the need and also, in the application of the cliché, has been used to imply elimination of the needs about which the feeling exists. The statistics of adult education do not support any such inferences. The statistics of adult education, for example, indicate that the people with the least amount of formal education participate the least; those with the most years of formal education show the greatest percentage of participation. The statistics are borne out by the frequent difficulty of recruiting among the educationally disadvantaged and the necessity to hire recruiters to obtain students. Obviously, the feeling of need does not exist for some persons whose needs, as the adult educator sees them, are evident. Organizers of adult basic education classes, civic affairs education, and other need-oriented programs have faced such a lack of response.

Persistence in justifying program development on the basis of "responding to felt needs" actually results in circumscribing the audience of adult education. The offerings continue to serve millions of adults in largely job-related or recreational areas of education but somehow failed to reach the 80 percent of the adults who apparently never feel the need for such educational assistance as is offered.

Clarence Faust may have hit the nail on the head when he said, at a meeting at New York University for adult educators some years ago, that education should not respond to felt needs; its function is to create felt needs. Possibly that is what community involvement does in the search for community needs, it creates the feeling of need.

Carol Kramer distinguished between "felt" needs and "real" needs as follows:

> The real need is a desirable element or condition that is lacking in, and would improve, a situation. Felt needs are what people with problems *recognize* as the elements necessary to improve their situations. It should be emphasized that felt needs *may also be real needs*, but that often they are not. Felt needs may be derived from symptoms alone rather than from true problems.[7]

Kramer identified a major flaw in the felt need theory by pointing to resultant efforts to cure the symptoms rather than the cause of a situation. She also defined the real need in terms of "a situation." an actual set of circumstances in which people find themselves.

Reality in defining need. Samuel Hand placed a similar stress on reality when he wrote, "Adult educators are finding that the degree of participation in and support of local adult education programs is proportionate to the extent to which these programs are geared to the real life problems, interests, and needs of the communities they serve." [8]

Eduard Lindeman, more than forty years ago, enunciated the principle that "the approach to adult education will be via the route of *situations,* not subjects." He defined the situation approach, usually known today as problem solving, as the method by which "the learning process is at the outset given a setting of reality." [9]

In the setting of the situation, which changes from community to community and from hour to hour, a fixed and restrictive definition of need will not provide the clarification which will enable the working adult educator to proceed with his job. Nor will such a definition produce a uniformity of response by adult educators or their agencies; nor will it resolve nagging doubts about the propriety or efficacy of a particular program.

Rather, the adult educator must arrive at his own understanding of the difference between need and desire and of the relationship between educational needs and other needs of people. He must evaluate the validity of the "felt needs" theory and, in time, must answer for himself the question of who determines the needs of communities. Such a clarification of his own thinking is essential before he begins the search for needs around which to develop educational programs for the adults of his particular community. For the adult educator, the meaning of *need* may be defined dynamically in terms of the twin thrusts of value-related pressures within the community and the individual.

FUNDING

Once the adult educator clarifies for himself the meaning of the word need, there are other obstacles to the determination of community need. First among them is funding. Whenever the determination of community needs is proposed, the need for money to finance a study is cited as a justification for inaction. Yet the lack of funds is not a valid excuse; money is not the answer. Even when funds are available, there have been deficiencies in the accurate determination of need and the subsequent development of educational programs to meet that need.

Business and industry, for example, devote substantial resources to designing and conducting educational programs to meet manpower and production needs, and the study of individual needs for job training purposes has received ample support. Yet one analyst of manpower planning pointed to the absence of accurate identification when he stated, "Although a great deal has been written about the importance of manpower planning, much less has been written of what such planning involves or how to engage in it." [10] When funds were available, something was lacking.

It is true that the resources of most organizations, or of committees within organizations, concerned with the education of adults are not adequate to support intensive research to determine community needs, and subsidies do not fall like manna from either private or public sources. Elaborate studies *are* expensive, and intensive interviewing is beyond the physical capacity of the typical staff or program committee. However, a constant probing for additional information and the utilization of existing sources of information are not beyond the resources and the ingenuity of most adults who are interested in educating other adults.

To those who must support their programs of adult education by fee income, the observation is made that they might be able to increase their enrollments and fee income by learning more about the real needs of the communities they serve.

Margaret Mead commented on a pervasive inability to predict change—a shortcoming which bears no relationship to the financial resources of the agency—when she spoke on manpower planning as follows: "Our predictions have always been too slow and built for too few. . . . Before we get it built, every airport we build is too slow for the planes that are going to come into it. Every student union in the country is too small for the enrollment before the roof goes on. Our continuous inability to predict the rapidity of change . . . is one of the things I think we ought to ask some questions about." [11]

Important as funding may be for comprehensive studies of community needs, the existence of funds will not guarantee accurate determination of needs nor will the lack of funds prevent the improvement of understanding and knowledge of existing needs.

WORDS OR ACTION

One of the major deterrents to community analysis is a fundamental philosophic conviction which denies the existence of a social action component in adult education. The trade union or the Chamber of Commerce which educates for political action does not confront this obstacle, but many organizations and individuals do. The roadblock consists of the traditional notion that "education" is "objective," and objectivity in such a context means that the educator is passively neutral, that he favors or advocates no point of view and no action. One of the clearest statements of the case against social action was made by John Diekhoff when he said, "The object of a school is to bring about certain changes in individuals; it is not an object of a school, *qua* school, to attract industry to a community, to mow the lawn in a neglected cemetery, or to secure the condemnation of a slum area." [12]

Yet it may be necessary for someone to lead the way to the lawn-mower, and the adult educator may have to cut the first swath to give relevance to his course on "Grass-cutting as an Art" or the "Care and Maintenance of Cemeteries"—whichever it may be. He may also attend and speak at a public hearing on the proposal to condemn the slum area.

In action situations, the adult educator faces a dilemma. No matter how well motivated he may be by a do-good idealism, he cannot solve other people's problems. Even if he wants the lawn mowed or the slum condemned, his mission is not providing the people with a solution. His mission is providing the information, the understanding, the techniques, or the organizational framework which may make it possible for those people to solve their own problems in a concerted social, political, economic, educational thrust. To enable them to achieve a solution, he may have to take part in social action, but he must understand the difference between participating as an action agent to help the learning process and participating in an attempt to use his educational role to impose a predetermined solution to a dynamic problem. The adult educator has his role as a teacher; separate from that he has his role as an individual citizen. Although the two roles may support a single objective, they are not identical.

Adult education may lead to social action, and the adult educator may encourage social action, although the action taken should be the conclusion of the group and not the will of the educator. However, the possibility of resultant social action is no reason to forego an educational program.

UNCHANGING PROGRAMS

Another obstacle to coming to grips with problems of the community is the static nature of many programs of adult education. For a variety of perfectly good human reasons, programs tend to become frozen into a pattern of repetition from year to year. For programs which operate on fee income, the pattern may be that of continuing to offer what has proven successful in attracting students in the past. In another situation, the reason may be a narrow construction of purpose such as whether instruction in trade union leadership should be restricted to steward training and grievance procedure instead of being broadened to include consumer protection and preparation for retirement. In another case perpetuation of the old content may be the easiest path. The test should be the needs of the community, and the needs of communities change. A few years ago there was a lot of concern with automation and with the obsolescence of both materials and people. Today communities face new challenges of drug abuse, ecology, and violence.

Many successful adult education programs, including some which serve broad geographic areas with large populations, provide no instruction, discussion opportunities, or counseling in such areas as child development, civic affairs, racial tension, or the myriad of other problems and adult concerns which appear to exist within those communities. The programs succeed because they continue to offer what has drawn students in the past, but they fail to meet needs in other areas.

Is it possible that national participation in adult education remains at a low level—one in five adults—because the existing programs have not identified what the other 80 percent regard as their real needs and interests?

EDUCATIONAL NEEDS

A final obstacle in the process of determining needs is confusion on the part of the adult educator over his role. Education is the function of the adult educator, and his role must be that of the educator. He must concentrate on the educational needs of his clients. Those educational needs are rooted in the personal, family, economic, political, and social needs or deficiencies of the clients, but the adult educator is not a social worker or a clinical psychologist or a banker. His task is to provide information and to provide learning situations which will make it possible for the contributions of other professionals to be more effective than they would be if the educational activity did not take place.

The adult educator can help the unemployed person, but the adult educator cannot solve the man's economic problems. The unemployed person needs $5,000 a year income to support his family in the inner city. The adult educator can help the man to learn to read; he can help the man learn the skills of a stock clerk; he can help the man learn how to fill out an application blank and go through an employment interview; he can help in a variety of ways—but he is not going to provide the job which will meet the economic need. The educational program may make possible the satisfaction of economic, psychological, and social needs, but the adult educator makes his contribution through the provision of education rather than by providing employment.

Consequently, the determination of need by the adult educator should lead ultimately to the identification of educational needs which exist within the total problem area.

Recognition of the obstacles which may stand in the way of need determination can be a positive factor in taking action to ascertain that need.

Who Determines Need?

Much of the tension between the educational establishment and the community at large results from disagreement over who determines need, and adult education is no exception. The efforts of neighborhood groups to have a voice in determining school policy are a common part of the urban scene today. Adult education faces the same challenge from its clients in all of the communities it serves. Does the educator prescribe or does the client determine both the need and the solution?

The true pattern of adult education is that of a partnership in which the educator and the participants—students, discussants, conferees, or whatever—jointly seek to identify the need and to develop the educational program which will help the community to meet that need. Unfortunately, a prevailing pattern of the educator, or the institution or agency, has determined the need and offered the prescription (a course, perhaps). The client has viewed both the need and the prescription in a different light and has often failed to respond to the proposed solution.

The prescription pattern is not caused by the smugness of the adult educators. Much of it results from the institutionalization of adult education. National or state organizations develop and encourage educational programs, and local sponsors offer the national package without exploring the need for tailoring it to meet local needs. An example is the tendency of university extension—in this case a statewide operation—to develop courses without seeking the advice of residents of the inner city, a tendency which has led inner city groups to be critical of the universities. "Canned" courses of the Foreign Policy Association, the Great Books Foundation, or the Carrie Chapman Catt Foundation have had less of an impact than their sponsors hoped because they were dropped on a local community rather than developed by the local community.

At times adult educators feel that their continuing contacts with representatives of the community give them an expert knowledge of the educational needs. Homer Kempfer surveyed 500 directors of public school adult education and found that they rated themselves first in terms of competency to identify the educational needs of adults. They gave second place to subject matter advisory committees and third to temporary advisory committees for specific problems or courses.[13]

If it can be assumed that the temporary advisory committees for specific problems were composed of members of the groups which faced the problems, then it was only in the third instance that the directors went to the community for help in determining community needs. What was true of Kempfer's 500 adult school directors has remained true in many adult schools and in many other clubs and associations which conduct and support educational programs for their members or constituents or for the community at large.

In the last analysis, it is always the client who makes the judgment about his own need and what will satisfy that need. The voluntary nature of most participation in adult education leaves the ultimate decision with the adult who either enrolls or stays away. Even in captive audience situations, such as some industrial or military courses, the client makes the last decision because he does not have to listen or to put the precepts into practice.

The role of the educator in this relationship is not greatly different from the role of the municipal official in his contacts with the community. Many a well-meant civic improvement program has been bitterly opposed by those it was intended to benefit. The lesson some city fathers have learned is that of involvement and participation of the community in the determination of the need and the planning for the improvement. The same lesson, which is a part of the theory of adult education, seems not to have been learned by all adult educators. Determination of need requires a meeting of the minds between the educational planner and his prospective clients.

Counseling. When the educational program is of an advisory or counseling nature rather than a lecture, class, seminar, or problem-solving group, there is even more danger of prescription. The counselor is cast automatically in an all-knowing role. Regardless of the technique or method used, the counselor must be constantly alert to the role of the adult in identifying his own personal needs and in helping to identify the needs of his group.

Ways of Determining Need

There are many methods for getting information about individual and community educational needs. The methods include surveys, community study, checklists, interviews, questionnaires, suggestion boxes, community representatives, advisory committees, contacts with community leaders, listening, and the use of available data such as census reports. Unfortunately, the determination of community need is a complex continuing process which does not lead to instant and lasting solutions. Kempfer, in his survey of 500 adult school directors, concluded that "how to identify these needs and interests is the perennial problem faced by all directors of adult education." [14]

The task may be illustrated by the following chart which relates present and future programs, purpose, planning, and the community in a simple system of the flow of information:

COMMUNITY ADULT EDUCATION PROCESS

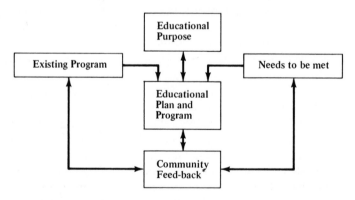

*Feed-back is more than evaluation and more than casual reaction. It is the total process of attempting to determine need, a process in which all sources of information and opinion are utilized.

Figure 1

One of the ways of determining need, not mentioned above, is the prescriptive process—by which someone decides what someone else needs. It is the process indicated by Kempfer's adult school directors when they said they were the best qualified to determine need. It is a process used widely by all persons who are planning educational programs for other persons. Arbitrary as the method may be, it is frequently accurate. For example, when there are large numbers of undereducated or illiterate persons, there is obviously a need for literacy training. When employees are raised to new levels of responsibility, there is need for training of various kinds. The first difficulty with the method is the problem of acceptance by those for whom the prescription is made. The second is that the method does not lend itself to the solution of complex or obscure problems.

Actually, all of the methods are valid under appropriate conditions. The chief difficulty is that the more intensive methods of community study and analysis are seldom employed despite the fact that they are practicable for most adult educators. The most commonly employed method is the survey, about which more will be said later. Malcolm Knowles suggested several practical, simple methods which included informal conversation, registration cards with space for entries pertaining to backgrounds and interests, and the installation of suggestion or question boxes where adults meet.[15]

The inescapable fundamental requirement to make any of the methods work is good communication by the adult educator within the community. His communication network must reach all segments and all levels of the community; otherwise, his program will reflect only the needs of individuals or groups with whom he communicates.

The role of communications in adult education was well expressed by Welden Findlay in a paper presented to the National Seminar on Adult Education Research:

[Adult education programs] function to identify existing needs of people —individuals, interest groups, communities, sectors of the economy, etc.— and to meet these needs by tapping existing sources of relevant information; they are, in essence, communication systems which, for their continuing viability, are dependent, first upon the continuing existence of sources of high concentrations of information relevant to areas of need within the system and secondly upon the ability of its professional personnel to identify important areas of need, to effect linkage with appropriate sources of information, and to guide the communication process toward need satisfaction.[16]

COMMUNITY STUDY

The most thorough method, and one which utilizes many of the other methods in varying degrees, is the full community study. Possibly the first proposal for community study in the literature of adult education was the procedure outlined by Gordon Blackwell to the members of the Association of University Evening Colleges in 1953. Blackwell said, "If you would know the needs and interests of your students, know the community." He also pointed out that there are community needs apart from the needs of individuals and that there are such things as community pressures.

Blackwell identified seven interrelated dimensions of the community which should be examined if program planning is to be aimed at the meeting of community needs. He emphasized that the seven dimensions were not watertight compartments and that he offered them as theoretical conceptions which might be "useful tools for understanding the community." He emphasized, also, the dynamic nature of the community and urged that the dimensions be considered only in a framework of social change; his outline was not a crystal ball. The seven dimensions which he suggested for study were the following:

1. *The population base.* He said, "If we are to understand the community, we need to know something about the human raw material that makes it up. Who are the people, what about their age and sex composition?" He included, also, the racial characteristics, educational level, mobility within the city, and migration into or from the city.

2. *The institutional structure of the community.* This he identified as "the complex web of organized social relationships which people have created in order to help them better meet their needs." He mentioned families, agencies, business and industry, the pressure groups, the civic organizations, and other special interest groups.

3. *The value systems.* Here his reference was to the value systems of the people, the things that they hold dear, the things that are high on their priority rating in the specific community. He suggested such qualities as neighborliness, hospitality, attitude toward government and its function, and their rating of security.

4. *Social stratification.* This he described as the way society layers the people of a community in ranges based on prestige.

5. *Informal social relationships.* He expressed the belief that the pattern of the network of interpersonal relationships is extremely important. He differentiated this characteristic of the community from the organized institutional structure and made particular reference to certain informal leaders who help mold opinion. Such an informal leader might be the shopkeeper known as the Mayor of Division Street. Blackwell suggested that the informal communications networks are what we often refer to as the grapevine.

6. *The power structure of the community.* He spoke of the "individuals behind the scenes who pull the strings that make things happen or can block things from happening in our communities."

7. *The ecology of the community.* This he defined as "the spacious

distribution of people and the other social aspects of the community, the way the community has been divided up in terms of functions, particularly social and economic functions." The ecology would include such community activities or characteristics as parking, transportation, location of institutions, housing areas, and recreation areas as well as the environmental factors which are so popularly described as the ecology of a community today.[17]

Samuel Hand also proposed community study as a direct aid to program development in adult education and offered three approaches to the study of the community. His first approach was the social welfare analysis of agencies, institutions, and services. His second was the study of the community as a social unit, an ecological approach which included the spatial and temporal relations of the people. His third was the problem-solving technique of using "the study itself as an educational process leading to social action." [18] Hand's suggestions appear in a Florida Department of Education pamphlet which also includes detailed checklists to help the adult educator make a thorough study of the history, the people, the economic structure, and the functional institutional operations of the community.

Community study is not a monopoly of the adult educator; it is a concern of practitioners in many disciplines, and some of the most helpful material comes from students in the other fields. For example, in the general field of educational administration, Wayland, Brunner, and Hallenbeck advocated study of the community for planning purposes. They said that the educational administrator must have an adequate knowledge of

(a) The values, mores, traditions of the community and important groups within it, and especially significant deviations from the norms of the Great Society. . . .
(b) The composition of the population of the community, its economic base, the pattern of social organization, the status and power structure.[19]

They suggested that data about the community be organized in the following three categories: (1) the geographical distribution of people and facilities, (2) the social structure, and (3) the institutional structure.

Checklists. Several of the writers who have been concerned with the determination of community needs have devised checklists. One of the simplest was drawn up by Otto Hoiberg, a community development specialist in the University of Nebraska Extension Division. His list consisted of only twelve items, such as business, education, cultural opportunities, recreational facilities, and the physical appearance of the community, and he rated the items on a four-step scale from "excellent" to "very inadequate." [20]

The most extensive set of checklists for analysis of a community is the compilation by Roland L. Warren for laymen and professionals in the field of social welfare. Warren deals with many aspects of the community, including its background, economic life, government and politics, institutions and agencies, communication, intergroup relations, and community organization.[21]

Sources of information. The prospect of a community study is frightening, but much of the necessary information is available and all available sources should be utilized. In addition to the census abstracts, essential information can usually be obtained from the local Chamber of Commerce, municipal agencies, departments of the state government, the county extension offices, the community relations departments of local industries, and librarians—to cite only a few.

SURVEYS

The most popular or most commonly used method of determining community need appears to be the survey or poll. Many persons seem to think that the survey is a simple method of obtaining information about educational needs, that the questionnaire or data sheet can be quickly prepared, and that the process may be easily completed. Warren devoted a chapter to "Organizing a Community Survey" and outlined a series of essential steps and decisions involved in the process. His suggestions apply whether the study is brief or extensive, whether it covers a whole community or only a part of it. He commented on the size and scope of the survey, its sponsorship, the cost, the organization of the survey committee, the job of the chairman, the preparation of the forms, the conduct of the field work, writing the report, and publicity and follow-up.[22]

There are dangers in the use of the survey. Questions must be perfectly clear. The typical survey provides a compilation of individual opinons. There is no way to register motivation. Despite such weaknesses surveys can be helpful.

To avoid ambiguity in the survey instrument, the adult educator can try to get expert help from people experienced in social research. Also, the instrument can be tested on a small group of potential clients in interviews which will permit questions to be asked and explanations given; thus the instrument can be improved.

Possibly the worst danger is the gap between interest as shown in a favorable response and the motivation required for participation in the program. Many adult educators have tabulated survey returns which indicated a high degree of interest in certain courses only to find insufficient response when registration night arrived. The only conclusion, when those surveyed failed to participate, was that the survey did not really discover a need.

The problem of survey reliability was discussed by Phillip Baumel in a Cooperative Extension Bulletin from Iowa State University in which he says:

In interpreting survey results, keep in mind that an opinion expressed on a questionnaire is only an opinion expressed at one point in time. It is not necessarily a commitment on the part of the respondent to act in a certain way or to support a certain issue when and if it comes to his attention again. Consequently, in interpreting the significance of answers to a community survey, it is usually wise to discount the extent of favorability expressed on certain kinds of issues. For example, a question on a survey may ask about opinions and desirability of school reorganization. Many may favor the general question. However, when and if this becomes a community issue and consequently more of the specifics concerning reorganization come out—such as location, particular schools involved, finances, building, etc.—many people who expressed a favorable attitude toward reorganization in general may be opposed to a particular reorganization plan. Consequently, as a general rule, ask specific questions.[23]

POWER STRUCTURE

One source of information about a community should certainly be the people described by Blackwell as able to make things happen or prevent them from happening. The term *power structure* became a part of the community worker's vocabulary because of Floyd Hunter's book on that subject, an analysis of a large community. Many persons believe that the power structure is the most important dimension of the community. While it is true that the power structure probably determines the success or failure of fund-raising campaigns and wields strong influence in political and economic matters, the concept of a small group of people who determine the needs and policies of a community is becoming outdated with the new, militant slogan, "power to the people." The ruling clique is still there, but its influence and effectiveness is being challenged by People Power activists.

The role of the power structure, however, cannot be ignored by the adult educator. It is still the people of the older power structure who authorize and administer tuition refund plans for their employees, who may grant or withhold time for participation in special educational programs, who may provide or obtain public or private financing of essential adult education adctivities, and who may encourage participation in adult education by other methods. The power structure must be understood if the community is to be understood.

Hunter's power structure consists of the following four elements, in order of their community importance:

1. business
2. government
3. civic associations
4. society activities [24]

Although most people may concur in the number one rating for business in order of importance, an adult education class of police officers in a large city unanimously contended that government was the primary element in the power structure. Subsequent conversations with community antipoverty workers produced the same contention that government had more muscle than business.

Possibly the most important finding to the analyst of the community may be Hunter's conclusion that the patterns of leadership and power in the minority community and the community at large are different. The power structure in the black, Puerto Rican, or Mexican-American community is not a mirror-like reflection of the white community's power structure. For example, Hunter pointed to a much stronger role of clergymen as power figures in the black community than in the city at large. His lesson to the adult educator is that he who searches to locate needs through the power structure must determine the specific power structure of the specific clientele before he seeks to utilize that power structure to help determine the community's needs.

Structural change. The power structure concept, of course, is valid only if there is such a structure. In a fluid society of dissent and protest, there may be situations in which no power structure exists: a dynamic condition of fluctuating change with the power shifting between the establishment and the dissidents, and moving in a confusing way from faction to faction within each temporarily dominant group. Consequently, the power structure concept, useful as it is as a guideline, may have to be utilized with more caution than was the case in 1953.

Also, from the eddies of change, the individual may emerge as a more powerful figure than he formerly was. If that is so, the adult educator must be not only perceptive but also flexible as he attempts to gain an understanding of the community's needs. He must be more willing to go to the community to gain the active participation of his clients in the planning process, which includes both determination of need and design of the program to meet that need.

COMMUNITY LEADERS

The notion of dealing with the power structure is not too different from the principle of going to the community's leaders for information about the community. In this sense the concept is not unique. Many adult educators know that you must start with the leaders in many situations to gain acceptance and support as well as to get their help in determining needs.

Cooperative Extension has always worked with the leaders of the agricultural community and with the power structure of the counties in which the agents carried out their educational activities. One of their reasons for going to the leadership was to obtain "legitimizers." In other words, if the leaders endorsed a program there were seldom questions about the authenticity or legitimacy of the enterprise.

A major study aimed at the identification of community needs in Tennessee involved interviews with selected citizens and community leaders. The procedure was described as follows: "[The study] sought to make a valid identification of community needs through interviewing the people in a community who could provide information on (1) the problems which existed in their area, (2) the nature and extent of each problem, and (3) the priority for solving these problems. Selective processes, such as stratified random sample by census tracts or districts of the study area, were utilized in determining local citizens to be interviewed. In addition, interviews were held with selected officials in each county, such as elected chief officials of counties and municipalities, county judges, school superintendents [and other elected officials as well as lay citizens]." [25]

One of the difficulties in going to community leaders is discovering who, among the so-called leaders, can really speak as a representative of a larger group. Indeed, many leaders in central city districts will state that they speak only for themselves in matters such as educational needs. When that situation is faced, the adult educator must take the time to deal with large numbers of potential clients.

Advisors. One adaptation of the community leader approach is the utilization of key persons as advisors, either as individuals or as members of advisory committees. The local directors of adult education surveyed by Kempfer suggested that needs could be discovered through utilizing "coordinators" in the local industries and throughout the community. The coordinators kept on the lookout for opportunities to develop adult education programs.

Advisory committees have been widely used, especially for specific projects. Cooperative Extension has utilized advisory groups for agriculture, home economics, and youth work. Such committees may be standing organizations, or they may be ad hoc groups whose term expires when the project is under way.

LISTENING

In almost every method of determining need, the art of listening is an important, if not the chief, factor. Coordinators and advisors have messages to which the adult educator must listen. Interviewers, counselors, and administrators must listen. The suggestions of participants and community leaders must be heard. Much can be learned by listening.

The most extreme case of listening as a means of determining community need was described by a state director of Cooperative Extension some years ago. He told of a county agent who shall henceforth be known as "The Whittler." According to the director, this agent was the best diagnostician of community needs he had ever known.

The agent's technique was simple and direct. He would go into a rural community and seat himself on the porch of the general store. He was a confirmed whittler, and he would take out his pocketknife and a block of wood and sit there and whittle. As he whittled he listened to the conversations within earshot. At the end of the day, it is alleged, he would know all that it was necessary to know about the needs of that community.

Conclusion

Much has been and is said about designing adult educational programs to meet the needs of people and their communities. Yet there is little evidence that many serious efforts have been made to identify such needs systematically. Too much reliance seems to have been placed on arbitrary prescription or on the inertia of institutions.

However, there are many ways to determine the educational needs in an area or among the members of an organization, and the successful adult educator utilizes some or all of these methods.

The educational "establishment" is under attack at all levels, including adult education, for a lack of relevance. The key to relevance is the identification of need.

Notes

1. Harry L. Miller, *Participation of Adults in Education; A Force-Field Analysis* (Boston: Center for the Study of Liberal Education for Adults, 1967), p. 3.
2. Paul E. Bergevin, Dwight Morris, and Robert M. Smith, *Adult Education Procedures* (Greenwich: Seabury Press, 1963), p. 14.
3. Horace M. Kallen, "Needs of the Individual," in *Purposes of the Evening College: Reflections in 1953*, James B. Whipple (ed.) (Boston: Center for the Study of Liberal Education for Adults, 1967), p. 15.
4. Bernard W. James and Harold W. Montross, "Focusing Group Goals," *Adult Education*, vol. 6, no. 2 (Winter 1956), p. 96.
5. Bernard W. James, "Can 'Needs' Define Educational Goals?"; *Adult Education*, vol. 7, no. 1 (Autumn 1956), pp. 19–20.
6. A. H. Maslow, "A Theory of Human Motivation," *Psychological Review*, vol. 50, no. 4 (July 1943), pp. 372 *et. seq.*
7. Carol Schlamp Kramer, "The Diagnostic Process in Adult Education" (Bloomington: unpublished M.A. thesis, Indiana University, 1960), p. 11.
8. Samuel E. Hand, *An Outline of a Community Survey for Program Planning in Adult Education* (Tallahassee: Florida State Department of Education, Bulletin 71 F-2, April 1968), p. i.
9. Eduard C. Lindeman, *The Meaning of Adult Education* (New York: New Republic, 1926), pp. 8–9. Reprint with new preface and notes, Montreal: Harvest House, 1961.
10. Eric W. Vetter, *Manpower Planning for High Talent Personnel* (Ann Arbor: University of Michigan, 1967), p. 3.
11. Margaret Mead, *The Changing Cultural Patterns of Work and Leisure* (Washington, D.C.: Manpower Administration, 1967), pp. 5–6.
12. John S. Diekhoff, *The Domain of the Faculty* (New York: Harper & Row, 1956), p. 165.
13. Homer Kempfer, "Identifying Educational Needs and Interests of Adults," *Adult Education*, vol. 2, no. 1 (October 1953), p. 34.
14. *Ibid.*, p. 32.
15. Malcolm S. Knowles, "Your Program Planning Tool-Kit," *Adult Leadership*, vol. 1, no. 1 (May 1952), p. 15.
16. Weldon E. Findlay, "On Identification of Critical Behavior and Related Major Concepts Relevant to the Training of Professional Leaders in Extension Education." Paper presented to the National Seminar on Adult Education Research (February 1969), p. 1.
17. Gordon W. Blackwell, "The Needs of the Community as a Determinant of Evening College," *1953 Proceedings.* (St. Louis: Association of University Evening Colleges, 1953), pp. 27–34. Reprinted with revisions in *Purposes of the Evening College; Reflections in 1953*, James B. Whipple (ed.). (Boston: Center for the Study of Liberal Education for Adults, 1967.)
18. Hand, *op. cit.*, pp. 8–10.
19. Sloan R. Wayland, Edmund deS. Brunner, and Wilbur C. Hallenbeck, *Aids to Community Analysis for the School Administrator* (New York: Bureau of Publications, Teachers College, 1956), p. 3.

20. Otto G. Hoiberg, *Exploring the Small Community* (Lincoln: University of Nebraska Press, 1955), pp. 16–17.
21. Roland L. Warren, *Studying Your Community* (New York: Russell Sage Foundation, 1955).
22. *Ibid.*, pp. 312–319.
23. Phillip C. Baumel et al., *The Community Survey: Its Use in Development and Action Programs* (Ames: Iowa State University of Science and Technology, 1967), p. 28.
24. Floyd Hunter, *Community Power Structure* (Chapel Hill: University of North Carolina Press, 1953), p. 11.
25. *The Identification of Community Needs in Tennessee, The Statewide Report on a Community Service and Continuing Education Program* (Knoxville: Tennessee University, State Agency for Title I, May 1967), pp. 6–7.

Selected References

SAMUEL, PHILLIP C. et al. *The Community Survey: Its Use in Development and Action Programs.* Ames: Iowa State University of Science and Technology, 1927.

ESSERT, PAUL L. *Creative Leadership of Adult Education.* Englewood Cliffs, N.J.: Prentice-Hall, 1951.

HAND, SAMUEL E. *An Outline of a Community Survey for Program Planning in Adult Education.* Tallahassee: Florida State Department of Education, Bulletin 71 F-2, April 1968.

HOIBERT, OTTO G. *Exploring the Small Community.* Lincoln: University of Nebraska Press, 1955.

HOULE, CYRIL O. *The Inquiring Mind.* Madison: University of Wisconsin Press, 1961.

KEMPFER, HOMER. *Adult Education.* New York: McGraw-Hill, 1955.

KNOWLES, MALCOLM S. *The Modern Practice of Adult Education.* New York: Association Press, 1970.

SANDERS, H. C. (ed.). *The Cooperative Extension Service.* Englewood Cliffs, N.J.: Prentice-Hall, 1966.

WARREN, ROLAND L. *Studying Your Community.* New York: Russell Sage Foundation, 1955.

CHAPTER THREE

The Functioning of Boards and Committees in Adult Education

LEONARD NADLER

Dr. Leonard Nadler is a Professor in the School of Education at The George Washington University, Washington, D.C.

THE USE OF COMMITTEES and boards is a hallmark of adult education. Since the tremendous expansion of adult education activities at all levels in the early 1950s, there has been a need for adult educators to work with a staggering number of committees and boards.

Frequently, the only way that funds could be obtained for adult education activities has been by developing committees and boards. In some instances, for legal purposes, a committee or board has been a necessary element of adult education programs.

Committees and boards are not merely legal artifacts. They are people. This fact has underscored the necessity for adult educators to be able to work effectively with groups of people in achieving individual and organizational goals.

Definitions

There are specific differences between boards and committees. Of course, in a particular situation the terms may be used loosely by those involved. For our purposes, a *board* will be seen as a legally constituted body. It will have been required either by the state law under which the organization is incorporated or to meet some other legal requirement. Essentially, the board is inflexible. The size of its membership and its functions are usually set forth by legal requirements or the bylaws of the organization, which have legal force.

A *committee* is a much more highly flexible arrangement, usually working within the framework of a board. It is possible to set up a wide variety of committees without the legal force implied by a board. As we discuss the kinds of committees and the nature of their work, it will be seen that the committee is a much more viable instrument for achieving both immediate and long-range goals.

There are various kinds of committees. In recent years new designations have emerged for what is essentially a committee. Among these are the terms *task force, project group,* and *action group.* It is likely that newer terms will evolve to describe what is essentially the same phenomena, a temporary organization of individuals endeavoring to achieve stated goals. There is a growing tendency in some places, particularly the United States, to become involved in temporary societies.[1] The changing needs of our society have underscored the desirability of creating various forms of temporary arrangements whereby individuals can join together to meet their mutual needs.

Carl Rogers has pointed out that "the modern human being wants to reduce his alienation, wants to be in personal contact with other persons."[2] Committees—and, to a lesser degree, boards—provide this opportunity for individuals. They can relate in smaller groups, have the feeling of involvement and achievement which comes from such relationships, and be fuller persons. In our larger voluntary membership organizations there is the constant problem of alienation. The organization grows in size, and grows away from its members. Business organizations have similar problems. The current efforts at organizational development (OD) are concerned with changing organizations as well as individuals. Among the more commonly used techniques in OD is the development of small groups of a temporary nature to probe for ways to make the organization more meaningful and relevant to individual and organizational goals.

HISTORICAL PERSPECTIVE

It is not possible to write a history of the specific use of committees and boards in adult education as it varies from organization to organization. However, certain trends are obvious and the reader is encouraged to leaf back through issues of *Adult Leadership* from its inception in the early 1950s to today. This magazine more than adequately reflects the trends in adult education.

In the early 1950s there was extensive use of committees and boards. Much of adult education was at the community level and training for board membership was an important factor. Committees abounded and, if anything, adult education leaders could claim to have been "committeed to death."

As we moved into the later part of the 1950s and the early 1960s there was less committee and board activity. When boards still had to exist because of legal necessity, a common complaint was that people would not serve on them. Inactivity of adult education in committees and boards at this time was unfortunate. The 1960s brought a new wave of social consciousness and involvement among the American people. Some elements of the adult education community were not prepared for this. However, stimulated by the Economic Opportunity Act of 1964, with its provision for community action, there was increased involvement and once again a proliferation of boards and committees.

The exciting story of the community action boards and committees of the 1960s is still being written. Their impact on American life is far from over, and whole groups of Americans have found ways of influencing their environment. Some of the defeats have been cited by Daniel P. Moynihan.[3] However, there are also some victories and many lessons to be learned. A book edited by Cahn and Passett [4] is appropriately subtitled "A Casebook in Democracy." The importance of the committee and board activity was that larger numbers of our citizens became involved. It also became apparent that there was a need for more than merely designating committees and boards. Training for leadership became a significant aspect of such membership.

With the advent of the 1970s we have a new generation—those born in the post–World War II era. They came to maturity during the early part of the decade and by force of numbers and enthusiasm have indicated very strongly that they "want a piece of the action." The use of committees and boards as one aspect of involving individuals in their own goal setting and task accomplishment becomes once more a very significant element of adult education.

Committees

Committees involve a unique form of participation in adult education. Not merely bringing together a group of individuals interested in working together, a committee must have a functional area and a purpose. There is a typical life cycle for a committee which is important if it is to be successful. Planning and understanding of these three aspects (function, purpose, and life cycle) are essential when using committees.

FUNCTIONAL AREAS

An overview of functional areas can be seen in Figure 2. It is not meant to be comprehensive, as individual situations will bring forth other functional areas meaningful to the organization or group involved. However, the functional areas identified are those most commonly found in vital and viable organizations. There is no hierarchy. They are purposely listed in alphabetical order and will be discussed in that order. At any particular moment in the life of an organization, one or more of these committees may be more essential. At one time most, if not all will be functioning.

An *activity* committee is one established to conduct a particular kind of limited task. It will have a fairly short life—to accomplish the specific task and then be dissolved. It may be established to raise funds for the organization or for a particular part of the organizational program. This is fairly common, as most of our voluntary organizations constantly need funds to accomplish organizational goals.

Even a private business organization may find that this becomes necessary; the activity committee may then be charged with the function of identifying new sources of capital.

Other activities are possible—finance is not the only purpose. An activity committee may be established to support a particular individual for local or national office. It could be concerned with cleaning up the community, or encouraging people to use fewer one-way bottles and cartons as an aspect of reducing pollution.

The activity committee has a specific goal and short-range objectives which can be identified and even measured. It can provide satisfaction for members who need to see tangible results of their efforts.

The *administrative* committee is probably the easiest to identify. Very few organizations can survive without committees in this area. An executive committee is part of most organizations. It is the operational group with a delegation from the board to carry out the ongoing operations of the organization.

Administrative committees are usually not places for creativity. This is unfortunate for in most cases the administrative committees spin off the other functional committees discussed in this section. When the administrative committees are considered less important, the leadership of the organization may be placed in the hands of more pedestrian members. Inevitably, such members prefer to stick to the book and are less likely to engage in risk taking; therefore, gradually, the organization does little but repeat its past history. Organizational leaders must find ways of making administrative committee assignments more challenging.

A *coordinating* committee can serve either internally, within the organization, or externally, in relation to other groups or organizations that are not part of the parent organization. Internally, the coordinating function may be among several committees, all responsible for different phases of an activity or program. They can benefit from being kept continually informed of what the others are doing. Such a coordinating committee is sometimes developed by having representatives from the other committees sit together. Within business organizations a group known as an executive committee is commonly used. In many cases it functions as a coordinating committee.

In our complex world today, with its proliferation of committees, various groups sometimes find themselves concerned with the same issue. In this case a coordinating committee can be made up of representatives of the various groups, all concerned about one particular issue. For example, if there is a felt need for a traffic light at a school crossing, we might find that a coordinating committee has been established which includes representatives of the local civic organization, the businessmen's organization, the PTA, the student government, and the police. In a sense, each member of the coordinating committee represents some other organization as well as himself.

TYPES OF COMMITTEES

FUNCTION	EXAMPLES
Activity	fund-raising campaign cleanup project
Administrative	personnel membership finance
Coordinating	with other community organizations with other committees in the organization
Dialogue	unstructured discussion of organizational activities
Inspection	of health and sanitary facilities of institutions
Judicial	grievances hearings bylaw revisions
Program	education leadership training
Study	of particular topics, as selected by members

FIGURE 2

In the search for meaningful relationships among people, a newer form of committee is the *dialogue* group. Such committees are not yet well known although they are beginning to emerge. They are typified by being less structured than most committees. For example, if a religious organization is seeking to improve its physical facility, it might establish dialogue groups of members who meet in a rather informal, unstructured fashion in the homes of the various members. They would meet to discuss the organization, their relationship to it, and the kind of physical facility that might be appropriate. The group does not prepare a report or make recommendations but, rather, the small group situation gives members an opportunity to share their ideas and their hopes.

On a more formalistic level is the *inspection* committee. Such a committee is formed when there is a need for an outside body to oversee the efforts of an institution or an installation. Some of the government schools, conducted for government employees, use a device known as a board of visitors. Essentially, this is an inspection committee which visits the school to review the facilities and curriculum as related to school objectives. Federal and state institutions in the health, welfare, and correctional field also utilize these types of inspection committees, composed of persons outside the organization who provide the inspection functions.

A variety of related functions are grouped together under the heading of the *judicial* committee. Essentially, this kind of committee is concerned with legal or semilegal events. The committee may be established by a union-management coalition to hear grievances. It may review the bylaws of either the business organization or the community organization in order to make recommendations for revisions. On our college campuses we are finding the use of a judicial committee extremely important in the form of student courts. They are not courts in the legal sense that they have the powers of courts in our land. They are more akin to the judicial committees that are providing a basis for communication within the organization, related to the application of certain of the organization's (i.e., the university's) regulations.

The *program* committee is probably one of the most popular. Most organizations have instituted kinds of programs to achieve their goals. These programs may be related to education, legislation, or production. In each case the committee has an ongoing program for which it has some responsibilities. It differs from the activity committee discussed earlier. The activity committee has a single function; when it achieves this it usually dissolves. The program committee is related to the ongoing and continuous aspects of the organization and will more closely parallel changes in administration or goals.

The last committee type that we shall discuss here is the *study* committee. This is a group of individuals within the organization who come together to explore a particular topic. Usually, this would be a topic selected by the members, but within the role of the organization. Such committees are sometimes called learning groups—but they behave in all respects much like committees. They have a parent organization, a determinable life, and the possibility of changes of membership. In some cases the study groups might come under the program committee—but organizations are finding that there is need for more flexibility than is found in the usual program operations. Study groups are a new kind of committee formation and we should be watching them closely as they develop.

PURPOSE

A committee should not be organized merely as a mechanism for involving members in the organization. The committee approach can provide this opportunity but the purpose is more important than merely establishing enough committees so that they will appeal to all the membership.

Committees should be established when there is a need. For some organizational activities the need for a committee is obvious. A review of the functional areas discussed earlier makes this clear. However, no matter what the functional area, there are a variety of purposes. These are listed in Figure 3. When a committee is established, its purpose should be clearly stated and understood by all.

The purpose provides limits but it can also provide new horizons. Whichever the direction, the committee members and their organization should have a clear set of mutual expectations.

When the purpose is *advisory*, this must be clearly understood. Such a committee must recognize that its advice is sought, which is not to say that the advice will be followed. The committee with this purpose calls upon the vast resources available within and outside the organization to get the best advice possible. It can call on the wide range of experience and expertise abounding in most of our communities and organizations.

The advisory committee may be assisting the board, an officer, another committee, or a group. The basic purpose of this committee is to listen to the problem or situation and to provide advice or suggestions.

A committee whose function is coordinating may have as its purpose the advisory role. Examples of such committees are cited by Burt.[5] He describes the use of advisory committees in cooperation between schools and industry in the area of vocational programs.

Being a member of an advisory committee can be frustrating to some of the activist-inclined practitioners of adult education. They are more inclined toward action than advice. If the purpose is not

PURPOSES OF COMMITTEES

ADVISORY

—to advise other elements of the organization

—to provide technical and professional resource persons to other organizational activities

FACT FINDING

—to gather data

—to determine the specifics of a situation or event

PROBLEM SOLVING

—to generate alternatives to a problem

DECISION MAKING

—to make decisions for the organization, usually based on advice, facts, and alternatives supplied by other committees

IDEA CREATING

—to produce innovative and creative ideas about a given area, with no responsibility for performance on the ideas

FIGURE 3

made clear, the activist committee member may be less than effective in his advisory capacity.

The *fact-finding* committee has as its purpose the gathering of particular information. This can be data related to budgetary expenditures, numbers of students who might enroll in adult education programs, or the position of a congressman on a piece of legislation. The function of this committee is to find the facts and to stop at that point.

Gathering the facts may not be easy. Usually, it requires special skills or access to specific sources. The purpose should be clear—the committee is only to gather the facts, and is not expected to go beyond that point. But the committee will also need to know the reason for gathering the facts, and possibly the intended purpose. To find the exact recorded vote of an elected official may sometimes be easy, as in the case of Congress. The *Congressional Record*[6] is the basic source. However, the fact-finding committee will also have to explore the ways in which congressmen are permitted to make changes in this record. Also, the questions a congressman asks in committee hearings will also be part of the facts which must be gathered.

If the fact-finding committee is dealing with a grievance, it may have to question a large number of people on all sides of the issue, as well as become familiar with the basic document which sets forth the rights of all the concerned parties.

A committee can be established with a *problem-solving* purpose. Such a committee may be an outgrowth of a fact-finding committee, or it may have been established with the specific purpose of solving a problem. In the latter case, it may also come close to making decisions but will frequently stop just short. In other words, it will propose alternative courses of action which might solve the particular problem.

There are many models for problem solving. Among these are the scientific or deductive method (involving several planned steps), the intuitive or inductive method, or the use of a force-field analysis. Whatever method the committee chooses should be directly related to this purpose of problem solving.

One of the commonest problems is that of involving membership. Too often the functional membership committee is not encouraged to approach it as a problem. Rather, it is encouraged to go out and increase membership, and therefore urged to mount a major drive. Too seldom does the committee approach it using problem-solving techniques. The end result desired is increased membership, but what is the problem? Is it not enough new members or the lack of renewals from old members? Until the problem is clarified, the membership committee may find itself merely going through some annual rituals concerned with numbers.

A *decision-making* committee is one which is expected to make specific decisions regarding activities of the organization. In many cases the decision may have to be ratified by the membership or approved by the board, but the committee itself is expected to make a specific recommendation on a decision. The committee may investigate its own facts, but it may also take the materials produced by other committees, bring them together, and then make a specific decision. This is very common on a task force committee where subgroups of various kinds have generated concepts which may be in conflict. It now becomes necessary for one committee to take this and make the appropriate decisions.

The decision-making committee may not be the same committee

which has to implement the decision. This highlights the necessity for a committee to relate its purpose to its function. The decision making may be done by an administrative committee, but then the implementation may be in the province of a program or activity committee.

It is sometimes helpful to organize a committee just to deal with facts or make decisions. The purpose of this committee is merely to create ideas and to engage in "way-out thinking." Such a committee may find it helpful to engage in brainstorming or a variation known as synectics.[7] One approach to the creative kind of committee is in the work done by Parnes and others in creativity.[8]

Such committees are used too infrequently. Yet they can be extremely helpful in encouraging the innate creative activity which lies dormant in so many people. In our society too many rewards are given for results, and not enough for ideas. In the absence of a restructuring of society, it is still possible for some groups and organizations to build in the recognition just for ideas. Our private sector has tried to do that for years through suggestion systems; however, these were based on individual creativity. We are finding that as people can stimulate each other, the small group or committee can be an effective instrument for developing creativity and ideas.

Readers who are committee members have probably had some difficulty with this section on purposes. They have been members of committees which operated in the area of more than one purpose. The problem-solving committee was also fact-finding. The idea-creating committee found itself making decisions. The advisory committee was also generating ideas.

This is usual and expected. The difficulty is that when multipurpose committees are organized, this should be clearly stated. The committee members and the parent organization should both be aware of the purpose. If the purpose is to change, this is acceptable if all concerned are in agreement. When either the committee or the parent organization without mutual agreement, alters the purpose after establishment of the committee, chaos and frustration must result.

Within a committee the shifts in purpose should be understood by all. If not, there is the danger of different committee members proceeding on the basis of different purposes. Such a committee is doomed to failure.

Some committees go through the formality of starting each meeting by restating their purpose. This may be too mechanistic for some but it does serve as a constant reminder of the purpose. It can save the time of committee members and contribute to a more successful committee experience.

COMMITTEES IN OUR ORGANIZATION

NAME OF COMMITTEE	FUNCTION	PURPOSE

Completed by: _____

(NAME OF INDIVIDUAL)

Date: _____

FIGURE 4

There are few organizations of any kind which function without committees. There are many of us who are members of more than one committee within a single organization. Many of us are members of committees in many organizations.

A challenge is presented in Figure 4. Can an organization list its committee structure and differentiate among the various functions and purposes? The reader is encouraged to try this within his own organization. The perception of various leaders in the organization as to the function and purpose of each committee is a good place to start. Then each committee member might be asked to respond using the same instrument. A review of all the responses will provide a significant way for an organization to review its committee structure.

LIFE CYCLE

A committee, much as any organism, needs a starting and stopping point. Usually, it is fairly easy to identify the starting point, but it becomes much more of a problem to identify the stopping point. A committee, once formed, may continue to function even though its origi-nal purpose is no longer vital or necessary.

The life cycle of a committee will vary depending upon the purpose, the organization, and the individuals. It is possible, how-ever, to indicate a generalized life cycle through which a committee should move. If it gets bogged down at any one of these points, it is then possible for those responsible for the committee to recognize that there are difficulties and to reexamine the committee's purposes, its membership, and its functions.

A typical life cycle is illustrated in Figure 5. A committee starts with *identification of needs*. It is unwise to organize a committee merely to involve members—the committee must have a purpose and function which is clear to all those concerned. The need may arise from actions of the governing body, the needs and interests of the members, or a local situation.

Very early, those responsible for organizing a committee should be sure that a committee is the appropriate response. There are other ways for us to effectively meet some of our needs without forming committees. However, once it has been determined that an organiza-tion has a specific need for a committee and for a determined func-tional type of committee, then the decision can be made and we are now ready to move on in the life of a committee.

A committee should not be asked to start its life without specific in-structions. The intent of these instructions is not to suppress the crea-tivity of the members or to direct the outcome of the committee's work. It is, however, important that the committee have a clear idea of the expectations of those who organized it, and of how the commit-tee relates to the overall functioning of the organization.

Committee Life Cycle

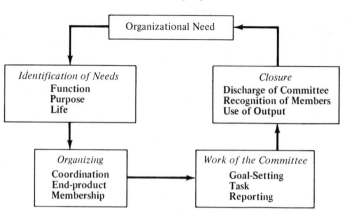

Figure 5

The purpose of a committee has been discussed earlier. This is important for we must be sure that those responsible for making the decision that a committee should be formed are in general agreement as to what this committee will do. If those who established the committee are in agreement as to its purpose, it is more likely that the committee will meet the specific need for which it has been created.

The life of the committee should be stated, to the extent possible. Frequently, in a membership organization, the life of the committee will parallel the life of the elected officers. If the officers are elected for one year, the committee is expected to have a one-year life. In other circumstances the committee's life will be determined by the fiscal year of the organization. If the fiscal year starts on July 1 and ends on the following June 30, then it is usually expected that the committee will have this same life. In other situations the normal calendar year of January to December may be the guiding factor.

Administrative committees are usually set up in a pattern which reflects the calendar of the organization. Program and activity committees are more likely to be limited to the life of the particular program or activity. However, none of this can be left to chance—or to the supposition that everybody knows what has been done in the past.

Vagueness as to life allows for too many misunderstandings. It is better to designate a specific time period whereby the committee will be considered to have finished its work, although there is always the provision for extending the life of the committee. Such a stated time is also helpful when it comes to inviting individuals to join a committee. They are more likely to accept such responsibility when they are aware of some kind of determinate life rather than merely an open-end situation. If the life span is unclear, members cannot know for what period of time they are committing themselves.

Now the committee can begin its own *organizing* phase. In addition to the total life of the committee, it is also helpful to establish checkpoints. This may be related to specific reporting dates with which the total organization is involved. For example, if there are quarterly progress reports, the committee may then be expected to relate to this time frame. It may be that the nature of the committee work indicates several major checkpoints at which time the committee is expected either to issue interim reports or make oral reports to the governing body which created it.

A committee is usually a part of something larger. Therefore, there is the need to coordinate the work of this committee with that of the larger organization. This coordination may be accomplished by having either the chairman or a representative of the committee relate directly to the total governing body. Another aspect of coordination may be worked out, such as minutes of the committee meeting being provided to a member of the board designated as ex-officio on all committees. At any event, there is an important relationship between providing an opportunity for committee members to be creative and self-directing, as contrasted with the need of the organization to have some feel for how the committees are functioning.

The coordinating function is also important to avoid overlap. A committee may start to function and then find the actual operation of one committee appears either to duplicate or conflict with that of another committee. It is not helpful to have these committees competing with each other, with the resultant waste of energy and frustration. This was evident during the days of the President's Task Force on the War Against Poverty in 1964 when innumerable committees were established with many overlapping parameters. Some of this was necessary by virtue of the newness of the activity and the inability of anybody to clearly establish parameters at that point. Indeed, it would have been self-defeating to have attempted to impose a rigid organization upon an emerging and very fluid situation. However, the managerial concept which pervaded the task force was that of "creative conflict." This meant that committees were set up having substantially the same assignments, in the hope that through this competition with each other they would perform at their highest level. It became counterproductive as soon as an individual discovered that others had received substantially the same assignment as he. Without the benefit of coordination, the results might tend to be determined more by individual relationships within the organization than by professional output. Many individuals left the task force who could have been productive if there had been a higher level of coordination between the different committees and the task forces.

When a committee is established, the purpose will also indicate the possible end product. Usually, it is not desirable to be too rigid in this. As the committee evolves and does its work, it may find other types of end products than those originally conceived. However, the expectations of these people designating the committee should be made known to the committee members. Are they expected to prepare a report, a pageant, a drafted piece of legislation, or a speech? The expectations of the parent body as to the output of the committee should be stated, but with the possibility that the committee members themselves may find alternative ways of sharing the end product with those concerned.

The instructions to the committee need not be arbitrary. They should be carefully written so as to express the intent of those organizing the committee but not so rigid as to crush the individual initiative of committee members. Where the committee finds that it takes exception to the instructions, the areas of disagreement should be brought out in the open and discussed as soon as possible. This will avoid the possibility of the committee continuing to do its work while deviating from the need for which it was originally established. All parameters of the committee should be understood by everyone concerned to the degree that any communication can be understood.

Too frequently, the *membership* of a committee is selected on the basis of who is available at a particular time—or whom we can encourage or coerce to accept this responsibility. When an organization must resort to this approach to the selection of committee members, there is probably some greater difficulty which cannot usually be solved through the normal committee process. Members should be carefully chosen for their ability to contribute to the basic purpose of the committee. It is also important to recognize that membership can serve other needs. For example, it is possible to identify individuals with high potential who have not yet been able to realize it within the organization. By involving them in committee work, we increase the possibility that performance will equal potential. Obviously, however, there is a danger in selecting a committee composed entirely of those with potential and none with a record of proven service. Those responsible for bringing a committee together should seek an equitable balance. The exact numbers of the performers and those with the potential will depend upon numerous factors, such as the purpose of the committee, the time in which the work is to be done, the loss to the organizational group if the committee does not perform effectively, and the need for involving other individuals.

Particularly in the decade of the seventies, when the baby boom of the post–World War II generation will be reflected in many more young people proportionately than we have had in the past, it is highly desirable that committee membership be shared with young people who have not previously been part of the organizational group. This is one way that the younger people can be encouraged to participate and bring about the changes which are so desperately needed by many of the organizations which use committees to reach their goals.

The question of size is important but difficult. Sometimes one hears that the best committee is made up of three people—one of whom is out of town and one of whom is sick! Though this is said about a committee in an organization, it becomes important to ascertain what this tells us about the use of committees in that organization. The leadership may still think of a committee appointment as reward and recognition, but the members may be seeing it quite differently. There is sometimes a tendency to determine size by a criteria leading toward decision making. A committee is sometimes composed of an odd number of individuals (as contrasted with an even number) so that when the committee votes there will not be a tie. This almost presumes beforehand that the committee is going to function as a legalistic group in which the power of a single vote can be extremely significant. If this is a possibility, there is some question as to whether a committee is the proper response to that particular situation.

Those responsible for identifying potential committee members have sometimes felt that they could use help from the psychiatrist and psychologist. Questions arise concerning the mixture of personalities and the motivations and drives which need either to be reflected among the committee membership or to be kept from the committee. The selection of members can very easily manipulate the anticipated outcome of the committee. Hopefully, for those who subscribe to democracy, the intent should be to assure that the committee reflects the variety of views on the particular issue for which the committee has been organized. Even on administrative committees there can be extremely different points of view concerning what seem to be almost mundane matters. Many a membership committee has found itself involved in more than merely increasing the membership of the organization. The composition of the membership of the organization can be severely affected by the nature of the committee and the way it reaches various parts of our population. What is being suggested is that the committee should not be "loaded" with a particular point of view but, rather, that committees be organized so that varying points of view are reflected and can be freely expressed.

Once the committee has been established, it must go through some initial stages of growth. One of the earliest is *setting goals*. As indicated earlier, the committee will have received instructions and its purpose will have been stated. Now the committee must restate the purpose in terms of the specific goals as seen by its members. It is dangerous to assume that everybody automatically agrees with everything set forth on the instruction sheet, or with the oral instructions to the committee. By taking the time to go through the process of group goal setting at the start, a good deal of useless effort can be reduced and the possibility of the deterioration of interpersonal relationships can be avoided.

Goal setting is not easy. The generalities under which the committee is organized are now reduced to specifics. The committee should allow itself sufficient time to engage in the goal-setting operation so that it is clear beforehand as to identified goals. Of course, there is always the possibility of the "hidden agenda," in which case it may not be quite so easy to identify the goals. Also, as the committee proceeds in its work, the goals must be continually tested to see that they are valid and reflect the ongoing interest and direction of the committee. Where it is ascertained that the goals selected by committee members cause a change in the basic purpose of the committee, they should return to the authorizing body which set up the committee and discuss it further. In going through the initial task of setting its goals, the committee clarifies certain issues which could be of immediate benefit to the organization.

With the goal-setting process, the work of the committee has begun. Now it moves on to the next stage of doing something about achieving its goals. This is the task operation period of the committee's life. Although the committee should be highly concerned with task, it should not ignore maintenance. These are two complementary functions which need to be present in almost any small group situation, but certainly in the functioning of a committee. The task function of the group is easy to identify, incorporating the discussions and actions the group takes as it works toward accomplishing its goal. However, we also know that it is important for a group to be equally concerned with the maintenance function or the interpersonal relationships which are so crucial when people work together on a common goal. See Figure 6 for a representative list of task maintenance functions.

Usually, the work of a committee results in some kind of report, project, or other final phase. There are very few cases where a committee should be permitted to merely function without in some way capturing its productivity and sharing its work with others who are concerned. This does not necessarily call for a volume of stenographic notes or an elaborate report. When the committee has finished its work, the total group to which it is responsible should be a little farther along in the particular area in which the committee has functioned. The highlights of the committee's accomplishments, as well as recognition of some of its frustrations, should be included for the guidance of the organization generally and as help to those individuals who may be following in the next sequence of the committee.

The content and form of the report are determined by the purposes of the committee as well as the projected uses of the report. If there has been a survey, it may merely be necessary to share this with various other members of the organization. If it has been a fact-finding group, the facts must be forwarded to those who can make the most use of them. In each case the function and purpose of the group may be the first guideline as to the nature and distribution of the report. But these should not be limiting factors.

Caution should be observed that the committee does not spend most of its time drafting a voluminous report which may be satisfying to some committee members but which will not result in the kinds of productive behavior for which the committee was originally organized. It is also a questionable use of resources if too much of the committee's time is consumed by preparation of the report. A com-

---

TASK MAINTENANCE FUNCTIONS

TASK

Initiating—proposing agenda items, tasks, goals, or objectives; suggesting new procedures or ideas.

Information Seeking—asking opinions, requesting facts, searching for relevant information about the topic under discussion.

Information Giving—stating beliefs, sharing opinions, offering data.

Clarifying—providing examples, restating information given by others, suggesting alternatives.

Summarizing—synthesizing related ideas, proposing a decision, restating positions taken by others.

Consensus Testing—finding areas of agreement, offering conclusion for group reaction.

MAINTENANCE

Encouraging—responding to others, being accepting of others.

Expressing Group Feelings—verbalizing the mood of the group, sharing one's feelings about the group, providing an opportunity for others to share their feelings.

Harmonizing—surfacing group conflicts so they can be worked on, reducing tension by reconciling disagreements.

Compromising—giving way to other positions in the group, admitting when wrong, willing to reexamine own status or idea.

Gatekeeping—helping others participate in the group, being alert to non-verbal cues signifying a need to participate, offering ways for others to share in the group.

Standard Setting—bringing implied group standards into the open, suggesting group standards.

FIGURE 6

---

mon practice, when a written report is involved, is to have the report drafted by a much smaller subgroup within the committee and then distributed to committee members for their reactions and approval. This can be time-consuming and may result in the surface indication that all are in agreement. At the same time, the report may not actually receive the attention and intense reading that it requires if it is to represent the consensus of the group.

When committee members are scattered throughout a wide geographical area, it may prove time-consuming to bring them together to review a final report. Sending it out by mail may fulfill part of the review function of the committee but it may then also require extensive correspondence which delays the report and lessens its effectiveness for the total organization. The use of modern technology can be helpful in this case. By sending out the report and then supplementing it with a telephone conference call, it may be possible to have the members of the committee provided with the opportunity to read the report and then to orally interact with each other as they discuss it on the telephone.

Modern technology allows for the possibility of other methods of reporting. Although a printed report provides for easy filing, it may not be the most effective vehicle for reflecting the work and the results of the committee. Other methods may be used very effectively for reporting and may be much more productive. For example:

Tape recording. Tape recorder and cassette tape recorders are found so commonly today that there should be little difficulty in using this as a media of reporting. It is possible on tape to have different members of the group give sections of their report and therefore capture, at least in part, the personality of each individual as he shares his thinking.

VTR. The Video Tape Recorder is less common, yet is increasing in its usefulness and availability. The committee may choose to report back by having a fifteen- or twenty-minute video tape recording of its final session or of its reporting session. This is shared with the members of the larger organization who can then capture more of the interpersonal dynamics as reflected in a real life presentation.

Projected devices. The overhead projector, the opaque projector, and the slide projector are all useful in presenting reports when the visual images are important. If there are statistics or other kinds of visual material which the entire group should look at, the reporting group may find that these devices can communicate much more effectively than an oral discussion.

Multi-Media. It may even be necessary and desirable to utilize a variety of other devices in order to communicate most effectively with the parent group. A professional production is not required. If attention is given to what we know about the most effective ways to communicate and a combination of audio-visual techniques is utilized, the report can serve the needs of the reporting group and the parent group.

CLOSURE

The work of a committee is not completed when it presents its report. This is part of the final process, but there are still some activities which must take place before it can truly be said that the work of the committee has been completed. In some situations the parent group which set up the committee should formally "discharge" the committee. This is not so much a legalistic step as a general affirmation to all concerned that this committee has now completed its function and therefore is no longer expected to conduct any kinds of activities as a committee. It is necessary that some specific activity be taken to discharge the committee just as a specific action was required to establish it. This lessens the ambiguity and confusion about the life of the committee, or about the fact that it has now been terminated.

Recognition should accompany discharge of the committee— although, unfortunately, this is too infrequently the practice. Particularly in those organizations where the committee work has been voluntary, the form of recognition is exceedingly important. As with most forms of recognition, it should not be paternalistic or demeaning. It should recognize the efforts of the individuals in an appropriate manner. This is not always easy to accomplish, particularly when the committee has a large and varied membership. However, some concepts of recognition should be borne in mind.

When an individual has been released by his work organization to take part in the committee, the work organization should receive specific and adequate recognition of this. The usual form is a letter to the committee member or his supervisor expressing thanks on behalf of the parent organization for the contribution made by the work organization through the efforts of one of its members. In a community group the recognition may take the form of a picture and/or news article in the local press expressing appreciation for the work done either by individual committee members or by the committee as a whole. When the work of the committee was long and arduous, a simple certificate signed by a prestige individual may serve as recognition. It has been a common practice among community organizations which rely upon committees for fund raising to have a certificate of appreciation presented. It is not uncommon to walk into an individual's office and find several such certificates gracing his wall.

In all cases the form of recognition should be appropriate. Nobody is impressed by an overstated letter of appreciation or a highly embossed certificate for a rather pedestrian committee assignment. This serves only to deprecate the work of those on committees requiring more involvement and more investment of time and energy.

In many cases the output of one committee becomes the input for another committee or activity. Usually, something needs to be done with the committee report, aside from merely filing it. It may be an administrative action, a vote by the membership, the establishment of a permanent group, or some other specific action that has resulted from the work of a particular committee. When this is the case, the original committee should have the ego satisfaction of knowing what was done with their work. They may merely be kept informed so that they know that the time and energy spent on their committee has not been wasted. Even when a report of the committee is listened to but then rejected by the parent group, committee members should know that this was the action. Then they will not be in the embarrassing position of questioning what happened to their report and eventually finding out that it had been tabled, hidden, or voted down.

Feedback to the committee members about the results of their final report can be helpful for their own information and education. It will also encourage them to take part in future committee activities when they know that their work will not be destined merely to gather dust on a shelf or in somebody's administrative file.

Boards

Although a board may to some degree go through the same life experience as a committee, the board is much more circumscribed by the laws which govern it and its actions are much more limited.

LEGAL BASIS

When a board is established, there has usually been some kind of legal action preceding it. If it is a board which is part of an established organization, the laws of the state in which it is incorporated may then determine the minimum requirements for membership on the board, and may also stipulate the specific actions which the board must take. It may even designate that the board must meet at least once a year or some other designated period of time.

When the board is set up pursuant to federal legislation, such as community action boards, some federal laws may then be applicable or there may be some specific guidelines or bylaws which had to be approved by the federal granting agency before the board could be approved. Notable among examples of this was the requirement by the Office of Economic Opportunity that a certain percentage of the board members must be from the area being served.

When one accepts membership on a board, one automatically accepts the legal restrictions under which that board must function. This does not mean that they cannot be changed, but they must be changed within the framework of law. The enthusiasm of individuals is wonderful but when one is a member of a board this enthusiasm is limited by some legal constraints. Rather than jeopardize the life and legality of the organization, the board members should either conform to the requirements or actively seek to have them changed. Ignoring legal requirements, no matter how good the reason, may ultimately serve as a hindrance to the effective work of the organization.

OPERATIONS

In many cases, a board has a prescribed agenda. This may be established by the legal form under which it is established, by the laws of the state, or by some other restrictive arrangement. This does not limit the areas the board can explore but sets at least a basic minimum that they must explore. In many cases the law requires that notice of meetings be sent out at some prescribed earlier date and also that the agenda be forwarded to members of the board at that time. This is important and helpful and should not be ignored.

In most cases a board is a decision-making body. It may utilize committees, not necessarily composed of board members, who prepare the various reports so that the board may act. When this has not been done, we find that the board consumes a tremendous amount of its own time in gathering data and performing other functions best done prior to the board meeting. As a result the board becomes frustrated in its actions. At the particular time it is meeting it does not have sufficient data or adequate time to digest the data so that decisions can be made. If the board does not make the decisions required by the nature of the organization, the entire organization is put in jeopardy. Certain work of the organization may come to a halt because the board has not been able to function effectively in making decisions.

A board, much like a committee, is made up of people. Therefore, the interpersonal relationships described earlier under the committee (task and maintenance) are also factors in the behavior of the board. The difference may be that the board does not meet as frequently as the committee and therefore finds itself caught in the trap of trying to make the most effective use of its time by hurrying to the task without having adequately taken care of its maintenance factors.

A practice of some boards is to take part of the meeting, usually at the start, to ask each board member to respond to a question such as "What is the most important thing that has happened in your life since the last board meeting?" Or another type of question that can be asked is "At the present time, what has you turned on?" Or "What are the goals in your life for the next six months?" Although the individuals may come to the board meeting representing groups or themselves, they are certainly individuals and the important values in their lives and the important goals they now have are obviously going to be important in the progress of the meeting. This is particularly important when the board meets only every six months or once a year.

MEMBERSHIP

The membership of the board is once again a matter that is legally decided. There are usually specific stipulations as to the minimum and maximum number. In some cases there is even a proscription as to where they may reside. When the board is incorporated under the laws of a particular state, it is common practice that at least one member of the board be a resident of that state. When setting up community action boards, as noted earlier, geography is an important factor. Such regulations should be carefully studied so that the membership complies with these regulations in establishing the board.

The duration of the board membership is, once again, normally established by laws or by other regulations and frequently there is even a carefully worked out procedure for filling vacancies should they occur during the term of the board. As the board is usually elected—rather than appointed, as in the case of the committee—it is likely that all members of the organization will have been involved in selecting the board members. This pertains whether the board is elected by stockholders or by community members. However, this does not cover all boards. There are still boards of education who are appointed by the mayor. Other types of boards such as public utility governing boards are sometimes appointed by the mayor rather than elected by the people. This practice varies from one locality to another and is usually a reflection of the history of the board in that particular locality. Frequently, to change the method of selecting the board requires elaborate legal procedures.

For many years a board was considered a rather separate body which met in secret and occasionally informed the public of its decisions. The tendency now is for open board meetings whereby any individual may attend, although he does not automatically have the right to take the floor and absolutely no right to vote on issues. However, the open board meeting is gaining momentum despite the problems of demonstrations and intervention with the normal processes of board operation.

Boards have also opened up their doors to nonboard members, due to the realization that it can be beneficial to have outsiders who can assist the board in solving a particular problem. This may be a person in the form of a resource person or in the form of a facilitator.[9] When a resource person is called into a board meeting, it is to give expert testimony or to lend his expertise to a particular problem with which the board is concerned—that is, the substance of the problem.

Recognizing the normal problems of interpersonal relationships, some boards have also invited in a process consultant. This person does not take part in the actions or deliberations of the board but, rather, is available as a resource should the board find that its interpersonal relationships are interfering with its successful operation. Obviously, the process consultant has no vote, and is a complete outsider focusing his attention on the method of discussion rather than its content. Although process consultants have proven helpful, this is not yet a common practice.

The Meeting

Both boards and committees have meetings. The essential work of both groups takes place in a more or less formalized gathering to which we can apply the term *meeting*. Although the board meetings are usually more formal than the committee meetings, there is a generalized procedure which affects both.

PREPARATION

Any meeting requires preparation. This goes beyond merely making an announcement. Indeed, if the preparation has not been adequate, it is very likely that the meeting will be less than successful. One of the first questions is whether this is a regular or a special meeting. Usually, boards have regular meetings that are determined at the beginning of the term of office of the board members, and usually all board members have been informed of the regular dates. This does not mean that they do not need some type of announcement, and this will be discussed later. However, the board members would want to know whether this is a regular meeting as previously scheduled or whether this is a special meeting.

Special meetings of boards can be called, but care should be taken that sufficient notice has been given when a special meeting is called. A committee has more flexibility in scheduling its meetings, but this should not extend to the point where nobody quite knows when the next meeting is to be called. Some committees find it desirable to plan two or three meetings in advance, as far as the dates are concerned. This is particularly the case when the committee is calling upon the resources of individuals who are active in a variety of organizations and therefore could have a conflict of dates. By planning two or three meetings in advance, it is possible to minimize the loss of good individuals because of conflicts with other previously scheduled activities.

Even when their dates have been established beforehand, it might be helpful to do a quick check of the members to see if all can come. As we are dealing with people, we have to expect the normal situations that occur in anyone's life. The minor tragedies of burned fingers, broken dishwashers, or unexpected visits by relatives are problems to which we all are heir. Sometimes a few selective phone calls can indicate beforehand that even though the meeting has been agreed upon earlier, it might be better to postpone it to a later date because several of the members will not be able to attend.

There should be provision for somebody, usually the committee or board chairman, to react to whether the meeting should be open or closed. That is, in addition to the regular members, should other people be allowed in? More to the point, should people be specifically invited because they can contribute to the work of the committee at this time? Sometimes this is done even though the individuals cannot commit themselves to the regular ongoing work of the committee or board. The nonmembers may be able to lend some small amount of time at a point when the committee or board can use their particular inputs.

The meeting should have an agenda. That is, the content of what is to be discussed and the sequence should have been explored beforehand. Particularly in the case of the committee, there should be a great degree of latitude in altering the agenda as the group meets. A board does not have quite this much flexibility. In the preparation stage the agenda should be tentative, and it is helpful to send it out far enough before the meeting to all those who plan to attend. They will then have time to react to the content of the agenda in terms of their particular needs and interests.

Many agenda items require the preparation of specialized materials. These may be reports, visuals, position papers, and other kinds of materials which will contribute to understanding of the points to be discussed. The preparation of these materials may be assigned to specific individuals on the committee prior to the meeting. At times a previous meeting may have produced certain materials or spun off a subgroup which has now produced materials to be reviewed at the following meeting. Care should be taken that materials reach participants in advance of committee meetings. It is wasteful to bring a group of people together and at that time give them material which they must take time to read. It is also unfair to have one or two persons who have prepared the material, knowing it very well, then try to digest it in a few minutes for the group. As the discussion proceeds, it is very likely that one will frequently hear, from a member of the drafting group, "But we already have that on page 27." Or, "You would understand this if you had read our position as stated on pages 32 to 41." To avoid second guessing and to save time, materials should be carefully prepared and put in the hands of committee members well in advance of the meeting.

The meeting itself should take place in the most appropriate physical facilities. Certain basic rules of physical facilities govern any meeting, such as air circulation, adequate light, accessibility, freedom from outside interference, and so on. However, it is not always possible to have the optimum facilities because of budget, time, and place of meeting. To the degree possible, the physical facility should lend itself to the topic of the meeting and the purpose of the group. A committee which is going to inspect a prison must expect that there will be a great deal of walking and restrictions on their freedom of movement. They may even find that at the termination of their walking visit there is a less-than-adequate physical facility in which to hold a committee meeting. On the other hand, it may be to their advantage to have the meeting right on the spot despite any physical inconvenience so that if additional questions arise personnel are available to respond, and there is an opportunity to reinspect a particular aspect of the facility.

Personal comfort of the committee and board members must also be considered. When the board is part of a large organization, it is not uncommon for food to be served as a part of the board meeting. Adequate provision should also be made for the coffee breaks which are an essential part of almost any American group meeting. The breaks provide not only for gastronomic rejuvenation but are an important part of the entire group process and be given particular attention.

In planning for the personal physical comfort of the participants, attention must be given to religious and health needs. If the group includes individuals who do not eat meat, any food served must then include provision for vegetarians. If some of the participants in the group do not take stimulants (coffee, tea, liquor), there should then be other beverages to meet their needs. Of increasing importance in these years is attention to smoking. Some individuals appear unable to function in a group situation without the constant reinforcement of tobacco. A delicate point arises when other individuals in the group —because of allergies, respiratory ailments, or personal preference— find the smoke offensive and unbearable. It becomes important, then, that this possible area of conflict be discussed early enough so that it does not become a major issue. If the smoke in the room becomes oppressive, some individuals may find they have to excuse themselves as their eyes tear and their throats tighten up. This may have nothing to do with the topic under discussion at the moment but it could be interpreted that way. Attention to the general needs of all participants becomes an important part of the agenda.

ANNOUNCING THE MEETING

For board meetings the announcements must be formal. For committees there are options which extend from formal announcements to very informal telephone calls. No matter what the form of the announcement, the intent is that it be effectively communicated to those who need to attend. Each group has certain standards which indicate the most effective and meaningful ways that such communications can be presented. When there is a close and ongoing relationship within the group, a formal announcement may be seen as needless and obstructive. It is important that the particular method of transmission, as well as the content of the announcement, be appropriate as related to the history of the group and the purpose of the meeting being announced. Sometimes the announcement can be a one-way communication—from the person making the announcement to the various members. More frequently, the members are asked to respond as to whether or not they will be able to attend a particular meeting. This form of acknowledgment emphasizes the fact that the communication has been received as well as providing data on how many of the group will be able to attend. Knowing this data prior to the meeting can be significant in terms of having a large enough group represented as well as the particular members who would be addressing themselves to specific agenda items.

It has been suggested above that other materials be sent out with the agenda. It should be emphasized that there needs to be adequate time to study the materials. However, merely sending out the materials does not guarantee that they will be studied. In addition, when the board or committee members are busy people, there is the tendency to put the materials aside so that they can be taken to the meeting. This does not insure that they are read beforehand. When it is essential that the materials be studied beforehand, some type of reaction instrument might be included. It might be a self-directed instrument in which the individual reader of the material can record his own reactions. It might be an instrument which requires that the individual respond in some way. This may be a short instrument—questionnaire, checklist, punch card—which is then sent back to the member who has the responsibility for announcing the meeting. This latter approach is extremely important when it is necessary that the materials have been adequately studied beforehand and that each member come to the meeting prepared to discuss specific items. It also allows the members to gather additional data, develop their own materials, or in other ways prepare themselves for the meeting. This avoids the possibility that during the meeting the member may feel that he has pertinent data sitting home in his files but he was not aware that it could contribute to the success of this particular meeting.

The announcement should contain specific information as to the length of the meeting. Most of our meetings are measured in terms of hours, but they may also be a matter of days, especially when the committee or task force has a particular function which must be accomplished within a specific time limit. Also, when individuals come from long distances, an attempt is usually made to reduce the travel time and expense by having a longer meeting. Those invited should have some indication of when they are expected to arrive and the outside limit as to when they will be able to depart. This should not be a signal that the meeting must continue that long even if the tasks are accomplished, but that unless unusual circumstances intervene the meeting will go no longer than the announced time.

The place where the meeting will be held must also be stated. If the board or committee is coming from a variety of distances, the place may influence the amount of travel time and money required and therefore be a factor in whether or not an individual can attend a particular meeting. Also, when the expenses are being paid by the organization rather than the individual, selection of a place can be extremely important in terms of the budget allocated to the board or committee for its meeting.

Boards and committees are finding it advantageous to "go off the ranch." (That is, to select a meeting place far enough away from the usual attractions of a city, but not too close to the individual's home office.) This diminishes the tendency for outside factors to interfere with the effective progress of the board or committee. Responding to this, specialized conference sites have sprung up throughout the country. An added factor when using such facilities is that at times there are different kinds of dress requirements. For example, most special facilities urge that individuals dress informally for the meeting. However, some also require that jackets and ties be worn for dinner. The particular dress expected should be carefully stated beforehand so that no member comes to the meeting without the necessary range of clothing that may be required or desired.

Leadership Training

Being a member of a board or committee consists of more than having the available time and having been elected or selected. It is now recognized that such membership involves the need for special training to meet the demands of these roles.

There are a variety of experiences available, and in some cases the organization provides them as part of its function. For example, when one is elected to the board of a local chapter of the American Society for Training and Development, he automatically becomes eligible for board member training. These sessions are held periodically throughout the country.

Interpersonal relationships are very important and board and committee members are sometimes provided with variations of laboratory training (sensitivity, encounter, awareness) so that their interpersonal relationships can be improved.

Much still needs to be done in this area. Too many organizations are still operating on the assumption that board and committee assignments can be handled by anybody. Perhaps they can—but they can be done better when appropriate leadership training is provided.

Notes

1. Warren G. Bennis and Philip E. Slater, *The Temporary Society* (New York: Harper & Row, 1968). This is a provocative statement regarding temporary groups and our democratic concepts.

2. Carl Rogers, "Involvement of the Psychologist in Social Problems," *Journal of Applied Behavioral Science,* vol. 5, no. 1 (1969), p. 6.
3. Daniel P. Moynihan, *Maximum Feasible Misunderstanding* (New York: The Free Press, 1969).
4. Edgar S. Cahn and Barry A. Passett (eds.), *Citizen Participation: A Casebook in Democracy* (Trenton: New Jersey Community Action Training Institute, 1969).
5. Samuel M. Burt, *Industry and Vocation-Technical Education* (New York: McGraw-Hill, 1967).
6. The *Congressional Record* is a valuable source of material. Obviously, most of it is concerned with what our elected representatives say on the floor of Congress (after some editing). In addition, there are usually insertions of vast amounts of data which would be helpful to many readers, and too expensive for most to research by themselves. It is available for $18 per year (published each day Congress is in session) from the U.S. Government Printing Office.
7. William J. J. Gordon, *Synectics* (New York: Harper & Row, 1961). This book presents the basic idea in clear form which is usable by any group seeking to improve its idea creating output.
8. Sidney J. Parnes, *Creative Behavior Guidebook* (New York: Charles Scribner's Sons, 1967). Presents exercises designed to increase individual and group creativity.
9. One way of looking at the different kinds of consultants that might be used by a board or committee is contained in Chapter 10 of my book *Developing Human Resources,* Gulf Publishing Company, 1971.

CHAPTER FOUR

Volunteer and Professional: The Role of Adult Education

HELEN M. FEENEY

Dr. Helen M. Feeney is Assistant Professor of Sociology and Coordinator of Continuing Education and Community Services at Queensborough Community College of the City University of New York, Bayside, New York.

IN THE UNITED STATES of America today there is a vast amount of activity and an equally great number of people engaged in, or related to, the adult education movement. Librarians, trade union officers, community center directors, managers, firemen, counselors, first aid instructors, evening school teachers, county agents and extension specialists, public health directors, clergymen, social agency staff, and even city, state, and federal legislators are all a part of this picture. "These practitioners," says J. R. Kidd, "have been trained in some other field than that of adult education but they are expected to display superior competence in many skills and fields of knowledge. Yet (few) . . . have paid much attention to adult learning." [1]

A police captain may be called upon to organize a series of discussions with diverse ethnic and racial groups in his precinct, a librarian desires to conduct a workshop on how to serve the functionally illiterate, or a labor union official working with a pressure group needs to train shop stewards and organizers in human relations techniques. All of these individuals are concerned in planning and conducting educational programs for adults but do not consider themselves "professional adult educators." Some of them will be setting up programs for staff and volunteer workers, for community groups or organizations with few, if any, professional staff, and often with people of diverse experience offering their services without pay. The latter may be part-time resource people or consultants, retired business executives, educators, physicians, writers, artists, and the like. Social agencies and community organizations in general have boards of directors or trustees who give generous amounts of time to policy-making and advisory service in order to further the purpose and work of a respective organization or agency. These people bring prestige and special skills to their volunteer jobs but are often in need of orientation to purpose, program, and personnel. How is this done? Who does it? Are educational guidelines available and where? What problems might be encountered and how are they handled?

In order to answer these and other questions that may arise in planning and conducting educational programs for adults, it is necessary first to look at the setting in which volunteers, staff, and professionals acting as resource people and consultants, perform.

The Many Roles of Volunteering

The men and women by the thousands who offer their time, talent, and skills as community workers, officers of service clubs, leaders of discussion groups, hospital and school aides, church and youth leaders, executive volunteers and fund raisers, are participating in a long-cherished tradition in America. They are giving service without pay, volunteering to work for, and with, the community or group, in order to provide an unmet need, to improve conditions, or to remedy a wrong. Many of them have been working in projects for as long as three years or more and expect to continue. Some give limited service, it is true, but many serve month after month, year after year, and would not do so if the experience were not personally satisfying. Some have found that working as a volunteer can lead to a paying job. They may have started volunteer work with no other goal then to give their services but later were asked to assume specific responsibilities and a schedule on an employed basis. Others have never before volunteered for community service and may never have felt any obligation to do so but are now helping with grass roots projects and ad hoc committees in their own neighborhoods.

Along with these people are the professionals who volunteer outside their own jobs—the trained social worker, county agent, hospital supervisor, clergyman, executive, nurse, and experienced organization president with whom other volunteers will work closely. Some volunteers will not work directly under a professional staff member but may call upon professional resource people or consultants for help in carrying out their respective volunteer jobs.

To work successfully with volunteers, certain skills and qualities are vital: sensitivity, thoughtfulness, interest in and concern for people, the ability to listen and to identify with them, and a genuine respect for their skills and their strengths.

Let us take a few examples.[2]

Mrs. Brown comes in to report for her first morning's work as a volunteer. She is in her late sixties and has recently lost her husband. You know from having talked with her that she feels completely lost, is desperately lonely, is unaccustomed to making decisions, feels she has no skills, and appears to be afraid of responsibility. In her place, you would approach the morning's work, as she does, with fear and timidity. What can be done to make Mrs. Brown feel that she is a responsible human being, who has come to give the most valuable thing she has—her time—to an important cause?

Perhaps introducing her to the other workers, indicating that this is Mrs. Brown's first day, that she lives close to Mrs. Jones, that she has come to help get the newsletter out. The explanation to Mrs. Brown about the work itself, which is necessarily routine, would embody in it the relationship of that work to the program, so that Mrs. Brown may see the value of her job in its true perspective. She is not just folding pages of paper. She is making it possible for the people in the community to learn what is going on. Here she is one of a company of people who are sharing in the same effort—the writers of the newsletter, the volunteer who cut the stencils, the people who made the news, those who ran the sheets off on the mimeograph machine, the volunteers who will address and stamp and mail them. The feeling of having a job to do, the sense of belonging, begins.

At 10:00 A.M., the coffee hour, everybody is ready for a slight break and conversation, including Mrs. Brown. She is getting used to her job; it goes faster now; she wants to learn more about what the others are doing. By lunch time she seems to be part of the regular staff. Would Mrs. Brown like to join Mrs. Jones and the secretary, who are sending out for sandwiches, or would she prefer to go out to a restaurant with Mrs. Smith and the file clerk? In either case, she has become a member of the group and feels her acceptance.

On her next workday, Mrs. Brown may be given another phase of the newsletter job to do. As time goes on, the agency will learn the things about her that can be counted on—her punctuality, her strong sense of responsibility, her inability to do a shoddy job, her quickness in learning. As she succeeds in one task after another, her willingness to tackle new jobs will grow; her potential strengths, unused before, will have a chance to develop. Within a few months Mrs. Brown may be in charge of the corps of people who get the newsletter out.

The next volunteer may be completely different. He is Mr. Graham, an architect, an exceedingly able one with a justifiably high opinion of his ability. He is a very busy man—much too busy to fritter away his time, he points out—but he does feel a sense of obligation to his community and wants to help in any way he can. A sensitive recruiter will know that this is not a man to put on a committee, that he is not at his best as part of a team. Instead, in an advisory capacity, Mr. Graham will be called on when there is a specific job to do; he will be performing an exceedingly valuable service, and he should be made to feel its importance to the purposes of the organization.

Suppose the next volunteer is Mrs. Sandowsky, a top-flight secretary before her marriage. Motherhood has made it impossible for her to continue her working career. She is not at her best as a housekeeper, feels dissatisfied and frustrated. She needs an outlet for her skills, and the organization needs her abilities. Flexible arrangements are made for Mrs. Sandowsky to come in daily for dictation, when she is out shopping. This is work which can be transcribed at home and returned the next day at the time of the baby's outing. Mrs. Sandowsky's letters turn out to be masterpieces of accuracy and beautiful typing. As the weeks pass and she takes on different kinds of secretarial work, it becomes apparent that she has a creative, searching spirit and a gift for organization and administration. Perhaps the agency's administrative and organizational problems can be shared with her. Perhaps she can be encouraged to develop new and more effective systems of operation. Ideas can always be developed at home and discussed with appropriate personnel at a later time.

Mr. Amato presents a different problem. He works at a job he dislikes because family responsibilities make it impossible for him to break away and start afresh at a smaller salary. He seems to be a thoughtful, clear-thinking, objective person. He likes people and wants to be useful, but he has no special skills and no time during the day. He thinks well of the idea of block organization through which neighbors work together to solve the problems common to their blocks. He even points out a number of problems on his own block that cry out for activity. But he does not think of himself as a leader. "You get someone else to start a block organization," he says, "and I'll help out." The director of volunteers believes that Mr. Amato does have leadership qualities, but he does not argue with him. Instead, the director asks whether he would consider getting a few of his neighbors together in his home to discuss the problems of the block? After an evening's discussion, they decide to have a general block meeting, at which Mr. Amato is made a member of the steering committee. As the block group develops and carries out a number of projects, Mr. Amato's qualities of leadership become increasingly evident. He establishes himself as the finest type of leader—one who stimulates others and brings out the potentiality for leadership in them rather than one who does all the work himself. Mr. Amato is selected to represent his block at the monthly meetings of all block leaders, and eventually becomes a member of the Board of Directors.

There are other examples as well. In a large metropolitan city, for instance, a semiretired businessman may offer his services to a newly organized volunteer bureau. He has had years of experience in the real estate field and the recruitment-interviewer assigns him to act as a coordinator between tenants and landlords in a controversial urban renewal project. While working in the rundown neighborhood, he becomes interested in a private social agency specializing in help to the aged. His talents as a liaison person interest the agency and he is offered a part-time job with them. Now he combines his volunteer work and his part-time job feeling a sense of renewal as he enters a second "career."

A college-educated housewife, volunteering to work on a local hospital newsletter, finds that she had the qualifications for a long-unfilled paid job on the hospital staff. She accepts it and manages to continue her volunteer work two evenings a week.

In one way or another, these people have found satisfaction in their work as volunteers and may even have found a way to another form of employment. But most of them feel the volunteer experience is the one that counts and may even express regret, as one woman did, when family and the job required that she relinquish her volunteer work, saying: "In some ways I was happier as a volunteer. There are certain regulations and restrictions when you are a paid employee."

Whatever the value of the contribution to a cause or a service, these volunteers became *involved* and found satisfaction in their work. They were part of something that was important, something in which they felt needed and wanted, and which encouraged their growth and development. Tricks and gimmicks are not necessary if the climate for involvement and freedom to grow exists. The form of involvement will vary in different organizations—hospitals, mental institutions, youth agencies, neighborhood associations, service organizations, or civic groups. The form of personal development will differ as well, for it may be growth in the ability to work with people, in developing patience and empathy, in deepening perception and understanding, rather than in the development of leadership qualities or learning new skills and techniques, important as these are. The principles, however, remain the same.

Building Sound Relationships

While it is difficult to list a specific set of instructions on how to work with the volunteer or lay "expert" who is offering his or her services as a consultant or advisor, there are some guiding principles [3] that will build worthwhile relationships among people and in organizations, social agencies, and the community at large.

1. *The first assignment should be simple enough to ensure success.* The jobs people are given to do must be within their skill and experience, especially in the beginning. A little success goes a long way in maintaining interest. Frustration at the outset may discourage many individuals, even to the extent that they will not return. On the other hand, care should be exercised in placing a highly skilled volunteer in a job that offers a challenge to him.

2. *People work best in a friendly, warm atmosphere, where their efforts are obviously needed and appreciated.* An agency can create such an atmosphere by seeing that the volunteer is made to feel a part of the working family, by expressing appreciation when it is deserved, by treating each volunteer as an individual human being, by remembering the small, thoughtful things that make each person feel that he or she is making a unique and special contribution.

3. *Volunteers must see the relationship of the job they do, however small, to the total effort.* While it may be boring to type cards for a file, the job becomes important when the volunteer knows how the cards are to be used, and when he realizes that his work will make it possible for everyone in the organization to have immediate access to a record of people who can be called upon for various kinds of essential work. Even in the most routine job, the volunteer can be given an opportunity to consider ways of doing it.

4. *Volunteers should be made to feel the importance of their contribution.* What, exactly, does the volunteer's work mean? Has it provided a service otherwise impossible? Has it opened the way for others to give their time and talents? Has it resulted in improvement to the community—what kind and in what way? Has it saved the organization money or released funds for essential uses? The volunteer has a right to know what his contribution means to the organization,

and the agency or organization has an obligation to communicate this.

5. *People work best when there is an opportunity to learn and to grow.* Interest stops when there is stagnation. People are unwilling to do the same jobs over and over again. Continued involvement demands new challenges, the provision of opportunities to try new methods and new skills, the kind of supervision that broadens horizons, the encouragement of potentialities for growth and development.

All people have strengths, although many are so modest or have so little self-confidence that they do not recognize their own potentialities. It is up to the volunteer supervisor or director to unearth these strengths and put them to use. In so doing, an invaluable service is rendered to other human beings and unsuspected gifts are released in the service of the cause or program of the organization or agency.

6. *Volunteers should be encouraged to make as many decisions as possible.* Growth is evidenced by the capacity to make intelligent decisions. One of the hardest tasks in an organization (particularly in a democratic, citizens' organization) is to refrain from making all the decisions. It may be simpler to do so, but it is wiser and healthier for the organization to encourage the volunteers to make decisions within their respective areas of competence. This does not mean, however, that untrained individuals should be allowed to make decisions in strictly medical or clinical fields, for example. But volunteers can comment upon and offer solutions to long waiting hours on hard benches for outpatients, on more suitable visiting hours for families, or on planning recreational programs in the wards.

There is a very fine balance between knowing when to step in and when to remain on the sidelines. Generally speaking, people can be trusted to act with maturity if you treat them as responsible human beings; if you give them the facts and a sense of direction about agency or hospital policy and programs, they will more often than not make intelligent decisions.

The people who work for an organization care about and are sincerely interested in what happens to it. It is important to keep volunteers, "outside" resource people and consultants, informed about developments in the organization, whether or not these developments are directly related to their respective jobs. The people who are contributing their time and their services will feel more intimately involved if they share with the staff knowledge of problems and crises as well as new programs and successes.

7. *Continued participation depends upon recognition and reward.* Volunteers and outside experts contributing their time, talent, and

skills must not be taken for granted. They do not owe the staff or the organization anything. They might be doing any number of things for pleasure or for profit. Instead, they have chosen to spend their time performing a service. Undoubtedly, that service gives them satisfaction or they would not have made such a choice. But your appreciation of the things they may have given up and your recognition of its value should be nonetheless real.

Rewards vary with volunteers. They may be concerned with self-expression, recognition, the need to feel useful and important, the desire for new knowledge, the need to meet new people, the feeling that leisure time is used for social ends, a desire to solve community needs. An agency should stress the meaning and value of the service rendered and provide proper recognition of it. If an agency is sensitively concerned about people and their feelings or about the growth and learning potential of individuals, it will not have to worry about the reputed problems of volunteer-staff relationships, about complaints on the use of professional terminology and rigid institutional procedures, or about so-called threats to the security of the professionals and other paid staff.

At times there may be failure in working with volunteers. Emergencies often limit the time for conferences, for example, or it may not be possible to assign tasks appropriate for a particular individual. Perhaps a staff member has had a long day of crises and aggravations or the personality problems of the volunteer have been too difficult to handle smoothly. But there is always an adult education role in working with volunteers and in that capacity we know that people can learn; that problems, if properly identified, can be resolved; and that, through effective group experience, individuals can develop mutual awareness and sensitivity to each other.

In the pamphlet *What Makes a Volunteer?* [4] Melvin A. Glasser notes the importance of the agency's obligations to its volunteers by building sound relationships between the professional staff and the volunteers. "Volunteers work best," he says, "when they feel that they are treated as equals by the professional staff—or as partners in a joint enterprise. The staff member is not superior because he is a professional and on the payroll. The volunteer himself may be a professional in another field or trained for a highly skilled service. A few professionals treat the volunteer in a spirit of tolerance or benevolence. . . . Volunteers are usually not playing at a job. . . . They resent being looked down upon as 'amateurs.' On the other hand, some volunteers seem to feel that their social or financial position, or their superior skills, give them the upper hand. The solution to this problem comes when both the professionals and the volunteers *are sure of their special skills and their jobs* and are thus able to work out a good relationship." (Italics added.)

The Professional as Volunteer

Professionally trained volunteers may spell the difference between an effective program and an indifferent one. The librarian, artist, or public relations man is usually pressed for time—whether on the job, working in the community, or endeavoring to spend more hours with his family. He may have offered his services for a project and had an unfortunate experience or, as is often the case, he may not feel challenged by the prospective volunteer assignment.

Yet many a professional—a pastor in a city parish, for example—may need to enlist the services of other professionals from his congregation or community because the church program includes a number of responsibilities for which neither he nor his curates have had training or even experience in handling.

These difficulties are not insurmountable, however, if the pastor can assure the specialist that his services are honestly needed, and if freedom to develop ideas and express convictions about the program are encouraged. Should the church's religious goals and the professional's techniques appear in conflict, a common meeting ground can often be found. Most people are happy to serve their church in an area where they feel competent. A banker can serve on the board as a trustee of investments; a librarian can supervise the parish information and library service; a public relations man (or woman) can assist in the preparation of the monthly bulletin or news publicity; an adult educator can recruit and train discussion leaders for a study group; a psychologist or an attorney can act as a consultant in a counseling program.

A number of colleges and extension centers have remedial specialists who volunteer to train home study tutors and reading aides in disadvantaged neighborhoods and many schools have retired teachers and principals helping in the classroom with children needing guidance in study skills and homework.

The clergyman, the educational administrator, or the police captain with an auxiliary corps of volunteer police patrols in his precinct must learn to work with these individuals as colleagues sharing a professional task or responsibility. All are citizens of the community and, as such, have a commitment to serve the community and its unmet needs. Each specialist is qualified for the task for which he has been recruited and, though one individual may give full time and be paid for his efforts on a regular basis while the other offers what "free" time he can and earns his living by his chosen profession or lives on a pension, each has a unique contribution to make. If this contribution is recognized and due respect given, there need not exist any sense of uneasiness or threat to job security. The pastor or the school administrator accepting the service will need to establish the climate for mutual acceptance and a commonality of interest. If a minister is emotionally insecure, a highly qualified volunteer may become a threat to his status as a leader in the community. A school principal, too, might wonder what could happen to his own positition if some volunteer "professionals" know more about educational policy than he does. If a chief librarian finds it difficult to work with people who want to think in new ways or act in a more experimental fashion, he may not find enough professionals of high caliber to volunteer for his community program. Sometimes a deep-rooted unwillingness to share responsibilities with others or to discuss new methods is rationalized as "It's a lot easier to do it myself." [5]

Sometimes there is difficulty in communication and nowhere is this more evident than across professional fields. There is an "in" language and a technical terminology in every profession and because one is a specialist in one field does not mean that either the language or the status position is transferable.

Sound relationships between the agency's staff and the outside professional who gives limited and unpaid service is a two-way street. A series of seminars or round-table discussions with both groups at the start of a cooperative endeavor may help to create better understanding and more unified goals. In most instances of this nature, an orientation to the agency's work or a short briefing session may appear to be all that is needed or all that most busy professionals are willing to attend. It behooves the agency staff, then, in their role of adult educators, to interpret the need for greater communication and request support for a longer peiod of "talking together" or getting-acquainted sessions. In addition to learning one another's roles and task responsibilities, the longer time factor allows for the development of positive attitudes toward each other and toward the agency or organization. If a sound educational groundwork is laid, future working relationships will withstand the pressures of emergencies and possible open conflict.

The "Ad Hoc" Consultant or Advisor

A great many organizations and community groups need help from outside advisors or consultants on a temporary basis. Who are these people specializing in a body of knowledge and who can be called upon to share it as a voluntary or unpaid service? The authors of a recent manual for community groups suggest the following:

1. From the professions: teachers, doctors, lawyers, scientists, social workers.
2. From the arts: musicians, artists, writers, architects, audio-visual and communications specialists, actor-directors, dramatists.
3. From the social sciences: psychologists, historians, economists, sociologists, statisticians.
4. From business, industry, and labor: personnel managers, education and training directors, sales and financial managers, engineers, technicians, designers, business agents.
5. From informal neighborhood groups: individuals who volunteer for tenant associations, local housing projects, senior citizens centers, playgrounds and parks, conservation projects.
6. From miscellaneous fields: recreation workers, community organizers, newspaper reporters, church leaders, librarians, military and defense personnel.[6]

In working with such outside advisors, especially on a temporary basis, it is important that the staff or officers of the organization or agency plan how to use and follow up on the skills and special abilities offered. A personnel manager of a large company, for example, may be asked to advise a committee desiring to employ recreational staff for a community project. As a personnel man, he can assist the committee by helping to clarify the jobs needed and the responsibilities entailed so that job descriptions can be prepared. He can provide information about salary ranges and sources of recruitment and caution the committee about state regulations on employment of minors, insurance coverage, and the like. As a busy officer in a company, he cannot, nor should he, *do* the job for the committee as he would in his own office. If the committee has planned carefully how it will use the limited time of this executive and has determined in advance how his advice and direction will be followed, the committee's work will then be productive and the executive will feel amply rewarded for his efforts.

The Board and Committee Member

Men and women who donate their time to leadership tasks in organizations as officers, board members, and committee members—whether elected or appointed—are generally defined as administrative volunteers. Usually, they are designated simply as board and committee members. A great number of these individuals who may be elected to the board of a community center, for instance, or who are appointed to serve on an advisory board for a local adult education program, want to be identified with, and feel a sense of responsibility for, the center or program they have been asked to support. Too often, however, board members complain of a sense of futility about the significance of their efforts. Reports are canned or predigested when presented at meetings, staff members are rarely known except for the executive director, the program and the clients or "consumers" of the program are even less known, and policy decisions are too often made on little or no factual information. The staff or a few officers appear to have all the knowledge and skills necessary to run the agency and unfortunately give the impression, usually by inference or attitude, that committee people are "amateurs" required by the by-laws to run the so-called public side of the operation. If all that is needed from a busy production manager facing an impending strike in his own plant is a signature on a document, why should he take the time to attend a meeting? If a member is asked to come to an Advisory Committee meeting when all the decisions have been made in advance, why should he bother?

Board members have a number of important duties to perform and one that makes great demands upon them is to understand, support, and interpret the agency's purpose and program. Very often this is the key to effective public relations and to successful personnel recruitment and financial support. This is true also of an Advisory Committee working with the Director of Adult Education in a public school system or a university extension program. Sometimes community understanding and even legislative support depend in large part on how clear and well informed the committee members are about the goals of the educational program, what services are provided, and where and how the money is spent.

As one writer has said: "People's attitudes don't change over-night. Let's face it: we must everlastingly inform and explain; we'll never get it made. We must use all the new media of communication, but let's not neglect the oldest—and I still believe the most convincing method—face to face conversation. Let's do it in the simple warm terms of the man on the street, unhampered by technical concepts and uninhibited by the language of experts." [7]

Direct Service and Membership Volunteers

Direct service volunteers are usually described as those who give their time to helping with program, conducting a social event, doing clerical work. They may be youth leaders, first aid instructors, hostesses in a hospitality center, information clerks at a reception desk. *Membership* volunteers are those individuals in an organization or club who are entitled to a voice in general operations or program planning. Usually, they have the privilege of voting for officers or delegates and may be eligible for elective office.

Both groups comprise the greater number of volunteers in a community. Their recruitment, placement, training, and development require both educational and supervisory skills. Discovering, motivating, training, and developing leaders for various kinds of activity and for diverse types of groups can be a challenge indeed for any organization.

For example, in the training of 4-H club leaders [8] we find:
New leaders want:

- explanation of their duties as 4-H club leaders
- information about the help available for doing the job
- training to understand young people better and how to work with them
- ideas about how to develop a recreation program
- personal consultation with the professional leader
- moral support from the trained personnel

Experienced leaders want:

- training in subject matter
- opportunity to share experiences with other leaders
- help with recreation activities
- help on how to obtain better parent cooperation

In order to meet the needs of these 4-H club leaders, the director of volunteers or training supervisor should have a knowledge of people and a comprehensive grasp of what the leaders should *know* and what they will have to *do*. This means an understanding of the full scope of a 4-H club leader and understanding of the educational process itself —how adults learn and how potential ability can be developed.

Volunteer training and development, once a new concept, now has widespread respect and support. Many individuals are engaged in agency training programs and are either developing materials or conducting actual training sessions. As trainers, as educators of adults, these individuals should possess the skills of teaching and guidance, together with the ability to communicate with varied and diverse individuals and groups. In their adult education role, trainers and supervisors should recognize the need for examining and improving content and methods in the training program. This is part and parcel of the evaluation process that should be undertaken by anyone concerned with the teaching of adults and should be undertaken on a periodic basis by all involved.

Supervision: An Educational Relationship

In addition to training, the direct service or program volunteer expects some guidance and supervision. The amount and degree will depend in large part on the task to be done and the ability and skills the individual brings to the job. It is the responsibility of the agency or organization to approach the supervision of volunteers as an educational relationship rather than as a management responsibility for overseeing work to be done.

If the educational or developmental aspects of supervision are kept in mind, there will be less personality conflict between volunteers and staff. Individuals carrying a supervisory role, however, will need to be aware at all times of the feelings of other staff toward volunteers. A highly qualified and able volunteer can often pose a threat to a new or even an experienced staff member. There is also the disappointment of the agency over volunteer "dropouts" or unreliable individuals who may require more time and effort than appears justified in terms of the work involved. These are "people problems," not volunteer or staff problems, and can be found in all groups. All supervisors need to recognize this factor and approach the task of supervising volunteers in terms of guiding people to do the best possible job in relation to what they have to offer.

If the supervisory task is considered an educational one, (1) the individual is allowed to maintain his or her personal integrity and self-respect; (2) the individual is given inceased motivation to work on the problem presented or the goal to be achieved; (3) the individual may be offered specific help on the task assigned or given a method or means to solve the problem or goal to be achieved. Both supervisor and volunteer worker may gain a greater confidence in themselves and increased ability to cope with their own difficulties as the result of such an approach.[9]

The educational relationship, then, becomes a problem-solving one for both supervisor and volunteer. In the process of conferring, discussing, and evaluating, alternate solutions may be considered and viewed from each other's viewpoint and from the viewpoint of the organization—be it social agency, service club, or civic association. In such an approach, the supervisor as well as the supervisee should be willing to change, to be influenced in some way by the relationship, and to seriously consider any ideas and suggestions offered.

Thus the relationship becomes a developing, maturing one for both individuals and, in the last analysis, for the organization itself.

The comment is often heard that volunteers "don't have the training or they can't be trained!" The myth that volunteers can not be trained to do certain jobs or to carry specific responsibilities has long been exploded. What needs to be borne in mind is that the training and development of volunteers is not to produce a professional but rather a well-informed and capable individual who can relate to the purpose of the organization and work effectively with his colleagues —volunteer and professional, administrator or group leader. As Cyril O. Houle notes in *The Education of Adult Education Leaders:* [10]

> Most leadership training, like most adult education, is self-directed. An individual confronted with the responsibility of becoming an educator of adults learns partly by the process of participation and partly by his own examination of that process. He studies books or pamphlets or manuals, he talks with others in a similar situation, he goes to meetings, he asks for supervisory assistance, he visits other programs, or he analyzes his own performance in terms of a standard which he has developed himself or adopted from some source. The quality of his learning depends in essence upon his capacity to teach himself.

Volunteers: Achieving Effective Service

It is well to remember that a volunteer job is a supportive one and that the volunteer supplements the work of staff and full-time employees but does not replace them. While the job itself may be a volunteer one, the commitment of the individual should have a professional dimension in the sense of being worthy of the effort expended. Whether or not the volunteer works full time or part time, it is important to make him feel as much a part of the organization as any full-time paid staff member. He should be a participating member of the agency, involved in its planning and program development to a practical and feasible degree.

Full-time employees usually have the advantage of established personnel policies to protect their working conditions. The volunteer must adapt to whatever work-related patterns exist and too often these are haphazard in design and minimal in execution. The result is an uneasy truce between staff and volunteer which sometimes develops into a climate of half-hidden hostility. The point of view of the volunteer is frequently disregarded, if it is given any credence at all. One large national organization studying this relationship, having wide experience in the recruitment of volunteers, describes the volunteer's work situation in this manner: [11]

- He works without pay.
- He usually works part time.
- He has other priorities.
- He has primary loyalties and goals.
- He does this particular work only because he chooses to.
- He receives no fringe benefits in the usual sense.
- He works under a different system of rules from those of paid staff.
- His rewards and penalties are different.
- His accountability is different in kind or degree.

Volunteers, then, have many concerns when working with full-time staff or professionals. Staff members, on the other hand, express doubts about the satisfactory contributions of volunteers because they are unpaid. Usually, these doubts come from staff unaccustomed to working with such individuals or from professionals who have not as yet developed ways of utilizing the skills and talents of unpaid workers. The complaints of staff range from lack of punctuality to outright disregard for an agency's policies. The gripes of volunteers range from being treated like children to having to feed the egos of professional staff members so they will not feel threatened.

While conflict between volunteers and staff does not exist everywhere, there is enough evidence to indicate the problem is a persistent one. What can be done to remedy this unfortunate climate? The following pointers may provide some useful guidelines for both volunteers and professionals:

Some Dos and Don'ts for Volunteers Working with Professionals

DO	DON'T
Expect sound guidance and direction from capable and willing staff.	Ask: "What do you expect of me —I'm only a volunteer!"
Expect general orientation, on-the-job training, and specialized help for the tasks you are asked to do.	Demand special privileges or allow yourself to be treated as a prima donna.
Request a clear explanation of your duties and responsibilities including a timetable of days and hours.	Gripe about your co-workers or agency policies.

DO	DON'T
Expect an assignment appropriate to your interests, training, special skills, and personal choice.	Spread gossip or rumors about the agency or its personnel.
Expect opportunities for rotating assignments as the need arises.	Feel guilty if you cannot give more time than agreed upon.
Be prompt in reporting for duty and dependable in the execution of the tasks assigned to you.	Disregard the agency's rules and regulations or create extra work for others by not following directions.
Notify your supervisor of any absences as far in advance as possible so your post can be covered.	Be intolerant of staff because they are on the payroll.
Expect the proper tools and facilities to do the job.	Stay away from training sessions because you think you know "all that stuff."
Respect the confidential nature of all information coming to you in the course of your duties.	Feel superior to staff because you have social prestige or a highly paid job elsewhere.
Expect to be counted on as a part of the agency's total staff and work with the professionals as a colleague.	Be late or absent at scheduled meetings because you "don't think they're important to your job."
Take all the training offered and continue to improve your skills while on the job.	Expect to be taken for granted or feel you personally *owe* the staff or the agency anything except performing a service to the best of your ability.
Expect to be asked to participate in some aspect of the planning and program development process of the organization.	Underestimate organizational policies and channels (they are needed for communication and productive results).
Expect some tangible form of recognition for a job well done.	Expect to have flagrant mistakes and inadequacies overlooked because you are a volunteer.

DO	DON'T
Increase your commitment as a volunteer by being enthusiastic about your job and by recruiting others.	Placate or flatter staff just because they are "staff."
Cultivate a genuine interest in people and, in particular, your co-workers and the individuals you serve.	Be noncooperative and nurse a "lone ranger" attitude.
Expect to feel free to make suggestions and to have your opinions listened to with respect.	Contradict or interfere with a professional's advice in the presence of a client.
Be flexible in revising duties and responsibilities when necessary.	Show favoritism to any client; nor accept gifts or money for any reason.
Be willing to ask for help and guidance when in doubt.	Be oversensitive to constructive criticism, especially from a professional.
Take the initiative in being friendly and helpful.	Imitate staff by using technical staff or professional jargon you do not understand.
Bring the thinking of the community and the opinions of co-workers to staff or agency meetings.	Be discouraged too easily by the problems and difficulties of the job or the people involved.
Be loyal and have a sense of humor.	Lose your sense of perspective of what is important and what is not.

Significant Trends in Volunteering for Adult Educators

We are now in the decade of the seventies and all too soon we will be in the nineteen eighties. The terms "changing times" and "rapid social change" have become clichés and, therefore, tend to be ignored. It is part of the role of adult continuing education to see that the volunteers who serve our organizations and our communities do not succumb to frustration or indifference because of a rapidly changing social climate. Volunteers have always had a sense of wanting to create change and of not being content to change merely because the world around them changes. So much is happening in our society, the causes needing help so urgent and yet so complex, that it is difficult indeed not to become submerged in a sea of seemingly futile effort.

This feeling of helplessness and personal inadequacy affects everyone but it need not overcome us if the power of voluntary effort for the common good is fully recognized. There are deep schisms between the so-called traditional volunteer—the middle-class, middle-aged woman walking in the middle of the road, on the one hand—and the militant marcher, picket sign aloft, following the "in" slogan of the day, on the other. The latter may be an adolescent or a bewildered anti-establishmentarian of indeterminate age. Both are stereotypes and serve no purpose in predicting the nature of the volunteer of tomorrow. We do not know what the role of the new volunteer will be; nor can we tell what his commitment to social purpose will be. But with some degree of accuracy we can say that the pattern of volunteering is not changing—it has already changed. In the United States and around the world there are young idealists, not satisfied with things as they are, taking positive and spirited steps toward molding the future. There are also the middle-aged and the elders, not content with changing as the world around them changes, determined to press on for improvement and into whatever might be. It is not a time for pessimism but a time for adventure for those who would be concerned about preserving a balance between individual conscience and the social good.

The "traditional" volunteer may still be recruited and will continue to fill a need in some places but the ranks of this group will undoubtedly diminish. Professionals seeking new categories of volunteers may be calling upon a former addict to help with a group therapy center, a retired executive to advise a disadvantaged minority on how to set up a small business, or a high school student to tutor a small boy in the neighborhood. The hours will not be set, the training will have to be flexible, the supervision more self-directed than in previous volunteer programs. The conditions of urban living, the problems of man's environment, the automation of a manual society—these are the causes and the movements that will attract volunteers and enlist their services. Students of all ages, welfare rights organizers, former professionals, handicapped persons, blue-collar wives, reformed alcoholics, and the independently wealthy need to be recruited for voluntary work—not just to give money or to sign petitions, but to give of their time and their energy as a personal commitment.

The volunteer worker of today wants "a piece of the action," whether it be in the program of the agency or the decision-making process itself. The volunteer of the future will want more of a piece of the action and this means a more direct role in developing program and in creating innovative ways of doing things. Wise and sensitive professionals will be aware of this and provide meaningful avenues for participation and for listening and acting on the ideas and opinions offered.

More and more of the training and development of the volunteer will be self-directed and, paraphrasing what Professor Houle once wrote, the quality of the learning will depend in large part upon the volunteer's capacity to teach himself. Providing the climate for this learning will be the important task of the professional. The volunteer as a citizen is offering his time, talent, and skills, in order to rediscover, however imperfectly, his own feeling of responsibility for society and a sense of common humanity for himself and his fellow man. Identification in meaningful tasks will help to overcome the depersonalization of an ever increasing cybernetic society. The experience of purposeful service and of making a worthwhile contribution of self will enable the alienated and the dispossessed to overcome a sense of isolation from an unending force over which he has no control. A desire to interact with other human beings for a purpose will be the clue for self-development. This new volunteer will not be easy to work with for he may be cynical in attitude and abrasive in manner. He may come from an affluent environment and he may come from a prison or a ghetto. Whatever the source of recruitment, this newcomer to the voluntary scene may appear ill equipped to handle the institutionalized or traditional way of doing things or of carrying out responsibility. Therein lies the challenge to the professional and to the agency itself.

A great number of persons and many diverse groups will be needed in the last decades of this century, and not all will fit into neat and well-delineated patterns. So many individuals will need help on all levels of society that organizations and staffs must face the arduous task of redefining job slots, work areas, and categories of service. Problems may arise, too, when long-entrenched institutionalism faces radical change. The creation of parish school boards and parish councils, for example, has significance for adult educators and community-minded leadership. When Vatican II issued its Constitution on the Church, the need became urgent for the participation of laymen in the work of local parishes. How would laymen and laywomen, long accustomed to the authoritarianism of the past, confront the difficult tasks of defining basic policy and making decisions by group consensus? Where would such leaders be found? What training would be needed? How would the customs and habits of centuries be reversed?

Religious leaders and parochial school administrators are now facing these challenging tasks and hoping to find the volunteer leaders who will effectively carry out the new responsibilities of their Church. The necessary organizational changes required are not enough to assure that the laity will make their rightful contribution unless the sociological and human relations problems are faced as well. In order to avoid disappointment and disillusionment, training and development in group processes, in reaching consensus, and in assuming responsibility for policy and decision making should be made available to these new participants on the religio-educational scene. Unless this is done, timid and easily persuaded parishioners may find it difficult to face articulate and independent pastors and equally well-informed and strong-minded Sister Principals. Parents of parochial schoolchildren, and indeed of all schoolchildren, need to learn the skills of effective participation on an informed and enlightened basis. Parent volunteers have an emotional stake in participation in school business and should not be frightened off by the professional know-how of administrators and teachers. On the other hand, as volunteers and as citizens, parents should also recognize their responsibility to become informed on the issues and to listen objectively when various points of view are presented. The pastor and his assistants, as well as the school principal and his teachers, face formidable tasks but ones they need not do alone. There are resources in the community at large—and particularly in the adult education field—to help in the recruiting, training, and developing of voluntary leadership. Community involvement, parish participation, neighborhood confrontation, and more local challenges by individuals and groups are on the calendar for the future. The result can be either chaos or community. Professionals who can work creatively in this changing scene may be able to assure that productive cooperation will be achieved.

While the manner of implementing social change may be of concern to many, interest in the welfare of others and of improving conditions has not become extinct. The professional and the community leader working with those who would help and give of their services need to bear in mind that minimal guidance is still necessary. As adult educators, both should keep their focus on the key concepts of flexibility, imagination, and sensitive awareness. We all bear responsibility for the common welfare and, despite increasing professionalization and specialization, the tradition of citizen responsibility and volunteer participation is a part of our American heritage. The task ahead, for both volunteer and adult educator, then, is to create a true sense of individual growth and development, and to open wider the doors for the informed participation of all adults who want to serve the social good of the community.

Notes

1. J. R. Kidd, *How Adults Learn* (New York: Association Press, 1959), p. 10.
2. *Working with Volunteers*, Leadership Pamphlet no. 10 (Washington, D.C.: Adult Education Association of the U.S.A., 1956), pp. 5–8.
3. *Ibid.*, pp. 10–12.
4. Melvin A. Glasser, *What Makes A Volunteer?* Public Affairs Pamphlet (New York: Public Affairs Committee, 1955), pp. 16–17.
5. *Working with Volunteers, op. cit.*, pp. 45–48.
6. Anne K. Stenzel and Helen M. Feeney, *Volunteer Training and Development: A Manual for Community Groups* (New York: Seabury Press, 1968), p. 152.
7. Thelma Whalen, "Board Members are People, Too!", *Adult Leadership*, March 1958.
8. *Working with Volunteers, op. cit.*, p. 33.
9. *Supervision and Consultation*, Leadership Pamphlet no. 7 (Washington, D.C.: Adult Education Association of the U.S.A., (1956), p. 6.
10. Cyril O. Houle, "The Education of Adult Education Leaders," *Handbook of Adult Education in the United States* (Washington, D.C.: Adult Education Association of the U.S.A., 1960), p. 118.
11. *Personnel Practices for Volunteers*, American National Red Cross (Washington, D.C., 1968), p. 4.

Selected References

ASSOCIATION OF JUNIOR LEAGUES OF AMERICA. *Placement Pointers on Volunteer Service.* New York: The Association, 1952.

AMERICAN CANCER SOCIETY. *A Training Guide for Volunteer Orientation.* New York: The Society, 1960.

AMERICAN NATIONAL RED CROSS. *Placing Volunteers.* Washington, D.C., 1965.

JANOWITZ, GAYLE. *Helping Hands—Volunteer Work in Education.* Chicago and London: University of Chicago Press, 1965.

KNOWLES, MALCOLM S. *The Modern Practice of Adult Education.* New York: Association Press, 1970.

NATIONAL FEDERATION OF SETTLEMENTS AND NEIGHBORHOOD CENTERS. *100,000 Hours a Week—Volunteers in Neighborhood Services to Youth and Families.* New York: The Federation, 1965.

NAYLOR, HARRIET H. *Volunteers Today—Finding, Training and Working with Them.* New York: Association Press, 1967.

STENZEL, ANNE K. AND HELEN M. FEENEY. *Learning by the Case Method:*

Practical Approaches for Community Groups. New York: Seabury Press, 1970.

TRECKER, A. R. AND H. B. *Committee Common Sense.* New York: White-side, and William Morrow, 1954.

U.S. VETERANS ADMINISTRATION. *You As a Volunteer: A Handbook.* Washinton, D.C.: Veterans Administration, Pamphlet 10-46, May 1957.

U.S. DEPARTMENT OF THE ARMY. *Handbook on Volunteers in Army Community Service.* Alexandria, Va.: Human Resources Research Organization, 1969.

U.S. DEPARTMENT OF HEALTH, EDUCATION AND WELFARE. *Using Volunteers in Court Settings.* J.D. Publication no. 477. Washington, D.C.: U.S. Government Printing Office, 1968.

CHAPTER FIVE

Getting Your Adult Education Program Started

GLENN M. PARKER

Glenn M. Parker is Director of the New Jersey Community Action Training Institute, a nonprofit corporation for opportunity, Trenton, New Jersey.

S O , N O W you're education chairman of a neighborhood organization or maybe program chairman of the local PTA. Do you really want to do something or are you merely in a "holding pattern" until you can get elected president of the organization? If you want to do something, read on. Incidentally, one way to ensure your election as president next year would be to get the organization's educational program off the ground.

Defining Your Job

The first thing on your agenda should be a reasonably clear definition of your job responsibilities. This will include what the group expects of you and, hopefully, something of what you want to do with this position.

Some national organizations, such as the PTA, have materials describing the program chairman's functions. It is general and can be adapted to meet local needs and your interests.

However, in most organizations you will have to develop your own job description. Begin by talking with the officers of your group and getting answers to some of the key questions about your job. Some questions you may want to consider:

- Am I expected to conduct a certain number of courses or programs during the year?
- Am I expected to conduct the courses or to set them up, getting "experts" to actually conduct the courses?
- Do I have to get approval of the content and other aspects of a problem before I proceed?
- Am I expected to make a regular report on my activities?
- Do I have a budget for the programs?
- What is the group's agenda and how can the educational programs be supportive of that effort?

You should also talk to other members of the group, last year's program chairman, and people who hold similar positions in other organizations. In addition, do some reading on adult education.

When you have completed all this talking, do some writing. Complete, as near as possible, the job description (Figure 7 on page 109). This will be an important exercise for you since it will set down in specific terms the "ground rules" of your job. It should also be submitted to the executive committee and other key members of your group. The other players need to know the rules of the game.

Defining the Community

The next step is to determine whom you are to serve. In other words, who is the community?

JOB DESCRIPTION

JOB TITLE: **EDUCATION CHAIRMAN**
(Program Chairman)

RESPONSIBILITIES: **(A general statement of the job's functions, including to whom the person reports or by whom he is supervised.)**

DUTIES: **(A list of the specific tasks to be performed.)**

BUDGET: **(A list of the amount of money, if any, available for use on educational programs.)**

FIGURE 7

If you are education chairman of a neighborhood organization, are your programs designed for

- only members of your organization
- everyone in the neighborhood
- only poor people in the neighborhood
- poor people throughout the entire city
- anyone interested in attending

These types of questions are important and should not be dealt with lightly. There are very distinct advantages and disadvantages to being restrictive in defining your community.

In the example given above, if your programs are only open to members of your organization you can

- gear the program to meet the members' specific needs
- have a smaller, more informal, and better learning, environment
- conduct it on a smaller budget

However, if you open the programs to everyone in the neighborhood or city-wide, you can

- bring needed education to more people
- use the program as a recruiting ground for new members
- bring together people with different backgrounds and interests

One way out of this dilemma is to first define your basic target group. After this is done you can determine your peripheral groups. For example, as education chairman of the American Association of University Women (AAUW), your target group would be the members of your chapter. Other groups you may want to reach include other women in your community, members of nearby AAUW chapters, and perhaps the general public (see Figure 8).

Once these kinds of distinctions are made it should be easier to proceed. Thus you may decide that a certain program—for example, a workshop in citizen action—should be open only to members of

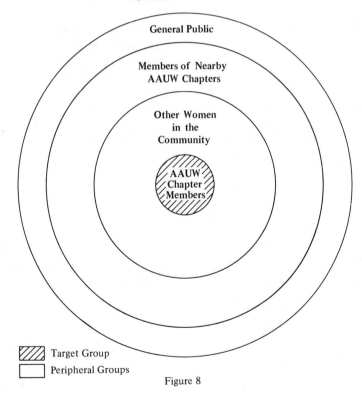

Defining your Community

Figure 8

your chapter. However, with another program—for example, a seminar in public education—you may want to attract the widest possible audience.

A good rule to follow is that programs which involve training in specific skills are most appropriate for your basic target group. Depending upon how you define your groups, the program may also work for your secondary group. Broad issue and discussion programs are appropriate for all groups.

Check Available Resources

Before you proceed, it will be important and helpful to see what else is being done in the community. It is quite possible that what you want to do is already being done by another organization which

- is doing it so well you may not be needed
- is doing it badly
- will see you as a competitor
- is willing to collaborate with you on jointly sponsored programs
- is willing to get out of the field and allow you to move in

There is nothing more discouraging for a community—whether poor or middle class—than to have the same or similar services offered by two organizations. There is only one legitimate excuse for duplication: When one organization is doing a poor job and refuses to get out. Many anti-poverty agencies, for example, conduct GED high school equivalency test preparation classes because the local adult school is failing in this area.

You may find that often organizations are unknowingly in competition with you. Thus members of the League of Women Voters may also belong to the Parent-Teacher Association. Unintentionally, you may therefore be competing for the time and effort of the same people. And, just as innocently, you may schedule programs on the same night or on successive nights.

The other side of the coin is that your check of other resources may turn up needed assistance for your projects. Often, groups and agencies may be willing to provide you with

- speakers
- materials
- facilities (meeting rooms)
- films
- publicity
- program ideas

Begin by making a list of possible groups and organizations which may be working in the same area. Some places to begin are suggested in Figure 9. Basically, you want to find out what they are doing and how they can help you. The first few people you talk with will suggest other groups conducting adult education programs in the community.

COMMUNITY RESOURCES SURVEY

GROUP	TYPES OF PROGRAMS CONDUCTED	RESOURCES AVAILABLE TO OUR GROUP
Adult Program, Public School System		
Extension Division, State University		
Extension Division, Community or Junior College		
Community Action Program		
Parent-Teacher Association		
League of Women Voters		
American Association of University Women		
AFL-CIO Central Labor Council		
Churches and Synagogues		
Chamber of Commerce		
Model Cities Program		
Public Library		

FIGURE 9

Assessing Needs

Perhaps the major criticism made against adult education programs is that they do not meet the needs of the students. This is especially true in low-income and minority communities. The problem is that rarely do educators ask the potential students what they need and want to know.

Adult educators often substitute their views on community needs for the real needs of the people. For example, in a low-income neighborhood a program planner will read census reports indicating a high degree of illiteracy and conclude that he should set up basic education classes. However, neighborhood women, if asked, might opt for sewing classes or a workshop in consumer fraud.

On the other hand, in middle-class communities, adult educators feed women a steady diet of "gourmet cooking" and "refinishing of antiques." Given the current interest in pollution, inflation, and Women's Liberation, many women, if surveyed, would probably request programs in political and community action.

"The times, they are a changing," is the classic line from Bob Dylan's song. People no longer want educators to plan for them. They want to be involved. The challenge, then, for the new adult education specialist is to help people plan for themselves.

And do not worry about the people who do not come to your program or who express little interest in continuing education. They will come around when their needs and your program coincide. Continuous recycling of the needs assessment process is therefore a necessity. However, in the meantime, begin with the people who have needs and want educational programs which you can provide.

It is therefore suggested that a survey of needs and interests be conducted prior to the initiation of any programs. The nature and extent of the survey must be carefully considered and well planned. In some cases you may not want to even conduct a survey since the data may already be available. This is true in some low-income communities which have been "surveyed and studied to death but nothing else." It could be dangerous to run a survey in these neighborhoods because the people feel sufficient information should already be available and now want to see some results. Check with the local Community Action or Model Cities program to see if the data are available.

Before you begin to construct the survey form, you need to know if it will be completed by an interviewer or by the person being surveyed. This will be determined to some extent by the size of your group and to some extent by the resources available to help you complete the survey.

If there are fifty people in your group you will probably want to interview each personally. However, if you have five hundred members you will probably mail them a questionnaire to be completed and returned to you. In the latter case, you may want to conduct personal interviews with a random sample of 10 percent of the membership or follow up personally with people who do not return the questionnaire.

No matter how it is administered, the form should be as short and as simple as possible. Make it easy on the person interviewed and on you later on when the data is tabulated. Use as many "closed-end" questions as possible but include a few "open-end" questions to give the person the opportunity of expressing his opinion, offering suggestions and/or ideas. See Figure 10 for a checklist to be used after your survey form is drafted.

CHECKLIST FOR SURVEY QUESTIONS

Use this checklist after you prepare your questions. If the answer is "no" to any of the following questions, do not use the question as worded. Rewrite it. If that does not work, omit it.

1. **Is the question absolutely necessary? Yes_____ No_____**
   Do you need to know the person's record in order to plan an adult education course for him?
2. **Does the question ask for only one answer? Yes_____ No_____**
   Do not combine two ideas in one question. Do not ask a husband, "Did you and your wife ever attend the adult program at city high school?" You are looking for two answers so ask two questions. "Did you ever attend the adult program at city high school?" "Did your wife ever attend the adult program at city high school?"
3. **Will the question you are asking get the information you need? Yes_____ No_____**
   If you ask a person if he favors adult education classes, his answer will not tell you if he will attend classes. Change your question to, "Will you attend adult education classes?"
4. **Do the people you are questioning have all the information they need to answer the question? Yes_____ No_____**
   If you ask a person if he will attend a GED preparation class be certain he understands what "GED" means.
5. **Does the question relate to the personal experience of the person being questioned? Yes_____ No_____**

If you are trying to find out where people favor classes being held, do not ask, "Do you believe adult education classes should be held in non-school facilities such as churches, community centers, and private homes?" You will get a better answer if you ask, "Would you attend adult education classes held in non-school facilities such as churches, community centers, and private homes?"

6. Has the question been worded to avoid embarrassment? Yes_____ No_____

You may get a better answer if you ask a woman if she is over 35 years of age instead of asking her how old she is.

FIGURE 10

CLOSED-END QUESTION:	Gives people several different answers to choose.
Example:	Have you ever attended a course conducted by the adult program at city high school?
	Yes_____ No_____
OPEN-END QUESTION:	A direct question that asks for recommendations or opinions.
Example:	What courses would you take if you could go to high school?_____

One way to conduct the survey is to use members of the target group as interviewers. This will result in more involvement at the outset, spread the work, and probably mean a more effective survey. See Figure 11 for an adult education survey.

Since it is important that you do not work in isolation from the membership, using some of them as interviewers will ensure participation during the early stages of your work. It will also mean that the burden of conducting the survey will be shared. And, finally, it should bring some more useful data since they should be able to more effectively relate to the target group.

In recent years professional adult educators have been criticized for their inability to reach students in low-income communities. One way to confront this problem is to use residents of the community in key roles. In a 1966 demonstration project, training made it possible for twenty-four poor people—most of them unemployed or on welfare —to provide educational experience to more than seven hundred adults living in six urban ghettos of New Jersey.

ADULT EDUCATION SURVEY

NOTE: The following questionnaire was designed and implemented by eight adult education aides who were working for Atlantic Human Resources, Inc., the antipoverty agency for Atlantic and Cape May Counties, New Jersey. The purpose was to find out what courses poor people wanted and when they should be given. The aides visited 2,722 homes, conducting 1,197 interviews in seven communities. The results of the survey helped the aides plan twelve adult courses—six in basic education, three in home sewing, one in typing, one in industrial sewing, and one in GED preparation. They decided on ten evening and two day classes. For a full description of the project see Barry A. Passett and Glenn M. Parker, "The Poor Bring Adult Education to the Ghetto," *Adult Leadership*, March 1968.

To Interviewer:

It is not necessary to talk to the head of the household. Talk to any adult living in the dwelling you visit. Start by introducing yourself and identifying the group conducting the survey. Then state the purpose of the survey. Answer question one BEFORE you start the interview.

1. What is the address of the person being questioned?
   Street_____ Apartment_____

2. The person answering question is: Male_____ Female_____

3. Marital Status: Married_____ Single_____ Widowed_____

4. Number of dependents_____

5. Age of person answering questions: (Check one)
   Under 20 years old_____ Between 30 and 50 years old_____
   Between 20 and 30 years old_____ Over 50 years old_____

6. Employment:
   Husband Unemployed_____ Employed_____ Earnings_____
   Wife Unemployed_____ Employed_____ Earnings_____

7. Do you get a pension, Social Security benefits, or other income?
   Yes_____ No_____

8. Circle highest grade completed by husband; draw a square around highest grade completed by wife.
   1 2 3 4 5 6 7 8 9 10 11 12
   Other:_____ (Explain)_____

9. Have you attended any classes since you left school?
Yes_____ No_____ If yes, where?_____
What course did you take?_____
Did you complete the course? Yes_____ No_____
10. If the courses you want were offered in your neighborhood, would you attend classes? Yes_____ No_____
11. What kind of course would you take? (List in order of preference)
1._____ 2._____ 3._____
_____
12. What hours can you attend class? During day_____
During evening_____
13. What day of the week can you attend class?_____
14. Would you like us to notify you when the courses begin?
Yes_____ No_____ If yes, please give me your name:
_____

Comments of Interviewer:_____
_____

FIGURE 11

As adult education aides, nonprofessionals could get to an adult poverty population that had not been reached by the school system.

Some of the trainees had high school diplomas—but many were dropouts. They had no experience in developing, administering, or evaluating adult education courses of any kind. By the end of the demonstration, the trainees had designed and were conducting more than fifty different adult education courses for disadvantaged people in their own neighborhoods. The courses included housing problems, sewing, typing, shorthand, Social Security benefits, and many other subjects.

One enterprising aide in Camden could not get target area residents to sign up for a history class. To get people interested, one night he held a three-hour session on the History of Jazz. Twenty-three people attended and nineteen decided to continue participating in classes on the history of blacks in the U.S. And a visitor to an afternoon shorthand class found every seat taken and had to stand in the rear of the room until the session ended.

The pilot project provided nonprofessionals with on-the-job training experience on how to survey a disadvantaged neighborhood to find out what kind of adult education courses the people wanted and needed. Then the aides were trained to use local resources to determine the courses that should be taught, to plan an adult education program, to recruit teaching staff, to assist in administering the program, and to help mobilize the community.[1]

It should be noted that the concept of using target group members as interviewers, recruiters, and even teachers is applicable to all types of organizations.

Although we have spent a great deal of time on surveys, they are not the only way to assess needs. Other methods are available and are often better. The survey is often used when there is little interest or specific need expressed by anyone in the group.

However, it is quite possible that a group within your organization may express an interest in participating in an educational experience. For example, the executive board may say, "We want to be trained." You can, of course, interview each member individually. However, you can also conduct a group-needs assessment (see Figure 12).

A group-needs assessment is a good way to predict how the group will function in a training session. Another method is to observe the group in a real meeting (see Figure 13). All these methods can be used in preparation for a program. Very often a group interview is followed up by a written survey form to reach people who were not present at the interview or who were reluctant to speak.

Now you have the important job of sorting the information into a useable form. The nature of this process will depend upon the type of data collected.

If you simply administered a survey questionnaire, the first step is to summarize the results. You are interested in determining the educational preferences of your group—that is, how many people are interested in a course in basic education or ecology or urban renewal, and so on.

GROUP-NEEDS ASSESSMENT [2]

Interview a Small Group

This method is helpful because the people talk to each other rather than to the trainer.

STEP 1: Have a meeting of the people you will be training. Divide participants into groups of threes or fours. Ask the small groups to talk together on the following: (give only one statement at a time)

15 min.—Where do you get your greatest satisfaction in your job? What do you like best about your job?

Next Statement:

15 min.—What gives you problems in your job? What makes you really frustrated? What do you dislike most about your job?

STEP 2:

15 min.—Have each trainee complete the following sentence on a piece of paper and then share with the small group:

If I knew how to:

1.

2.

3.

I would be more efficient and effective in my job. (Ask the small groups to list their most important training needs.)

STEP 3:

15 min.—Now, in the total group, share lists and discuss training needs. Give your observations and comments, too.

During Steps 1 and 2 move around, listen to discussions. Take notes unless this discourages them from talking freely.

FIGURE 12

CHECKLIST FOR OBSERVING A MEETING

1. Does the meeting seem to be well planned? Is there an agenda? Was it sent out in advance of the meeting?
2. What methods of procedure are used? Are they effective?
3. What is the extent of participation in the meeting? Do a few people dominate?
4. How are decisions made in the meeting?
5. Are the group resources used effectively? Are there committees, task forces, and so on? Do they seem to work?
6. Do people seem to know what is going on? Do they seem to have sufficient information and/or skills to effectively participate? If not, what do they need to learn?

FIGURE 13

If you find that at least ten people are interested in the same subject, check to see where they live. If they live in the same neighborhood, you are set to go. However, if a few people live in different parts of town, you may need to check and see if transportation will present a problem for them.

Let us assume that twenty-five people want a course in Spanish and twenty people want a program on drugs in suburbia; should you select one or try to conduct both programs? One way to answer that question is to decide if you have the skills and resources to do both.

GUIDE TO ANALYZING TRAINING NEEDS DATA [3]

What Things Do the Trainees Want to Improve?

The trainees will be the most enthusiastic about training which helps them with what they want to improve. People learn best what they want to learn. What are people most dissatisfied with in their knowledge, actions and relationships with each other? Are there any areas all the trainees want to improve? Are their ideas of what improvements are needed the same as your ideas about their training needs? Do you have the abilities to help them in these areas?

What New Skills or Ways of Acting Will the Trainees Need to Accomplish Improvements?

If they want to understand some things or improve their relationships with each other, are there any specific changes in behavior you think they will need to learn?

Trainer's Experience and Abilities

What training do you think the trainees need most? Is it what they want? Do you have the abilities to give them this training? Can you get the resource people and materials to help you do this training?

Time

Is there enough time available for you to help people learn what they want to learn, what their supervisors want them to learn, and what you think they need to learn? What training can you accomplish best in the time you have?

FIGURE 14

Here is where your survey of available resources may again be helpful.

It is quite possible that another organization already runs a program in the same subject or would be willing to set one up. For example, Spanish could be handled by the adult program of the local school system or community college.

You may decide to run both programs but you need not set up both simultaneously. Begin with the course which is easiest from your standpoint. After that one gets off the ground, begin work on the second and schedule it to begin at the conclusion of the first.

The summary and use of the data from a needs assessment, as outlined in Figures 12 and 13, can be more difficult. Try to isolate the things people want to improve, relate them to the skills needed, and match them with your skills, resources, and available time. Figure 14 presents a guide to handling the data.

Plan Your Program

Once you have assessed and analyzed the needs of your group you are ready to plan your program. But, first, let us change it to *their* program and say it is being planned with them. It is suggested that, when possible, you bring the results of your assessment back to the group and help them use this data to plan a program.

Here you will present a summary of the results indicating the major needs and interests and a suggested program based on those needs. You should ask for reactions and suggestions for improvement. This should result in some changes in the program and, hopefully, a signal to go ahead with your plan.

You are now able to proceed with the knowledge that it will be "their program and not just one that you dreamed up." This should help to build a commitment to the program and make your job from now on a good deal easier.

1. *Set goals.* As a result of your assessment process you should be able to set some goals for your program. They need not be in highly technical terms.[4] However, you should list some expected outcomes of the program. In other words, as a result of the program:

- What will the participants know or know more about?
- How will organization function more effectively?

Your goals should be clear, specific, and set in terms of the participants and not the instructor. Do not try to "cover the waterfront." It is not likely that in one evening the group "will be able to understand the welfare system."

2. *Prepare curriculum.* After you set some goals, you need a method for achieving them. The curriculum is the "road map" for getting to where you want to go. It indicates the subject of the session, the learning techniques to be employed, and the length of the session. For example—

Prejudice and Discrimination (3 hours). Using a film and small group discussion, this session deals with types of prejudicial and discriminatory behaviors and attitudes. The instructor opens the session by outlining the goals and introducing the NET film *Where Is Prejudice?* Following the film showing, the participants are divided into groups of eight or ten and asked to identify types of behaviors and attitudes exhibited in the film and relate them to their own experience. At the conclusion of the session each group reports the results of its discussion. The instructor summarizes the types of behaviors and attitudes as an introduction to the next session which deals with positive action.

Preparing a curriculum is an important exercise for you since it clearly defines your direction. It is also helpful for people you may use to conduct the session. In the above example, if you used discussion leaders in each small group it would be helpful if they had a curriculum in advance of the session. They could prepare their approach, perhaps some stimulating questions, and certainly see the film if they were not familiar with it. It is also important that the participants have an idea of where you are going.

One note of caution: for some people the term *curriculum* implies something fixed and unchanging. Not so. It can be changed both before and during a program if the situation requires a change. Again, in the above example, the participants may become so incensed by the film that they want to discuss their own feelings or move immediately to plans for positive action in their community.

3. *Select training resources.* The resources you will need consist of two general types: people and materials.

People resources are speakers, trainers, consultants, discussion leaders, or other individuals who assist in the conduct of your program. Usually, they are people who possess a special expertise in a particular area. For example, you would call in an outside speaker to handle a program on the Women's Liberation movement. However, you might want to have several speakers—usually called a panel—to discuss various aspects of the movement. In another session you may have two people debate the usefulness of the movement.

If your object is to train your board in effective decision making, you will want to use a trainer who not only knows his subject but is able to train other people to master it.

Locating good people resources is a big part of your job and there are no fast answers on how-to-do-it. The best source will be other groups in the community conducting adult education programs. As mentioned previously, when you survey other groups to see what they are doing, check out their people resources. Some organizations may even have a "consultant pool" list which they may be willing to share with you. See Figure 9 for a list of other organizations.

And, finally, do not forget your own organization. There will certainly be people in your group who will have special knowledge and skills which you can tap. This is also another way of building an interest in education programs in the organization.

Materials resources include a wide range of items from pamphlets and other printed materials to films, slides, tapes, and other audio-visual aids. To run down all that is available is a job. If your group is affiliated with a national organization, begin by contacting the national office. For example, both the AFL-CIO and Office of Economic Opportunity headquarters in Washington publish film catalogues. Libraries in your area can also help—both the public library and those on the nearby college campuses.

If your group is devoted to one area, write to organizations and agencies specializing in that subject. Housing groups should contact the local and state housing agencies, as well as the U.S. Department of Housing and Urban Development in Washington. You should also get on the mailing list of the Government Printing Office in Washington.

Review all materials before they are used in any program. This means reading a booklet to ensure that it is relevant to your subject and will be easily understood by the participants. This means viewing a film for the same reasons.

One of the worst things to do is to give participants a kit of materials "so they will have something to take home." Never give out materials without either using them in the program or explaining their purpose and suggesting that they be read after class. If you do not attach any importance to them neither will the participants.

In the same vein, never show a film just "to fill some time" and never use a film without an appropriate plan: an introduction which includes the name, length, purpose, and brief summary of the film. In some cases you may want to ask the participants to look for specific things as they watch the film. Your plan should also include a design for discussing the film after it is over.

4. *Locate a meeting room.* Typically, selecting a room in which to

hold a program is considered a routine aspect of the educator's job. It normally amounts to "I'll need a room to hold twenty people and some coffee and donuts." But there is more to it than that, as experienced hands know from bitter experience. The following quotes indicate the frustrations that can arise from failure to thoroughly check out a room:

"The plug was too far away and we didn't have an extension cord so we blew the film session."

"The nearest restaurant was six blocks away so our lunch break took two hours instead of one—and the service was poor because the restaurant was not prepared to have thirty-five people descend on them at the same time."

"Within an hour the room was smoky and stuffy and you couldn't open a window because it was 20 degrees outside."

5. *Supplies and equipment.* Depending upon the type of program, you may need a variety of supplies and equipment to ensure that things run smoothly. What you need will depend upon the content and format of your program. For example, if you plan to have four groups discuss a film and report back to the total group, you will need at least four marking pens and a sufficient amount of flip chart or newsprint paper, and do not forget the masking tape if you plan to post the reports on the wall. A film showing naturally requires a projector and screen and, just to be sure, an extension cord and extra projector lamp. Some other things you may need include:

- writing paper
- pencils
- name badges
- registration/attendance forms
- evaluation forms
- tape recorder

6. *Design and evaluation system.* If you take the time and trouble to go through all the previous steps, you will surely want to know how well you did—that is, to determine the effectiveness of the program. And, to put it another way: To what degree were the program's objectives met? The evaluation system should also tell you which things went well and should be repeated next time and which things failed and should be omitted. There are several basic sources of evaluation information.

The participants. Whenever possible, you should get the opinions and attitudes of the participants in the program. Usually, this will come at the end of the program. However, if the program is rather long, it should come at various points during the program.

The easiest method for obtaining this information is a questionnaire which is completed by the participants. It should ask whether the program met their needs, how well they liked the speaker or trainer,

EVALUATION FORM

NOTE: These questions represent our request that you help us evaluate this program. We need this information in order to improve the quality of future programs. All information received will remain confidential. There is no need to sign your name.

1. Was the program related to your needs and interests?
   No_____ Somewhat_____ Very much_____
   Comment:_____
2. What do you consider to be the most important thing you learned in this program?_____
   _____
3. Will you do anything differently as a result of this program?
   No_____ Yes_____ If yes, what?_____
   _____
4. What was the best feature of this program?_____
   _____ What was the
   worst feature?_____
5. I would like to return for another program which starts where this one left off?   Yes_____ No_____
6. Here is a scale indicating how you might feel about the program. Circle the number that is closest to the way you feel about the program.
   BAD 1 2 3 4 5 6 7 GOOD
7. Please list below any subject not included in the program which you feel should have been covered and which you would like to have included in a follow-up program.

FIGURE 15

whether they will do anything differently as a result of the program, and what could have improved the program. See Figure 15 for a sample evaluation form. An alternative or additional method is to have an oral discussion with the total group in which you ask the same questions and record the responses on tape or newsprint or both.

A more difficult method is to test the participants both before and after the program to determine the amount of factual information acquired as a result of the program. This is appropriate for a training program when your goal is to have the participants learn new facts. It may also be used in basic education courses.

Since many of your objectives will call for the participants to do something differently as a result of the program you will want to see if, in fact, some changes do take place after they get out of the class. This is what educators and trainers call "behavioral change." There are some methods for doing this by observation and reports. For example, if you were training a board in decision making you might observe them in action both before and after training and note changes in behavior. The checklist in Figure 13 might again be a helpful guide.

The speakers or trainers. Your people resources should also be asked to record their evaluation of the program. Plan to speak with them after the session and, if possible, ask for a written report. You will want to know their feelings on:

- the extent to which the goals were achieved
- the strong and weak points of the program
- how it could have been improved

You. Do not forget to record your reactions to the program. Since you planned it, your feelings on how well it came off are important. You will review the extent to which the goals were met, the strengths and weaknesses of the program but do not forget to also rate the speakers or trainers and the meeting room.

7. *Keep a record.* At the conclusion of each program prepare a brief report summarizing the key information. The report should be submitted to the leaders of your organization and put in your education program file. You will want to refer to the file as you plan future programs and next year's program chairman will surely find it useful. You may also want to share your reports with other educators in the community. The report should include:

- brief description of the program, including the objectives
- the number of participants and other information which might be useful
- date(s) and length of the program
- location of the meeting room
- evaluation of results
- general conclusions and recommendations

Advisory Committees

To begin with, most advisory committees do not work. Therefore, consider carefully their value.

A working committee can provide useful program ideas and feedback on current programs. It can also lead you to new resources and serve as an effective spokesman for your program in the community.

They usually do not work because their task is never made clear and they are never given useful work to perform. Often, committees die for lack of interest, although sometimes they get energetic and want to *decide* rather than *advise*.

The composition of the committee ought to be weighed in favor of the consumers (students) of your service. However, other educators and members of the so-called "power structure" should be invited to serve. A good mixture is healthy for the program and the life of the committee.

At the outset, the task of the committee should be spelled out in some detail. Specific responsibilities of each member should be explained. The meetings should be brief and well planned. Materials related to the program should be mailed to the committee between meetings.

Beyond committee composition and meetings, consideration must be given to the time involved in having an advisory committee. It must be staffed. That is, someone must pay attention to the needs of the committee and ensure its proper functioning. And this takes time. Therefore, only suggest an advisory committee when you are ready to do it right.

The End and the Beginning

A good deal of material has been outlined in the preceding pages. Therefore, a word of caution is necessary: do not wait to master all the areas discussed. Begin by doing the things with which you feel comfortable.

And do not feel your first program must solve the community's most pressing problem. Your first program should (1) meet a real need and (2) be one which you are able to accomplish. Build your skills and confidence and move on to the tough ones. Attack the problems that are solvable is a truism that bears repeating.

Notes

1. Barry A. Passett and Glenn M. Parker, "The Poor Bring Adult Education to the Ghetto," *Adult Leadership*, March 1968, p. 326.
2. Adapted from *Community Action Training's Handbook for Trainers* (Trenton, N.J., Community Action Training Institute, September 1968).

3. Adapted from *Community Action Training's Handbook for Trainers, op. cit.*

4. For those interested in the more sophisticated aspects of effective goal setting, see Robert Mayer, *Preparing Instructional Objectives* (Palo Alto: Feron Publishers, 1962).

Selected References

Community Action Training: A Handbook for Trainers. Trenton: New Jersey Community Action Training Institute, 1968.

CRAIG, ROBERT L. and LESTER R. BITTEL (eds.). *Training and Development Handbook.* New York: McGraw-Hill, 1967.

MALCOLM S. and HILDA F. KNOWLES, *Introduction to Group Dynamics.* New York: Association Press, 1955.

MILES, MATTHEW B., *Learning to Work in Groups.* New York: Teachers College Press, 1969.

NYLEN, DONALD et al. *Handbook for Staff Development and Human Relations Training.* Washington, D.C.: NTL Institute for Applied Behavioral Science, 1969.

SMITH, ROBERT M. (ed.). *The Handbook of Adult Education in the United States.* New York: The Macmillan Company, 1970.

CHAPTER SIX

Adult Education Projects
in Small Group Settings

L. L. PESSON

Dr. L. L. Pesson is Professor and Head of the Department of Extension Education at Louisiana State University and Agricultural and Mechanical College, Baton Rouge.

H O W C A N a small group be handled so that a desirable atmosphere for a program can be developed? What are some ways that interest can be kindled within a group? These are questions that many people ask themselves as they are faced with the problem of working with a group in a leadership situation. In this chapter, hopefully, you will find explanations of some concepts that will be useful in helping you think about these problems. These concepts are intended as guides in facing problem situations rather than as recipes which will produce exact results each time they are used.

The focus of the chapter is on the small group situation. In this context, the small group is defined as one in which there are perhaps no more than twenty to thirty people. The people who are part of the group would have a reasonable chance of getting to know each other within a short period of time. This is also a group which will continue to be with each other on occasion over a period of time so that relationships among individuals are developed.

The chapter is organized around four main topics. The first part stresses a few useful notions about *groups* as a unit. In the second part the *leader* as a part of the group is given some attention, while the *program* forms the basis for the third part. The final or fourth part looks at the *learning* process in a small group situation.

The Group

Whenever two or more people get together, there is the likelihood of a group forming. To begin, we can ask ourselves the question, "when is a group a group?" Just because several people are gathered together, it does not necessarily mean that a group has been formed. A group becomes a group only when members begin to share one or more common *goals* together. Goals are the links which hold the chain together, the chain being the people who are part of the group. As an illustration, an adult discussion group at a church has as its common goal learning more about one's religion, coupled with some good fellowship. These goals constitute the force that makes it a group. When these goals for one reason or another, are no longer in force, the group ceases to be a group. Whenever an individual quits identifying himself with these goals or the reaching of these goals becomes unpleasant, his participation will drop off.

One fundamental task of any person working with a group is to aid the group not only in setting goals but also in reaching goals on a continuing basis. This requires a conscious effort on the part of the leader to consider the reasons for the group's existence and to get agreement from the group for these reasons, being careful to match individual desires with group goals as much as possible. When these two come close together, the chances are that the group will be a strong one. Goals are the binding forces that hold a group together, and anyone working with a group must recognize this to achieve maximum effectiveness.

GROUP PROCESS [1]

Whenever a group forms, certain processes go on whether we realize it or not. Understanding something about these processes is helpful in getting the job done well. Each group has certain functions that must be performed for the group to continue to exist. These *task functions*, as they are often referred to, represent the things to be done. Foremost among these is the production of satisfaction for the group as a whole and for the members who are a part of it. This satisfaction can come either from the product of the group's effort, even if it is only an intangible thing like being proud to be a part of it, or from the personal reward that comes from being with a group to which one feels a spirit of belongingness or from which some pleasant experience is derived.

For a group to be an operating unit, there are certain other necessary tasks. Someone has to perform the task of introducing new ideas to the group. Periodically, this is a necessity; otherwise, the group may get into a "rut." Coupled with this is the task of clarifying or elaborating so that the group can grasp the meaning of a newly introduced idea, for example. Another related task is that of information or opinion seeking and giving. This back-and-forth-type banter among members is very important to group development. Without this, it is very hard to develop the feeling of unity or pulling together that is so necessary for a healthy group. Yet another task appears at this point; the task of consensus taking. By some process the group must sift through the different opinions and come up with some degree of agreement. While doing so, a summarizing task must be performed so that the issues or points facing the group come clearly into focus.

It is evident now that there are a number of task functions to be performed within the group. Different people may be required to do different tasks. Some are good at coming up with ideas while others are useful at clarifying meanings. These differences are essential, emphasizing that varying types of people can help form a stronger and more interesting group. A group full of idea men could very well end up in feuds over which one had the best idea, to illustrate the point.

The task functions, particularly when well performed by different members, help develop a stronger group and this contributes strongly to goal achievement.

Every group, as it forms and develops, comes to have a definite *organization* or *structure*. Group goals are a major factor in this structure. To illustrate, one or more individuals are always looked up to in each group. This process of giving a special place to these people is most often related to the person who can contribute more toward reaching goals. If one is a gifted athlete, it may be quite easy to become an influential person on an athletic team because one can contribute a great deal to the success of the group. On the other hand, if one takes all the glory for himself, it can lead to problems because the individual is putting himself above the group, causing group frustration and preventing goal achievement. It is important to emphasize that those individuals in the group who are good at performing task functions are more likely to be recognized in the group as important members. This gives a form or structure to the group in terms of holding it together.

Another important process is the *building and maintenance* function, the process of keeping the group alive. Involved are such items as participation, communication, coordination, and socialization: taking part in what is going on, knowing what is being done and why, working together toward the same goals, and identifying oneself with the group and what it stands for.

Up to this point, we have looked at group processes. These processes are all related to group goals, with goals the binding forces that hold the group together. The leader's function is to make sure that the group sets its goals and then makes forward progress. In so doing, three important sets of processes have been identified. First, the leader must be concerned with the task function, the things that must be done to achieve goals. Next, he must be aware that a structure or organization develops within the group, and that this structure is related to the earning of status or position in the group, based on the ability to contribute to goal achievement. Third, the group must be kept alive and this can be done best by making sure that people take part, that they know what is going on, and that they have a chance to work together and identify themselves with the group.

This forms a large but necessary order for the person who works with a group in an adult education program. The success of such a voluntary program, however, is related to the process of forming an effective group. If people come and feel unwanted or realize nothing worthwhile from a session, they are not likely to be seen again at such an activity. Whether it involves a Sunday school class, a working committee, or a civic group, the meaning is the same. An effective group is a must and effective groups are formed only when the processes described are operating well.

GROUP EFFECTIVENESS

What are some factors that affect the effectiveness of a group, both in getting the job done and in keeping the members coming and involved? First and foremost, the *satisfaction* of the individual members of the group is most important. The goals that are achieved must be important to the individual member in some way or another so that satisfaction is obtained. Two concepts are very important in this regard: group unity must be developed and the atmosphere or climate of feeling within the group must be good.

The first concept, *group unity*, refers to the degree to which each individual identifies himself with the group and is willing to share with the others the things that the group stands for and believes in. Group unity is related to the degree to which the individuals in the group interact and relate to each other. This also means that a feeling of belonging to the group is developed by the individuals, based upon a feeling of acceptance by other members of the group. Group unity is also related to the usefulness or value of the group as seen in the eyes of a larger community. A highly respected group may show strong unity because of its usefulness and value to others in the community. This helps members to identify themselves strongly with the group.

A second important concept related to effectiveness, *group climate*, refers to the general feeling or atmosphere within the group. Is the general feeling one of enthusiasm or apathy, friendliness or hostility, pride or indifference? This general feeling is influenced by a number of factors. Among the more important ones are the general morale of the group and the degree to which friendliness is expressed among members. In relation to general morale, the most important consideration is the extent to which there is a climate of pride in being part of the group. Being a part of the group is good. There is a definite hope or expectation that participation in the group will bring good and useful results. Friendliness, as the idea suggests, relates to a climate of permissiveness and tolerance among group members. It is fun or at least pleasant to be a part of the group. Fuss and argument among the members of the group must be kept to a minimum.

SOME PROBLEMS WITH GROUPS

We have looked at some basic ideas about groups. We have fo-cused on some concepts that help us to understand more about what happens when we get a group of people together. These ideas help us to explain why some groups work so well and others fall apart or operate very poorly at best. Some problems that do occur involve apathy or indifference, indecision, or disagreement. How can one handle these kinds of problems? What can be done to over-come them?

Using the basic concepts identified so far, it is possible for us to come up with some ideas about the handling of such problems. As an example, let us take a look at a group situation involving apathy. The members just do not care. What can be done? What is the problem? The concepts expressed so far can give us some inkling of the prob-lem. What are the group goals? Do they represent something that is useful and important to the group as a whole and to the members in particular? If the goals are not important and useful, what goals might be useful and appealing to the members? Do the goals need changing? How can the members be aroused? These are practical questions that each of us must face.

One of the common tools used in trying to get groups to respond is *pressure*. Can pressure be used effectively? If so, how can it best be applied? All of us feel pressure to a greater or lesser degree as we participate in groups. The question is how to use it to best advantage.

Sometimes the pressures in groups [2] are clearly defined. For exam-ple, in a family, comments among members imply that certain family members should alter their behavior. Husbands pressure wives and wives pressure husbands. Both discuss ways they want their chil-dren to change and they set about to organize a system of checks and balances for changing their children's behavior. In such instances all the people involved recognize at least some of the forces in play.

A class or training group, designed to make the members more sympathetic supervisors, also expects to induce changes in the behav-ior of the members. In a therapy group the very purpose is to create changes. In religious groups considerable effort is devoted to making people change their behavior.

We all recognize these pressures in groups when we are told rather directly, in one way or another, that we should change. But just as real as these clearly defined forces are the unwritten or implied psy-chological pressures which may never be consciously recognized at all. There are feelings generated both by what the group does and by how it goes about its business. In certain groups we find ourselves beginning to behave as though certain things were expected of us, even though others in the group may deny they have attempted to influence us. Even a do-nothing-care-nothing group exerts an influence, for groups tend to make members over in the group image.

1. List three groups to which you now belong. Include the group you like best and the one you like least. The "like least" might be one you would drop if you could without embarrassment. How long have you been a member of each? How did you happen to join?
2. Taking each group, state what you feel are its goals. How complete is your sympathy for these goals? Are these goals the ones which actually determine the group life as you see it?
3. What pressures do you feel in each of these groups? How are these pressures produced?
4. What would the "ideal group member" be like in each of these groups? How would you have to change to conform to this idea? Do you feel any pressure to change in this direction?

Group pressures do not always tend toward desired change. People participating in a group do not always find themselves changing at all. Let us cite two reasons.

Incomplete membership. No two people in a group hold identical membership cards. People join the same group for different reasons. The reasons may not coincide with what the group offers. For example, a person may join a religious organization because he likes the opportunities to socialize which the group provides. Yet the major concern of the group, and the one which affiliating with it suggests, is for the members to explore their values. This exploration the social joiner may resist.

Or suppose a committee is established to do something constructive about community recreation. The committee is composed of representatives from parents' groups, each major community organization sending a representative. Although each representative has a certain identification within his basic group, he now finds himself a member of the new group. He will hardly alter radically his interests and activities to accommodate the new group's goal. Yet he cannot resign without disturbing the relationship which he covets within his basic group.

Most groups combine, in less striking fashion, many and diverse elements. As such, they cannot command 100 percent identification of the members. If a person holds only a 10 percent membership investment in a group, he is not likely to respond to the efforts to change which the group tries to master.

Crosscurrents in group operation. What goes on in a group may produce countercurrents which prevent or distort the direction of the force for change. For example, members of a group may be uncomfortable about their stereotyped social or religious prejudices. The group may have been designed with the explicit purpose of altering the members' behavior as it relates to these prejudices. Yet, in many of these mixed groups where there would be a possibility of mutual acceptance across the line of prejudice, we feel ourselves tighten and tense up. We find, against our hopes, that we are less and less understanding of the very ones we wanted to understand. Our sensitized stereotypes have become the commanding group force. We are losing ground in our objective.

Similarly, we may join a group in order that, through experience, we may become better or more active participants in any group. Yet the attitudes we find here may make us so anxious that we hardly talk at all! It may be that the fear generated by a process of mutual criticism which the group uses is not acceptable to us. The method freezes rather than relaxes us, and our group goal is lost.

As you studied the three groups which you were asked to think about earlier, did your analysis of your own memberships turn up items both pleasant and unpleasant?

Some groups are appealing. Others are irritating. Where do these pleasant or irritating aspects or impressions or experiences come from? To what forces are they a reaction? What makes us feel positive or negative about a group? What is the source of the impact which a group has upon its members?

The leader as a group force for change. Leaders are always important in the life of a group. Sometimes they make us uncomfortable by virtue of their passivity; at other times their assertiveness irritates or satisfies us, depending upon us and how we feel. The whole pattern of a group can change when the leadership changes. Since each of us has his own set of needs, no one of us reacts to the leader's behavior in the same way. But we all do react.

There are many ways in which the leader exerts force. Feelings are set up by the way he does things. The tone of his interpersonal relationships is another way. The delinquent gang leader and the religious leader have at least one thing in common because of the position they hold in their groups, because they are recognized leaders and others respond by trying to pattern their lives after the leader's image. Thus the leader constitutes a very potent force.

As you review the groups you analyzed, did you find the leader a potent force? How?

Group code or customs. Sometimes the group force is felt through the group code or customs. Certain group procedures, commonly held values or opinions, and specific ideas dominate the activity. These may be wrapped up in a document called the constitution; more likely, they are a cumulative effect of the interaction of the members and of the procedures which have grown up over the group's history. Many groups formalize and structure the business of accepting each step of a course of action. Certain people may be the only ones who may accept responsibility or make decisions. People listen when certain members talk; they ignore other contributors. There may be severe limits placed upon what topics can be talked about. In contrast, other groups may be quite relaxed, not even demanding membership for voting. There are groups which have a power hierarchy and a rigid line of succession.

How would you say your three groups rate on this category of force potential?

Social structure of the group. How members interrelate in any group composes another set of forces which operate and are felt by members. Committees, cliques, friendships and enmities, factions and splits all leave waves of pressure. How people congregate and seat themselves, how they vote, and even whether or not they attend a meeting are the result of the web of social relationships which have developed. How much mutual acceptance or rejection do the members feel for each other? How "equal" is the membership? Are there first- and second-class memberships?

As you look back over your three groups, what would you say about the forces generated by the social structure?

Program content as a force in group life. To what purpose is the group dedicated? There may be topics and subjects which are taboo, and these can operate as a limiting factor or as an expanding one. For example, if a group is dedicated to perpetuating racial separation, we do not find in it a liberating force to encourage our acceptance of other races. A mother's child study club is not the place to increase anyone's appreciation of opera. What kind of a force is injected by goal content limitations? Do these limitations suit the membership and do they provide a channel for the members' efforts to change? Or is it a pot luck, anything goes type of group, in which there is no definition of what changes are part of the group intent?

To sum up: Groups can have within them conditions which help members to make positive changes. There may be a purposeful design for change within the total group membership or incidental factors which change only a given group member or a number of members. Changes are not always in accord with the desire of the group or of the member. Since we react to the forces that play upon and against each other in a group, we need to understand what they are. Our feelings of personal accomplishment or our failure to change as we wish are related to this play of forces.

The Leader

This section focuses on the leader, the person who must stand out front and make an impact on the group. In the previous section some ideas about groups were presented. It is now logical to consider the processes by which the leader can relate himself to the group, developing acceptance to the point that there is a mutual relationship of trust and respect. The actions of the person in the leadership position are important in that they can make or break the relationship that is so necessary. Some concepts useful in looking at the leader's role are presented in the hope that they will increase the understanding of the leadership process.

SOME CONCEPTS OF LEADERSHIP

What is meant by leadership? There are at least two main schools of thought. One suggests that *leadership* is the act of influencing others, that when one individual can move another to action leadership is then taking place. A second definition, that of *democratic leadership*, identifies leadership as the process of aiding a group to set and attain goals. While there are some philosophical differences in the definitions, both are useful for the purposes of this chapter. In either case the essential meaning is that a process of influence takes place. It is useful for us to look at some notions that will help us to examine the process so that greater insight will result.

First, it is important to recognize that each person is different, and that these individual differences result in a wide array of capabilities and personalities. These differences can be characterized as *leader styles*, at least at the opposite ends of the "totem pole." On the one hand, we can think of the relationship-oriented person whose primary concern is to develop and maintain good relationships with the people with whom he is working. All else is secondary. This style is best represented by the "public relations" man as the extreme case. The emphasis is on avoiding any situation that will cause problems. The opposite extreme is represented by the task-oriented person. His only concern is to get the job done properly. He is not concerned about people, or about the effects that what he is doing will have on them. If their toes are stepped on, "so what?" The job must be done well and anything that gets in the way is kicked out.

These two characterizations represent extremes but do illustrate the fundamental differences in the way people operate. In reality, very few people are at either extreme; most are somewhere in the middle, tending toward one side or the other. It is important for each person to recognize his own particular style and its limitations. A particular style fits a person for a special kind of situation. Often, complementary styles are good: one to keep peace and the other to get the job done. Much depends on the group and the kind of situation it faces. Regardless, the essential idea is to recognize one's style and to use it to advantage, remembering that in the haste of getting the job done one must not step on too many toes or vice versa.

In a very interesting book on leader effectiveness, Fiedler [3] suggests that there are three major factors in looking at the requirements in any leadership situation. These factors are leader-member relationships, task structure, and position power. All three have a definite bearing on the kind of leadership needed and the response of the group to the person in the leadership position. Each of these ideas will be examined separately and they will then be looked at together.

The first of these ideas, *leader-member relationships*, deals with the kind of relationship that exists between the leader and the group. Do they accept each other? Respect each other? Is there a spirit of cooperation and togetherness in working toward common goals? Do they trust each other? These questions highlight strongly the meaning of this idea, emphasizing that a relationship of good quality is essential for an effective leadership situation.

The second idea is *task structure*. This concept is concerned with the degree to which the jobs necessary for goal setting and goal achievement are well defined and organized. Has attention been given to outlining the jobs to be done, who is going to do them, and who will see that they are done properly? It can also include the responsibility for providing adequate recognition for jobs well done. Also, processes like coordination and communication must be helped along so that everyone knows what has to be done, when it has to be done, and for and with whom. This concept implies an orderly process of movement toward the group goals with a minimum of confusion and frustration.

The third idea is *position power*. This concept focuses on the degree to which the leader or the position the leader occupies has control and influence over the behavior of the members of the group. As an illustration, an adult leader working with students in a youth group has much more power than a volunteer in an informal group who agrees to lead in a project, such as arranging for a group outing of some kind. Power may increase with time, particularly if the leader is very successful in helping the group achieve its goals. Even though it may be only small at first, if he is really successful much power can result because of the success. The power that lies with the individual or the position is related to the ease of getting things done. It is easier for one with power to get things done, but this power can be misused if one is not careful.

The three concepts outlined here—leader-member relationships, task structure, and position power—each affect the leadership of any group. The best situation may well be when all three factors are at their best. Leader-member relationships are very good, everything is well organized and understood, and the leader has a strong and positive influence. This utopian situation seldom occurs in real life so all we can do as leaders is to work toward this goal. The three ideas do provide us a useful way of thinking about leading a group. Each group leader must be concerned with developing good relations with the group and within the group. An atmosphere of unity and friendliness must be promoted so that a more effective group can be developed. Thought must also be given to task structure. Things should be well planned, organized, and carried out with as little confusion as possible. Agreement should be reached, but it is important to remember that agreement might come easier if the leader has a plan of some sort to begin with. Just to walk in and say "What do you want to do" may bring the house down with an argument. There is a starting point and a common base to begin with that may make it easier to get on with the job of moving the group to where it wants to go.

With respect to position power, one has to recognize the amount of power present in the particular leadership situation. In an adult literacy class, for example, the teacher as a leader will probably have strong influence over the group, especially because of the great effect he can have on the group. On the other hand, the volunteeer who is attempting to lead some of his friends in an adult discussion group may find that his power is negligible. In these kinds of circumstances, leader-member relationships and task structure become much more important.

LEADERSHIP FUNCTIONS

In achieving the desired situations mentioned in the section on leadership concepts, leader-member relationships, and task structure, it is possible to think in terms of ways to do these things better. Ross and Hendry [4] suggest a double-barreled approach, dividing leadership functions into what the leader must be and what the leader must do. This division will serve as the basis for the present discussion.

First, let us take a look at the things that a leader *must be*. There are two rather basic styles of leadership, the relationship- and the structure-oriented styles. Recognizing the fact that each person tends to be more of one type than the other, it is still important to look at some characteristics of the more effective leaders. Some of the more important ones suggested by Ross and Hendry [5] are:

- identifying with the group being led
- being acceptable as a leader to the group
- being a considerate-type person; being helpful and concerned with the group's welfare
- generating enthusiasm and cheerfulness; being friendly and talkative with the group
- showing stable emotions; controlling one's temper

Other characteristics related to effective leadership include:

- the desire of a person for a leadership role
- the ability to do the job well
- a consistent way of doing things
- good intelligence
- self-confidence in getting the job done
- the ability to share with others in a general sense

All of these points suggest that a person must be concerned with the effect he has on others. He must be conscious that his actions strongly affect the relationship which can be developed with group members. Thus each person in a leadership position ought to take a look at his modus operandi and rate himself in terms of the suggested points.

It is also possible to take a look at the things a leader *must do*. For after all, if nothing is done, nothing will happen. Ross and Hendry [6] again suggest things a leader must do for leadership to be effective:

- Help the group to pull together, suggesting that a feeling of unity must be developed within the group.
- Create a pleasant atmosphere, developing a feeling of agreeableness.
- Aid the group in analyzing problems and give the help needed, including setting goals.
- Assist the group in achieving the goals that are set.
- Help initiate new ideas and new projects; keep things from becoming boring.

- Make sure that everyone knows what is going on.
- Establish a structure for the group; see that interaction occurs among group members.

In looking at leadership functions, one last and important point should be mentioned. This is the rather fundamental question of the purposes of the leader. Is he concerned primarily with his own advancement or that of the group? Do his own goals come first? Is he using the group to satisfy his own goals or does he submerge his own goals to those of the group? Groups, very frequently, have a way of sensing that they are being used, although this is not completely true. It does force a person to look at his own motives and consider them in light of the group's goals. Can the two coincide reasonably well together?

The Program [7]

The process of planning the program of any educational effort is fundamental. One must decide where he is going before he can get there. This holds true for an adult education program as well. The purposes the group seeks to attain must be well defined or the group may never know whether it got there or not. It is obvious that the central core of what is to done hinges on the purposes the group is to reach. Unless these purposes are clearly defined, it may be difficult to determine exactly what activities ought to be conducted with the group.

In a discussion of this fundamental decision-making activity, Tyler [8] suggests four questions that must be answered. What educational purposes does the program seek to attain? What educational experiences can be provided that will likely aid people to achieve these purposes? How can these educational experiences be organized so that learning will be effective? How can one determine whether these purposes are being attained? These questions highlight strongly the necessity of the first step, deciding what purposes to seek. Therefore, the important question facing us at this time is how to make these decisions objectively and meaningfully.

PLANNING CONCEPTS

Planning is a decision-making process. It is a conscious effort to look objectively at the situation, whatever it is, and come up with an estimate of what needs to be done, eliminating the less important and focusing on the more important problems and needs. This is especially critical for adult education programs. Under normal class-room conditions students must come to class. On the other hand, in an adult education situation the potential learner is there because he wants to be. If his time is wasted, he is not likely to return—at least not regularly. It becomes doubly important to tune in on felt needs and problems or, if they are unfelt, to bring people through a process so that they do recognize them as the basis for an educational program.

Education is concerned with bringing about desirable changes in the behavior of people. The planning process, as a result, is concerned with identifying the changes that people need to make if they are to face life better. How can this process be made as good as possible? A useful idea in this connection is the conception of *planning*. It can be thought of in four stages. First, there must be some determination of what is possible. What should be the situation in the community? What should these people be able to do in order to operate more effectively and improve their situation? The second stage then involves a look at the present situation. What is it really like there? What are people doing or not doing? This gives rise to the third stage, comparing the present situation with the desired situation. The result is that some gaps or needs are identified, and these gaps or needs are the differences between the present and the desired situation. Stage four involves an evaluation of the merits of one gap or need, compared with other gaps or needs? Which of these gaps are most vital? Which ones will do the most good?

Let us take a look at an actual situation. An adult women's discussion group is being organized for the purpose of helping a group of women from a slum area learn more about their role as home-makers. Using the four-stage planning model, the decisions about the purposes of the group can be made more objectively and easier. In looking at what is possible or needed, such things as feeding the family a well-balanced diet, using family planning techniques, and raising children properly are desirable. The second stage refers to the determination of the present situation. Are the diets of the family satisfactory and do they understand and use family planning techniques? Again, these are examples of the kinds of questions to be answered. If there are sizeable gaps between what they should do and what they are doing, then gaps or needs are suggested. The fourth stage involves the decision on which of the potential goals or objectives are more important. Is it more important to focus on nutrition or family planning problems? If there are needs in both areas, which is needed most or which appeals to the people themselves more? This may be the place to start the program.

The four stages are tools for analysis that can help a person consider carefully the situation, emphasizing that all sides are looked at as much as possible. In thinking through this idea further, another companion idea is very helpful. This is the concept of *sources for objectives* as suggested by Tyler.[9] He identifies three main sources: the learners themselves, the specialists or experts in the various areas of concern, and the situation facing people in the community.

The potential learners need to be studied so that their present situation can be pinpointed. What sorts of things do they do? What problems do they have? Getting this kind of information makes it easier to relate what is being done to what ought to be done. To illustrate further, the definition of education used in this chapter indicated desirable changes in human behavior as the basic idea. The present behavior patterns of the learners themselves must be identified as the basis for deciding upon the things that need to be changed. If people are already doing the things they ought to be doing, there is then no need to fool with the matter any further. Other useful things can be given attention.

The use of specialists as sources of program objectives relies on their detailed knowledge about the program area or the people to reach or both. The specialist may be important in determining what is possible or what ought to be done. He can also be useful in problem solving since he usually has a very detailed knowledge about the kinds of situations under consideration. By bringing his knowledge and experience to bear on the problem in question, it is possible to get a more accurate assessment of the situation and some possible courses of action, particularly if the necessary course of action is in doubt.

Looking at the community as a source for objectives, the prevailing situation can give rise to some important objectives from at least two aspects. First, what does it take for a person to be able to cope with the situation in the community? Second, what are some problems that the community itself is experiencing?

As an illustration, a community recently faced a water problem. The solution required community action, with the people required to organize themselves to solve the problem. This took unified action of the community, and leadership was necessary to achieve this unity.

INVOLVING PEOPLE IN PLANNING

The idea of involving people who are to take part in a program in making decisions about the program has been received widely in adult education circles. The idea implies that if people are involved in making decisions, they will be more likely to want to do something about the selected problems. It is a question of people recognizing a need or problem and agreeing to do something about it, whether accepting a new idea or a new way of doing things. Therefore, we are concerned with using a process through which people come to realize that their present behavior patterns are inadequate or outmoded and that they must be thrown away and new patterns accepted.

In the planning process, the idea that people can more accurately pinpoint their problems, needs, and interests is also fundamental. This is not to suggest that people always know what their problems are. Often they do not. What is suggested is that if people are brought through a systematic process of looking at the situation realistically and analytically, they will tend to put their finger on some of the more basic problems. On the other hand, if they are put into a situation in which they are simply asked to list their needs and problems, they are likely to react by naming the smaller things, which are often less fundamental. As an illustration, many people fuss about the cost of living: high prices, high labor costs, and so on. It may be that the real problem facing them involves aimless and wasteful spending caused by not having a family budget.

It is important to consider the kind of people to involve in planning a program. First, the target audience must be defined. Who needs to be reached? What groups are we aiming for? When this is done, it is then possible to decide upon the individuals to involve in the planning process. Opinion leaders should be sought, and these leaders should be representative of the entire audience group, however diverse. People look to people whom they know or with whom they can identify. Some respected person in the neighborhood or some local or area celebrity may earn their admiration. In terms of involvement in planning, however, it is practical to recognize that the neighborhood leader types are the most likely candidates.

It is very realistic, consequently, to look systematically at the potential target audience and attempt to identify key leaders who might give support to the program and who can contribute useful ideas about what is needed. If these people are not known, others can be useful in suggesting potential participants. It is not a process of involving four or five close friends in a planning session. The chances are they feel and think like you and know many of the same people. So it becomes a waste of time. To illustrate, if a community-wide adult literacy program is being conducted, it is necessary to identify those areas in which people who need help are likely to be found.

Once this is done, some identification must then be made of leaders they respect and an attempt made to involve these people in the planning process.

When planning is done for a small group only—for example, a group of thirty—it is possible to involve the whole group in planning. If this is not practical, an election can be held to select a planning committee. A lot depends on the group composition and character. At any rate, the procedure used must be systematic so that the group purposes and goals are determined objectively, keeping in mind needs, interests, and problems. The entire purpose of involving people in planning centers around the awakening of the desire to make a change in the people concerned.

The planning committee [10] is a good way to get people involved. When a committee meets for the first time to work on a new problem, it helps to begin in a way which orients the members (1) to one another, and (2) to the common task which they have been brought together to perform. Some biographical bits from each committee member might be a good starting point, followed by a discussion built around the questions:

What are the ingredients of a good program?

What can each member of this committee (using his particular skills and experience) do to help build a good program?

After the committee works out a list of the elements of a good program, further discussion can bring out the realtions between these elements and the resources of individual skills and experience available in the committee. Suppose that the committee has agreed that one element of a good program is that it deals with the needs and interests of the members. The committee might try to see this and other aims in relation to such questions as:

Which people in the groups have skills or talents that can be used in the program?

Which people are members of circles of friends within the larger organization?

Which people represent points of view on subjects of interest or controversy that should be considered in the program?

Which people have contacts outside the group with which our group should be familiar?

There are several advantages, in addition to orientation, in discussing the program in relation to committee personnel. Such discussion can:

Reveal skills and interests not ordinarily associated with particular persons.

Reveal areas in which the committee may need some reinforcement.

And most important, provide a basis on which the committee can build an agenda for future work and delegate responsibilities to committee members in relation to their skills and interests.

PROCEDURES IN PLANNING

Certain procedures in planning are helpful in arriving at good decisions about programs. These procedures are merely guides since it is not possible to say that each thing must be done at a specific time, followed by other steps in sequence. For planning to be an orderly process, nevertheless, certain procedures are useful.

A thorough *determination of the situation* is a first step. Whatever information is useful should be assembled and studied objectively. The sources for objectives, listed earlier in this chapter, are useful guides in determining the kinds of information to collect. It would include the things people do, their characteristics, the situations they live in, and their attitudes and beliefs relative to the program under question. All of these ideas relate to the potential learners themselves. Questionnaires or surveys are means of getting this type of information. Specialists are useful in outlining what is possible: new ideas or practices that may help under the conditions. They can also help interpret the information that is collected.

The program planning committee itself is normally well acquainted with the group it represents. Keep in mind, however, that factual information focuses attention in an objective fashion. It keeps people from "getting off the track" by talking about their own "pet peeves" or "pet projects."

A second stage refers to the *identification of needs and problems.* This means that the information that is collected must be analyzed properly? What do the data mean? This interpretation must be made so that the data can be translated into something meaningful. When the present situation is compared with the possible, based on objective data, it is then possible to note the potential needs and problems. Often problems are not what they appear to be on the surface. The analysis of data can help to pinpoint problems that are not easily seen on the surface. To illustrate, some recent work with low-income families indicated that the nutrition problems relate to lack of fruit and vegetables in the diet. It is not a problem of total food intake. Rather, it is a problem of eating the wrong kind of food; eating too many carbohydrates and not enough vegetables. This is a natural sort of thing, especially when one does not appreciate the importance of eating vegetables, and it emphasizes the point about focusing specifically on the real problem.

The planning process should result in a *decision about the objectives or goals to be sought.* In a sense, this decision is a value judgment since in the final analysis someone has to decide what is to be done. In adult education this decision should be made as objectively as possible, and this is why the planning process is suggested. The objectives or goals selected represent a forecast of what things could or should be like as a result of the program, whatever it might be. The accomplishment of these things should be meaningful and worthwhile to the involved people. Thus objectives serve as guiding beacons to the activities of the program.

These goals and objectives [11] should be clear and understood by all. A little time spent by the planning committee in defining the objectives of the group can do much to save confusion and increase the quality of the product when later on, it begins to build its program.

Many organizations have stated objectives. These objectives, in combination with those that come from information on the needs and interests of the members, form the outer and inner bounds of the group's objectives. In the actual operation of groups, these objectives present themselves in an interwoven network so that some may become hidden from plain view. A helpful means for unjumbling the many possible objectives is to classify them as follows:

1. Those based on the needs and interests of members as individuals. Such as:

- to become a better parent
- to develop better speaking habits
- to make some new friends

2. Those based on the needs and interests of the group or organization. Such as:

- to increase our funds
- to get more members
- to develop better public relations

3. Those based on the needs and interests of the community, the nation, or the world.
Such as:

- to learn about housing conditions in our city
- to promote industrial peace in our state
- to further international understanding

When we talk about objectives for individuals we are talking about education. And the purpose of all education is to produce changes in human behavior. In their final statement, objectives for individuals should contain two halves—behavior and content. For example, the objectives of a parent-teachers' program might be charted as follows:

- To develop knowledge of the characteristics of children 6–10 years old.
- To develop knowledge of the history and purpose of our organization.
- To develop knowledge of the structure and operation of our school board.
- To develop understanding of the forces affecting child development.
- To develop understanding of the forces increasing and decreasing participation in our organization.
- To develop understanding of the forces influencing legislation affecting our schools.
- To develop skills in working with children to assure proper development.
- To develop skills in building better programs.
- To develop skills in organizing voters to work for better educational legislation.
- To develop attitudes of respect toward children as persons.
- To develop attitudes of good will toward people.

There may be changes in other areas, such as the development of values appreciation and interest.

An alert planning committee will usually derive many more goals than can be accomplished within the time available so it must rate the goals according to priority, sifting out the most important and holding over the rest.

In working to achieve one objective—developing skills in working with children, for example—other important objectives are also achieved. It would be hard to imagine the development of such skills in a parent or a teacher without the accompanying development of appropriate attitudes, knowledge, and understanding.

The committee can relate several goals to one another and to the objectives of the organization. For example, the overall purpose of our Parent-Teacher Association is that of providing a better school environment for children. With good program building:

the overall objective   of providing a better school environment for children

becomes related to

the individual objective   of becoming a better parent

which becomes related to

the organizational objective   of increasing cooperation between parents and teachers

which becomes related to

the community objective   of understanding more about federal state and local legislation affecting school operation.

The Learning Process

The primary function of any adult education program is that of changing people, creating desirable changes in people through well-designed learning situations. If this purpose is not accomplished, all the rest of the activity is then to no avail. The group can be a good one, the leader can do his job well, and a good program can be planned. Unless it has an impact upon the behavior of the people for whom it is designed, it is an exercise in futility. The focal point of the entire activity of any educational program must be on learning or changes by the people involved. In this section, as a result, we will examine a few useful concepts about learning and their usage. We will also study some useful methods and techniques.

OBJECTIVES AND LEARNING [12]

Planned education programs should be based on objectives. These *educational objectives* become the bases for selecting the material to be taught and the methods and techniques to be used, both focusing on the desired behavior to be achieved by the learners. As indicated earlier, the objectives selected have been carefully conceived after a thorough analysis of the situation. The material to be mastered and the behavior to be developed by the learner in relation to the material are the keys to planning of the learning situation.

We can think of the behavioral aspect of an objective being expressed in three ways: thinking, feeling, and acting. These three areas can be thought of as follows:

1. *Thinking.* This is the intellectual or cognitive aspect of behavior. It involves the thought processes that go on in the human mind, consisting primarily of concepts of ideas with which to deal with problems.
2. *Feeling.* Involved in this area are the affective behaviors, particularly values, with values defined as the degree of worth attached to an idea or a set of behaviors. Emotions are also an important part: hate, love, like, dislike, and so on, and other personal factors such as interests.
3. *Acting.* Acting involves overt behavior, the things we actually do or say. Needless to say, how we think and what we value most has a profound effect on our behavior. Skills in doing things are an important part of actions, of course, and the skills we use are affected by our intellectual conceptions and the values related to these conceptions.

Let us illustrate these ideas further. Not long ago in a workshop on program development a group, involving a number of home economists, was asked to identify what they thought was a good breakfast, nutritionally, in order to illustrate the planning concept. Prior to this, they had been asked to indicate what they had eaten that morning. Using their own standards, the group evaluated the breakfasts they had eaten that morning. Eighty percent had eaten a poor breakfast. Analyzing, we can say that, intellectually, the home economists understood nutrition. They did not value it as highly as being slim and sleek, so the desire to be attractive won over the intellectual conception of what a good breakfast ought to be. So, from an action standpoint, the intellectual and emotional processes both have an influence on the kind of behavior exhibited by the person and, according to circumstances, one or the other can have a larger influence. Most people operate on the intellectual rather than the emotional level, and for this reason this section about learning focuses primarily on the intellectual standpoint.

Concepts are the basic units by which people think. We can define a concept as follows:

- an idea—something you can see in your mind
- a conceptual picture of what and why
- a tool for thinking and learning
- an intellectual framework for problem solving
- a major area of attention in a discipline

As we can see from this definition, the explanation for human intellectual behavior is based on the concept. If one wants to think about the problems of human nutrition, one must think in terms of a very fundamental concept, that of a balanced diet. What does a balanced diet consist of? It consists of proteins, carbohydrates, vitamins, minerals in the right quantities for a specific person's needs and situation. As we see, concepts are ideas that can be used to think about problems, to come up with the correct answer at the right time and in the right place.

Intellectual behavior can be thought of at two major levels; *knowledge* and *understanding*. By knowledge, we mean knowing that something exists, recognizing it, being able to define it. Its existence is known and recognized by a person. Let us take the concept of a satellite. It orbits the earth. We all know that. We can describe it. We can define it. But do we understand what is involved? Could we design a satellite? Scarcely, unless one happens to be an expert in this sort of thing.

By understanding, we are talking about being able to think with a concept, being able to apply it to new situations, being able to extend it out from the basic idea and enlarge it. It involves the ability to come up with the right concepts, if necessary, and to apply them in a new situation. Let us suppose that some person raises a question and says his group will not respond to him. How can he get them to do something? The concepts about the group expressed in the first section are useful ways for thinking about such problems. By using these concepts, he may be able to come up with some ways to gain a response from the group.

If we apply the ideas of knowledge and understanding to our own particular job as adult educators, it gives us some idea of the learning experiences that we must help people undergo in order to perform our jobs with maximum effectiveness. This reminds me of a situation that occured not long ago. A friend of the family, who had attended a short course of sixteen hours of instruction time on soil fertility conducted by the county extension agent, and who had had only a primary school education, was all aglow about the learning he had received. He reported to me, "Now I understand what Mr. X has been telling me about depth and placement of liquid nitrogen fertilizers." Although he had heard many times that he ought to follow a certain procedure in regard to depth and placement of the fertilizer, he had never been able to grasp the concepts involved, primarily because no one had ever put him in a situation that really helped him learn. It was a source of pride for him to be able to understand what happened to the fertilizer when it was placed in the soil, and the factors that would increase the efficiency of plant by using the fertilizer properly. He was also a better farmer as a result because now he understood something more about plant nutrition.

The focal point of designing good learning situations rests on two very important emphases: the material to be learned and the behavior to be developed as a result of the learning process. If the basic concepts involved in the material can be identified and used as the basis for outlining the material to be learned, learning is then easier. If the concepts are explained and handled in such a manner that people can learn to understand and use them, learning will be easier and more effective. So the upshot of this section is that a good learning situation for people is the result of a well-thought-out teaching plan.

SOME CONCEPTS OF LEARNING [13]

Education, as outlined, is the principal function of the adult educator. The question arises as to the manner in which we can most efficiently and effectively design and organize learning experiences for the people with whom we are working. Consequently, we can think of some concepts about learning that can be helpful to us in accomplishing our task better. Some selected ones that seem most useful are:

Practice. A person has not really learned a new behavior until he has had a chance to put it into practice. Whatever the behavior happens to be, whether an idea or a specific practice, some opportunity must be provided for the learner to come face to face with it. If we think of girls learning clothing skills certain selected skills can be demonstrated from here to eternity, but learning does not really take place until the learner herself is faced with the problem of doing it.

Reinforcement. A person needs to find out whether or not he is using the idea or the practice correctly. He needs some feedback to determine the correctness or wrongness of what he is doing. It is one thing to talk a person into preparing a family budget, but another thing to determine if the job is being done correctly. This is what is meant by reinforcement.

Follow-up is also a part of reinforcement. How can we help people remember what they have learned so that they can apply it at a later date? Written materials of all kinds are always very useful for this purpose and serve a reinforcement function.

Satisfaction. Learning must be accomplished by satisfaction for it to be most effective. It reminds me of the old farmer who was interviewed a few years ago about the reasons why was he still using an old variety of corn instead of one of the new hybrid varieties. His reply indicated that he liked big ears with straight rows and, besides, his corn always won first place at the county fair. It was pleasing to him to raise pretty corn that won blue ribbons. After all, as he indicated, he did not need much corn anyway. It was a hobby, primarily.

This concept is especially important to us as adult educators. Our audiences are voluntary, and they must be reasonably satisfied or they will not come back again. The attitude that we take can definitely have its effect. Part of it reflects on the response of people to us as individuals but we should do as much as possible to make learning satisfying. This is not to suggest that satisfaction is necessarily equated with pure pleasantness, jokes, or foolishness. Satisfaction can be derived very strongly from clear, well-presented, and well-explained learning experiences conducted with directness and expediency. As my wife remarked once after attending a training meeting for volunteer leaders, she was disgusted because much too much time was spent on the philosophy of the program and praise for them as leaders, and much too little time on teaching them what and how to do so that she could work with her group better.

Learning curve. It takes time to learn. Just because we have said something does not necessarily mean that people have grasped or understood what we have said. The learning curve indicates that at first learning is very slow. After a time there is a sudden increase, followed again by a period of slow increase in learning. The old adage, "It takes time for it to sink in," is more true than some of us realize.

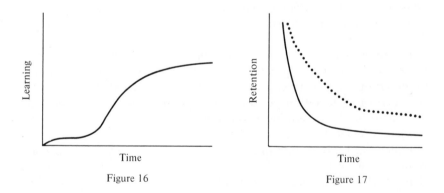

Figure 16   Figure 17

Retention. By retention is meant the extent to which the new behavior is incorporated and retained within the person's repertoire. The retention curve, as you will note from the black line in the illustration, goes down very quickly under normal conditions. One research project indicated that after two years college students remembered less than 20 percent of what they were taught.

Under other circumstances the curve can be flattened as illustrated by the dotted line. Concepts will be remembered much longer than facts. More efficient learning experiences—involving practice, reinforcement and follow-up, satisfaction—have a much more lasting effect, compared with experiences that focus on remembering a lot of specific facts.

Possibility for use. Material which is highly applicable to a person's problems or felt needs will be received and learned much more readily. This is particularly true as long as it does not conflict strongly with some basic values or concepts held by the person. If it does conflict strongly, it will likely be rejected, even though it may be highly pertinent to the problem. Food habits are a good example of this. They are deeply ingrained in people and are not easily changed. Even though people understand something about good nutrition, they cling strongly to old habits. Cigarette smoking is also a good illustration. Most people know that it is bad for the health, but the strong emotional quality of smoking keeps many at it.

Going back to the original idea of the possibility for use, it does enhance the potentiality for learning and acceptance if the learning experience is related to people's problems and is within their background of experience. Ideas too far removed from a person's problems or experiences have little relevance to them. We can use Christ as an example. His teachings in the Bible were most often in the form of parables. By relating the concepts he taught to the realities of living, he was able to effectively instill in his disciples and followers the fundamentals of Christianity which have endured until this day. The parable of the injured man, a Jew, who had been waylaid by a robber and who was passed up by a Pharisee but who was assisted by a Gentile, a foreigner and nonbeliever, is a lasting example of charity and love—basic concepts of Christianity. By relating it to experience, Christ was able to effectively portray the concepts he was attempting to instill in his followers.

Based on the concepts we have discussed in this section, it is also possible for us to derive a few very basic principles that can guide us as we go about the business of designing and organizing learning experiences for people.

1. Many different learning experiences can be used to produce the same behavioral change. This is another way of saying that there is no "school solution," to use the military terminology of the ideal way to do something. Learning experiences should be adapted to the group, to their situation and experiences, and presented in a manner

which is satisfying to them as well as suited to the capabilities of the teacher. For one group, an informal meeting held in the home community may be best, while yet another group may need to be approached formally in another setting.

2. There is no one best method or technique to use in teaching. Different methods and techniques are suited to different kinds of situations. It depends on whether we are teaching concepts or skills and the complexity of them; it depends on the level of the behavioral change being sought (knowledge-understanding); and it also depends on the familiarity of the group with the material. A good teaching program would feature a variety of methods and techniques.

3. Learning experiences that appeal to more than one sense at a time are generally more efficient. For example, the use of visual aids to accompany a presentation makes learning more efficient. We not only hear, but we also see, and this aids learning.

4. Repeated exposures of people to an idea, particularly if it is presented to them through a variety of ways, enhances the learning process. Be careful, however, for these things sometimes can be overdone. This implies that for major objectives, there should be some continuity and sequence in our teaching program. By *continuity* we mean that over time the same general idea must be emphasized, perhaps in different ways and through different methods. By *sequence* we mean that we should start with the more fundamental and simple parts of the idea involved in the practice or skill and gradually build up the knowledge and understanding of the people, making sure that one level is mastered before we move to the next level.

TEACHING PROCEDURES [14]

Two fundamental ideas are involved. One relates to the concept itself and the second relates to the behavior being sought with respect to the learner in relation to the concept. Keeping this in mind, it is possible for us to think of the learning process as follows:

1. For efficient learning, the concept or concepts must be identified, the knowledge needed by the learner defined, and the material organized into appropriate learning units. As an illustration, let us take nutrition. If we are focusing on the concept of a balanced diet, we must then consider the information about a balanced diet needed to clarify the meaning, including subsidiary ideas like proteins, carbohydrates, and so on. It reminds me of a former co-worker in Asia who taught proteins to illiterate villagers with the idea, meat makes meat. It is an oversimplification, but it does get across the concept

in the sense that it indicates that certain foods provide certain necessary nutrients in the diet.

2. The first stage in the learning process is knowledge acquisition
or information getting. The concepts involved need to be introduced
and the way in which the concepts can be utilized must be presented
so that the learner can become familiar with the information and
know what is being talked about. Generally, the results of this stage
are the recall and recognition of the information.

Motivationally, this is an important phase because the learner must
come to recognize the usefulness of the information to himself. Involved at this stage is not only the presentation of the knowledge,
but also the awakening of the desire to learn and to use the information.

3. The second stage in the learning process is that of moving toward understanding. This gives us a key in identifying how far we
want to go. As a bare minimum given by the nature of our job, we
want people to be able to think with and use ideas. This means we
must emphasize the application or use of the concept by people.
Of necessity, appropriate learning experiences must be planned
that will achieve this end. If we recall the concepts of practice, reinforcement, possibility for use, satisfaction, and the learning curve,
these serve as guides to the kinds of methods and techniques that
can be used. The learner must be put into a situation in which he is
forced, if necessary, to deal with the ideas in terms of his own case
or at least to make a mental extension of it to his case. Repeated
opportunities must be provided that will allow the learner to deal
with the concept in new situations, and additional information
must be presented to expand his understanding of the idea so that
a deeper and deeper appreciation will be developed.

4. Finally, aid the learners to evaluate the adequacy of their behavior. They must know the correct behavior and be able to determine their short-comings; otherwise, the job is not complete.

SOME USEFUL METHODS AND TECHNIQUES [15]

Deciding which methods and techniques to use in achieving a
specific educational objective is one of the important tasks of the
adult educator. How can the group be aided to master the material
being taught and achieve the desired behavior about the material?
There is no one best method or technique. The approach must be
acceptable to the group, it must enable the leader to put over the

material effectively, and it must be done in such a way that effective learning takes place. The adult educator should refer to some of the concepts presented in this section as guides for judging the effectiveness of learning.

The good teacher has a *plan*. The kinds of methods and techniques that will be used must be carefully thought out in advance. Good teaching does not just happen; it occurs because the leader has planned in some detail how he expects to lead the group toward the preselected objective. He must use good techniques and proper methods to accomplish his mission. The following discussion of some methods and techniques [16] will be useful in thinking through the approaches to be used in the teaching plan:

Clinic. Most people talk about a clinic as a means of diagnosing the difficulties or of analyzing the components of a particular situation and then finding different working techniques or procedures to try. Many groups use role playing, a film or filmstrip, or a case study as a basis for analysis or as a kickoff to discussion. People who are trying to understand how rumor spreads have looked at pictures or diagrams and then, without referring to the pictures again, described what they saw or answered questions about details. A paragraph which had been read to them and which they then attempted to recall and repeat or a short sentence whispered from one person to another and finally stated aloud would have been other ways to begin analyzing what rumor is like. After they have seen a demonstration or some other kind of kickoff, those who take part in a clinic session are likely to go into a question-and-answer period or a general discussion before they attempt to formulate any hypotheses or suggest any procedures.

Forum. Any meeting given over to general public discussion of some particular issue or closely connected group of issues. Usually, there is a platform-audience orientation, and audience participation is often limited to asking of questions.

Film forum. A forum in which a film is used to present information. Someone may explain what the purpose of the film is and suggest how it can be used; he may also call attention to particular things in the film to watch for. After the film has been shown, audience members may comment or raise questions. The purpose of a film forum may, of course, be to evaluate a specific film.

Panel discussion. A lot of groups like to use a panel meeting to pass along information or to present a problem. Half a dozen people, more or less, may be asked to present different kinds of information or different views of a problem. These people, who constitute a panel, are usually seated behind a table at the front of the room. A leader or chairman introduces them one by one to the audience and indicates the nature of the problem to be discussed. Each panel member then gives his information or states his views or the views of the organization he represents. Since discussion among the panel members and question and commentary between panel and audience usually follow a panel presentation, the panel speakers should not talk too long. Thus they should get together before the panel session to get an idea of the position or set of mind of each.

Symposium. Like a forum and panel meeting, a symposium centers around a group of speakers. It is more likely to have less audience participation than either of the other two types of meeting and sometimes the members of the audience do not enter into any discussion or ask any questions—they listen to what the speakers have to say and store what information they can for later use. The speakers at a symposium are in basic agreement with regard to general content or overall problems of the meeting and attempt to aid the audience to develop a full and detailed understanding. The number of speakers at a symposium varies according to the number of aspects of a subject or points of view to be represented and according to the amount of time available for the meeting.

Workshop. The workshop centers around a specific core of problems or area of interest. Those who attend work intensively over a brief period of time upon particular problems they decide upon within the limits of the overall problem or area. The long-term workshop (or institute)—one, two, three, six weeks—usually emphasizes group practice or rehearsal situations in which special group techniques such as role playing, sociodrama, case studies, and so on may play an important part. A lot of people use the term *workshop* (or conference) in terms of a general meeting that discusses a problem or problem area and then breaks down into smaller groups, each concerned with a single aspect of the problem. When a workshop runs for several days or longer, these small groups will from time to time report back at general meetings. These general meetings give people a chance to see how the workshop is progressing and an opportunity to change plans for the remaining sessions. A single meeting is sometimes said to use a workshop technique when there is a similar intensive consideration of a problem, especially if part of the time is spent in subgroups.

Discussion groups. Most people find it easier to talk to a few than to a large number. They find it easier to speak informally than to make an address or even a report. The buzz group, a good warm-up device, is a way of setting up face-to-face communication within a large audience and of getting the general thinking out. It is a subgroup of four to ten people drawn from a larger group or audience. It serves the function of enabling all the people in a large group to participate in planning, of setting a course of action, of talking something over thoroughly to an extent they could not do if they tried to work in a single unit. Usually, buzz groups report their thinking or recommendations to the total group by asking one person to summarize their discussion and to indicate minority as well as majority opinion. What is said in the reports may be noted on a blackboard or newsprint pad and used as a basis for further thinking. Buzz groups are formed pretty arbitrarily—odd-numbered rows of people in an audience turning around to face even-numbered ones, the chairman or discussion leaders passing down a central aisle and indicating to the audience roughly how they should divide into groups, and so on. It may make a convenient transition between a panel and the rest of a meeting.

A particularized version of the buzz group evolved by Professor Don Phillips of Michigan State College, the Phillips 66 technique requires that for discussion purposes an audience break up into groups of six each. In a small audience members may count off by sixes. In larger audiences three people in the first row may turn to face three in the second, three people in the third may face three in the fourth, and so on. When the groups of six have been formed, each member of a group introduces himself to the others in his group. Each group then appoints one of its members as spokesman. The spokesman gets from each member his views or comments and then asks the group to decide which one or two of these to present to the whole audience. At the end of six minutes the whole audience or meeting is called back together, the spokesmen present the comments or queries from their groups, and these are recorded or reacted to by the chairman. Because of the time limitations, the Phillips 66 is particularly useful as a starter, although it may be used as a follow-up device to get audience reaction to a speaker or panel.

Role playing [17] is a relatively new educational technique in which people spontaneously act out problems of human relations and analyze the enactment with the help of other role players and observers. Role playing is a general term referring to the spontaneous acting out of roles in the context of human relations situations. It deals with the interactions of people with other individuals or groups as carriers of some specified cultural role, such as supervisor, leader, mother, father, employee. These situations always involve more than one person and deal with problems a majority of group members face in executing their roles.

Why use role playing? The growing interest of all kinds of groups in role playing makes it the more important that we answer this question clearly. Part of the answer is that role playing is novel; it is an absorbing group activity; and it provides opportunities for much more active participation by group members than do many other educational methods. These are good reasons, as many groups still suffer from rigidly narrow range of methods or from methods which do not highly involve the members. But they are by no means the most important reasons for using role playing.

A major advantage of role playing as an educational method is that it can bring out data about human behavior and human relations not made available by more traditional methods. Written records or lectures may give a group useful data and may stretch the boundaries of the group's previous experience, but the data they bring is limited by the fact that it must always be presented to the group through the medium of words. It cannot provide the group with direct common experience of what is being talked about. Role playing caters to the whole person of the learner. He not only hears about a problem or tells about it; he lives through it by acting it out—he experiences it emotionally and then uses this experience to produce and test insights into the problem and generalizations about ways of dealing with it. He may also practice what he has learned until it becomes a part of himself. Thus individuals, through role playing, may develop new skills for dealing with problems in human relations. Furthermore, role playing allows groups to get case material which, unlike the written or even the filmed record, can be tailored readily to fit the specific needs and situation of the particular group that is going to use it. For example, workers' education groups can do role playing on handling grievances, discussion groups on handling overtalkative members, and so on.

Because role playing helps people to get insight into their own and others' feelings, it has been widely recognized as a method of helping people to broaden their understanding of and to empathize with other people—to see things from the point of view of the person on the other side of the table (or tracks, or globe).

Another value of role playing is that it allows many attitudes and feelings that fundamentally affect group processes—but are usually left unexpressed and subjective—to be brought before the group for review. Thus role playing can serve as a method for illustrating and objectifying many of the causal and dynamic factors in group process and human relations that are frequently ignored. Role playing can also serve as a method of presenting information about what particular individuals in a group have been doing—for example, when a subgroup wishes to show its parent group what it has been doing rather than just to tell about the results.

But the most important value of role playing is that, because it is a way of presenting human relations problems in the context of a classroom training group or social laboratory, group members can experiment with their behavior, make mistakes, and try new skills without chancing the hurts that experimentation in real life situations may involve. In this artificial environment the learner can try out new behavior in the presence not of judges, but of co-learners.

CHECKLIST OF TOOLS FOR LEARNING [18]

Types	*Special Purposes and Uses*
HUMAN RESOURCES	
Speaker	Presents knowledge and experiences systematically with personal touch. Can be inspirational. Can interact with audience through questions.
Debate	Presents opposing points of view. Focuses on points of controversy. May clarify issues.
Symposium	Presents several points of view or kinds of experience systematically.
Panel	Shows several minds at work cooperatively on a problem. Presents information functionally.
Group interview	Develops information in relation to specific questions.
Book review	Combines thinking of an author with interpretation of reviewer. May stimulate further reading.
Chalk talk	Clarifies information and develops understanding of relationships through visual symbols.
Dramatics	Presents knowledge and experiences with emotional overtones. Places ideas in situations.

Types	*Special Purposes and Uses*
HUMAN RESOURCES	
Consultant or "Resource Person"	Makes special knowledge and experience available to a group in terms of its own needs and problems.
Demonstration, recital, performance	Provides a direct common experience. Permits interpretation of process through words and illustration of words by process.
PRINTED MATERIALS	
Books	Present knowledge and experience systematically and thoroughly. Make thinking of best minds of all times and places available at convenience of reader.
Pamphlets	Provide knowledge and experience in special areas in condensed form. Inexpensive.
Study guides	Provide progressive learning experiences toward predetermined goals.
Discussion guides	Enable inexperienced groups to move their thinking in directions set by others.
Manuals	Give instruction in performance of skills.
Newspapers, magazines, reports, periodicals, catalogs.	Provide reports of current events and contemporary ideas. Readily available. Inexpensive.
Bibliographies, reading lists	Provide overview of literature available on selected subjects.
AUDIO-VISUAL AIDS	
Blackboard	Permits creative and simultaneous illustration of ideas by speaker. Especially valuable for listings. Highly flexible.

CHECKLIST OF TOOLS FOR LEARNING [18]

Types	*Special Purposes and Uses*
AUDIO-VISUAL AIDS	
Motion picture	Provides wide range of knowledge and experience. Condensed and selected. Makes possible visualizations of realities otherwise out of reach. Conveys movement.
Slides, slide films, opaque projections, stereographs	Permit personal interpretation and expansion of visual experience. Visual images can be enlarged greatly and held indefinitely.
Charts, graphs	Especially valuable in communicating statistical ideas.
Maps, globes	Permit visualization of geographical relationships.
Photographs	Provide permanent visual records of local situations.
Exhibits, bulletin boards, diorama models, mock-ups, specimens	Provide concrete examples of wide range of objects. Permit organization in terms of functional operation, developmental sequence, categories, and so on. Can be examined closely.
Puppets	Permit creative portrayal of situations.
Radio, television	Provides rapid reports of contemporary events. Makes available the ideas and talent of national figures.
Phonograph records	Make available to all groups national talents in music, dramatics, and speech. Can be stopped at any point for discussion.
Tape recordings	Make precise records of groups or individual performance. Available for later detailed analysis.

Types	Special Purposes and Uses
GROUP ACTIVITIES	
Field trips, excursions	Provide first-hand observations of situations.
Pageants	Enable groups to portray historical events and to get a greater emotional identification with them.
Role playing	Enables group to develop insight into cause-and-effect relationships and test ideas for producing change in human relationships.
Discussion	Permits maximum use of experiences of individual group members as resource for group.
Arts & crafts activities	Provide creative self-expression, translation of ideas into objects.
Skits	Permit creative illustration of ideas and situations.

Notes

1. For a more detailed explanation, consult a book on group dynamics such as George Beal, J. M. Bohlen, and J. N. Raudabaugh, *Leadership and Dynamic Group Action* (Ames: Iowa State University Press, 1962).
2. This section on pressure is taken basically from an article by William Morse, "Pressures in Groups," *Understanding How Groups Work*, Leadership Pamphlet no. 4 (Washington, D.C.: Adult Education Association of the U.S.A., 1955).
3. Fred E. Fiedler, *A Theory of Leadership Effectiveness* (New York: McGraw-Hill, 1967).
4. Murray G. Ross and Charles E. Hendry, *New Understanding of Leadership* (New York: Association Press, 1957).
5. *Ibid.*
6. *Ibid.*
7. For a more thorough discussion of program planning, see L. L. Pesson, "Extension Program Planning with Participation of Clientele," *The Cooperative Extension Service*, H. C. Sanders, ed. (Englewood Cliffs, N.J.: Prentice-Hall, 1966).
8. Ralph W. Tyler, *Basic Principles of Curriculum and Instruction*, Syllabus for Education 305 (Chicago: University of Chicago Press, 1950).
9. *Ibid.*

10. The discussion on the planning committee is taken from Malcolm S. Knowles, "The Planning Committee," *Planning Better Programs*, Leadership Pamphlet no. 2 (Washington, D.C.: Adult Education Association of the U.S.A., 1955).
11. The discussion on goals and objectives is taken from Malcolm S. Knowles, "What Are Your Goals?", *Planning Better Programs*, Leadership Publication no. 2 (Washington, D.C.: Adult Education Association of the U.S.A., 1955).
12. For a discussion of this topic see Tyler, *op. cit.*
13. For discussion of learning see Herbert J. Klaussmeier and William Goodwin, *Learning and Human Abilities*, 2nd ed. (New York: Harper & Row, 1966).
14. *Ibid.*
15. For a discussion of methods and techniques, see Harry L. Miller, *Teaching and Learning in Adult Education* (New York: The Macmillan Company, 1964) and Sanders, ed., *op. cit.*
16. This material was taken from Homer N. Calver, "Some Program Patterns," *How to Use Role Playing and Other Tools for Learning*, Leadership Publication no. 6 (Washington, D.C.: Adult Education Association of the U.S.A., 1955).
17. This material is adapted from Grace Levit, "Learning Through Role Playing," *How to Use Role Playing and Other Tools for Learning*, Pamphlet no. 6 (Washington, D.C.: Adult Education Association of the U.S.A., 1955).
18. Taken from Elbert W. Burr and Donald P. Smith, "Check-List of Tools for Learning," *How to Use Role Playing and Other Tools for Learning*, Leadership Pamphlet no. 6 (Washington, D.C.: Adult Education Association of the U.S.A., 1955).

Selected References

ADULT EDUCATION ASSOCIATION OF THE U.S.A. *Planning Better Programs.* Leadership Pamphlet no. 2. Washington, D.C., 1955.
——. *Understanding How Groups Work.* Leadership Pamphlet no. 4 Washington, D.C., 1955.
——. *How to Use Role Playing and Other Tools for Learning.* Leadership Pamphlet no. 6. Washington, D.C., 1955.
BEAL, GEORGE M., JOE M. BOHLEN, and J. N. RAUDABAUGH. *Leadership and Dynamic Group Action.* Ames: Iowa State University Press, 1962.
FIEDLER, FRED E. *A Theory of Leadership Effectiveness.* New York: McGraw-Hill, 1967.
KLAUSMEIER, HERBERT J. and WILLIAM GOODWIN. *Learning and Human Abilities*, 2nd ed. New York: Harper & Row, 1966.
MILLER, HARRY L. *Teaching and Learning in Adult Education.* New York: The Macmillan Company, 1964.
ROSS, MURRAY G. and CHARLES E. HENDRY. *New Understandings of Leadership.* New York: Association Press, 1957.
SANDERS, H. C. (ed.) et. al. *The Cooperative Extension Service.* Englewood Cliffs, N.J.: Prentice-Hall, 1966.
TYLER, RALPH W. *Basic Principles of Curriculum and Instruction.* Syllabus for Education 305. Chicago: University of Chicago Press, 1950.

CHAPTER SEVEN

Planning Conferences, Seminars, and Workshops for Large Groups of Adults

QUENTIN H. GESSNER

Dr. Quentin H. Gessner is Supervisor of Conferences, Extension Service, The University of Michigan, Ann Arbor.

T H I S   C H A P T E R represents an effort to discuss adult continuing education in the group setting. Group meetings, of one type or another are an important part of our way of life—for example, political, business, and church conventions; forum and lecture series; adult education programs; university lectures; high school assemblies; trade association and banquet meetings are all standard forms of group gatherings. In the United States alone, millions of people attend thousands of group meetings each year to become better informed and to prevent their obsolescence. Such programs are known as conferences, workshops, seminars, institutes, and so on. The term *conference* is used frequently throughout this chapter synonymously with seminars, workshops, institutes, and so on. These conference-type programs can and should continue to be utilized as one technique for providing continuing education for adults in our society.

In terms of background you might think we would know more about conferences than we do since, historically, conferences have been around for quite some time. Apparently, both Plato and Socrates used the conference to develop interest and content for their students and, three centuries before Christ, Aristotle made use of conference techniques. In fact, conferences have been around as long as man himself. Brief and perhaps rather inconclusive research indicates that the first conference occurred in the Garden of Eden, attended by a serpent and Eve, the mother of mankind. It is recorded in Genesis 3:5 that the serpent advised Eve, "Your eyes shall be opened, and ye shall be as Gods, knowing the good and evil." As a result of this conference, Eve ate of the forbidden fruit and you know what a mess we have made of things since. The fact that the first conference speaker was a snake, and that his advice was bad, seems to have had no long-term damaging impact on the conference business.

It is easy for one to develop the opinion that many conferences are a "hit-or-miss" proposition, poorly planned and nonproductive. The mere existence of a conference program does not mean it is educational nor does the fact that it is held on a college or university campus place it in that category. However, conferences can be meaningful and successful for the participants, and they certainly can be productive. To achieve these goals, conferences must be well planned and properly administered.

Conference planning offers an interesting situation. On the one hand, we find the person suddenly faced with the responsibility of planning, conducting, and evaluating a conference without the foggiest notion of where to turn or how to go about it. On the other hand, another person in the same situation, also without conference planning experience, may not have a care in the world because "after all, anyone can run a conference!"

Therefore, for the new or uninitiated person charged with the responsibility for planning, conducting, and evaluating a conference experience, the following information is provided;

1. Definition: What is an educational conference and what are its components?
2. Who are the participants? What roles can they play to make a conference successful?
3. Planning the conference: options and alternatives.
4. Specific guidelines for conference planning.
5. Administrative details of conference planning.
6. Summary.

Definition: What Is an Educational Conference and What Are Its Components? The term *conference* is frequently used to describe a wide range of activities. William M. Sattler and N. Edd Miller identify "a conference as any meeting, assemblage, or gathering of people, formal or informal." [1] Halbert E. Gulley suggests that a "conference designates a large meeting sometimes referred to as a convention or workshop." [2] Howard Y. McClusky has defined a conference as a "planned and orderly series of educative experiences designed to achieve an educational objective." [3] This last definition clearly exemplifies the need for planning a progression of activities designed to provide a cumulative educational experience for participants attending an educational conference. Thus a conference may be viewed sequentially as consisting of three major components:

1. The planning component which determines the form or structure of the conference.
2. The program component which is the actual conference experience.
3. The evaluation component which includes the participants' perceptions of the conference experience.

Paradoxically, you should plan backward. Think about the major components of a conference in terms of participants' evaluation of a program (evaluation component), which will obviously result from their conference experience. The conference experience (program component) is meaningful in light of the participants' attitudes, expectations, learning abilities, needs, and experiences. This means the planning is crucial and depends upon the attitudes, experiences, and expectations of the planning committee (planning component) and, most of all, upon an empathic understanding of the participants.

In addition, other important factors are the interpersonal relationships among planners, the objectives they establish for the conference and the planning process itself, the participants' objectives, and the objectives established by the speakers for their presentations.

The conference planner should, at the very least, be aware of the major components and some of the factors involved in planning, conducting, and evaluating such a program.

Who Are the Participants? What Roles Can They Play to Make a Conference Successful? Generally, conference participants represent a cross-section of many occupational, professional, and socioeconomic backgrounds. The degree of variety among participants will depend primarily upon the subject under consideration.

Some will attend to increase their education, to gain information, to solve a problem, to resolve conflict, or to discuss specific areas of interest. Also, participants may attend because they have been told by a superior to do so or because they have a desire to get away from job responsibilities for a few days. Some conference participants attend a program for social reasons or visibility purposes. A planning committee should give consideration to the reasons why potential participants attend a program. If they fail to do this, the program may prove to be unsatisfactory from the attendees' point of view.

For example, an unfortunate situation developed in a recent conference because the program planners had not adequately considered the experience and sophistication of the participants. In this program medical doctors were to provide information related to the initial emergency care of accident victims to ambulance drivers, policemen, and firemen. Their presentations were at a level beneath that of the participants' expectations. Many persons in the audience had more experience in emergency situations than the speakers. One ambulance driver had delivered sixty-three babies over a fifteen-year period, all under emergency conditions. Child deliveries by the speaker had been in a sterile hospital delivery room. The result was that speakers did not provide new or meaningful information for the audience. Of course, feedback from the participants indicated frustration and a generally negative reaction to the program. Had the program planners involved some of the potential participants during the planning stage and learned of their past experiences and program expectations, the problem might not have developed.

The general planning principle: *Determine who the participants will be, and identify their needs and expectations in relation to the proposed program.*

Conference planners, through consideration of the participants' role, will be able to plan their programs more effectively. By increased awareness of what is expected of them, conference participants can develop greater cooperative interaction and participate more fully in the program. Individual participants, by paying attention to their own behavior, can help make the conference more efficient and satisfying. For example, if the program is geared to problem solving, participants can fullfill the following roles suggested by Alfred W. Storey.

1. *Clarifier.* Helps make group goals clear and thereby improves the probability of a rational choice.
2. *Informative giver.* Assists the group on problems of fact. Gives authentic information when it is useful.
3. *Orienter.* Assists the group by defining its position with respect to its goals by summarizing what has occurred, by pointing out any departures from agreed upon goals.
4. *Coordinator.* Clarifies the relationships among various ideas and suggestions.
5. *Energizer.* Prods the group to greater activity, tries to stimulate greater interest and satisfaction.
6. *Encourager.* Praises and accepts contributions of others, has a warm friendly attitude toward other group members.[4]

Planning the Conference: Options and Alternatives. Harleight B. Trecker has defined planning as the "conscious and deliberate guidance of thinking to create logical means for achieving commonly agreed upon goals. Planning always and inevitably sets priorities and calls for value judgments. The alternative to plan is no plan."[5]

Experience has persuaded me that systematic planning for conferences is more the exception than the rule. Many programs seem to be planned with what can be called a shotgun approach. In this loose type of planning, committees suggest speakers or topics to use in forthcoming programs. A typical pattern is for a committee to suggest speakers the committee members have heard speak at other programs they have attended. Another planning committee likes to invite entertaining speakers to cover subject areas that each member individually believes need to be covered. In this procedure, the planning committee assumes that it is best for all participants because of their own personal interests.

Another problem which emerges when a committee plans by this approach is a lack of continuity with other conference programs of their organization over a period of years. The programs tend to be yearly one-shot programs rather than a series of connected short-term learning experiences designed to provide a continuing education program for the participants.

In an attempt to provide such a continuing education experience for its membership, a state association of assessors initiated a three-year plan for its annual conference. The plan seeks to provide within a three-year period the basic information a new assessor needs to carry out his responsibilities. In the first year, during a one-week institute, basic details of assessing are studied; in the second year, more complex materials are covered; and in the third year the basic training is completed. From that point on, hopefully, the individual is prepared to study more detailed areas of the profession. Such planning provides continuity and a systematic training process, and it maximizes the effectiveness of the instructors' and participants' time and effort.

Another approach often used by conference planning committees is first to select a theme and then to decide what the program content should be. Or a committee may decide on subjects that are popular at the time. Unfortunately, these methods do not necessarily meet the needs of the participants and tend to ignore the reasons for bringing them together. They also ignore who the conference participants are and do not take into account the backgrounds and experiences they will bring to the conference situation.

From this discussion it is obvious that there are many ways one can initiate conference planning. But, before deciding on a particular route to follow in planning a program, the conference planner should be aware of additional factors that can influence the design of the program. Here are some options and alternatives for the conference planner's information and consideration:

- "camel back participation" concept
- styles of leadership roles available
- learning principles that can be applied in a conference situation
- program formats available to the planner

CAMEL BACK PARTICIPATION

Leroy H. Marlow in his article, "The Camel Back of Conference Participation," suggests the theory that "true participation during a conference is, in reality, 'Camel Back' activity with two, three or perhaps four noticeable 'peaks' of participation." [6] Marlow indicates that conference participation does not necessarily increase as the program progresses, but suggests there are peaks and valleys of participation during the conference experience.

From my experience, when conferences last several days or longer, one must pay particular attention to how the program is structured in relation to the time allocated for the meetings, coffee breaks, social activities, and free time.

Timing and rhythm in scheduling are important. It has been suggested the "mind will absorb only as much as the seat will endure." This time-honored statement is good to remember when planning a program. Much depends on the type of program format one is developing but, generally, the planner must remember that conference participants need to have intermittent breaks during the day, free time for themselves, and perhaps a social activity to refurbish their think tanks. These "relaxers" are best scheduled when "valleys" might be expected in terms of participant fatigue, lack of motivation, or interest.

STYLES OF LEADERSHIP
IN CONFERENCE PLANNING

The style of leadership one may wish to follow is another option available to the conference planner. William M. Sattler and N. Edd Miller suggest that styles of leadership can range from maintaining tight control over the conference planning committee to allowing considerable individual freedom. The control versus freedom continuum can be shown as follows:

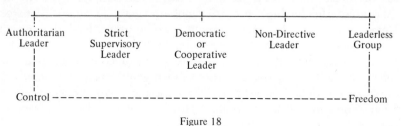

Figure 18

The characteristics of each leadership style differ quite markedly from one to another.

Authoritarian Leadership. In this role the conference leader will dictate both the way in which the conference is conducted and also the decisions that are reached. This person dominates the group, refusing to share leadership with others because he feels the entire conference needs his own type of firm control and central direction.

Supervisory Leadership. The person who assumes this role is less autocratic, more considerate and friendly than the strict authoritarian. He is concerned that the program is his personal responsibility, and is committed to predetermined conclusions.

Democratic Leadership. The democratic leader is primarily interested in having all planning committee members show initiative and take part in group decisions. He attempts to keep the lines of communication open at all times, promotes cooperation, and assists the committee members to share ideas and mutually resolve problems.

Nondirective Leadership. This style of leadership calls for greater permissiveness by the leader. The group members learn to guide and direct themselves and are generally responsible for making the decision of what to discuss and/or which problem to resolve. This leader influences the group through personal encouragement and implied help.

Leaderless Group. In this situation the leader is practically nonexistent since the group members are given the opportunity to practice self-direction. The nondirectiveness of the group allows for greater permissiveness than the other leadership styles described. A T-group which operates within a relatively unstructured situation with no imposed direction is an example of a leaderless group.

The leadership style you decide to use will depend upon such factors as your personality, operating style, organizational structure, and so on. Several limitations are noteworthy. For example, if you use authoritarian leadership, group members may become alienated. Democratic leadership may in reality evolve into a leaderless group. The leaderless style cannot be recommended, given the time limitations usually imposed on persons assuming a conference planning role. Inevitably, someone has to establish goals, make decisions, and organize the details necessary for conducting a conference program. Such action may lead to conflict. However, it may be necessary for conflict to occur before decisions are made.

It is important to remember that the leadership style used may change frequently in a group situation. Perhaps the best plan is not to adopt any one style exclusively, but to utilize the appropriate characteristic of each style called for at the proper time in the planning process.

LEARNING PRINCIPLES

Persons responsible for conference planning should see a short-term program as a *learning experience*. Therefore, to develop a program that is meaningful and rewarding for the participant, one should make use of adult learning principles that can be applied to the conference situation. Several suggested principles for use are as follows:

1. People learn best those things which are of interest and importance to them.
2. People learn best when they have the opportunity to share in the planning of the methodology, policy, and responsibility of their learning experience.
3. People learn best when they have the freedom to express their feelings and opinions about the things which they are learning.
4. People learn best within an accepting, friendly, and unthreatening atmosphere.
5. Learning should be aimed at achieving the goals of the learner and in helping him move toward their attainment.
6. Learning should deal with the experience of the learner.
7. Learning will depend upon experience since past experience determines how the new experience is assimilated.

It is important to understand learning will not occur by chance. Principles like those just enumerated must be considered during the program planning stage and conditions must be created that will enable learning to take place.

TYPES OF PROGRAM FORMATS

Most meetings have, within a broad definition of the term, an educational purpose. They seek to share or provide information to an audience for problem-solving purposes, decision making, or bringing about change in the individual or the group. They disseminate information, technical data, or policy statements. Or the meetings could be for discussion of individual, group, or community problems. Depending on the program purpose and objectives, the conference planner has a number of formats available to him:

Panel. A panel is a discussion, generally informal, which is held before an audience and involves a free interchange rather than prepared speeches. The distinctive feature of the panel is the communication pattern. A small group of experts discusses a problem in a conversational exchange of ideas. This format is quite frequently used in public discussion. However, the panel can be used as a reaction group to a prepared speech or to stimulate the audience prior to a question-and-answer period. Generally, the physical arrangement is to have the panel seated in front of the room, as illustrated:

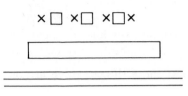

Figure 19

Symposium. In a symposium situation a group of experts or well-informed persons deliver prepared speeches for the benefit of an audience. Following the talks, questions may be asked or a panel of peers may discuss the content of the message. The same procedure is generally followed for each speaker. The symposium method is often used for scientific meetings when technical papers are presented. For example, an international symposium discussing the problem of noise generated by supersonic aircraft might use as speakers a representative of the U.S. Air Force, a spokesman from the Federal Aviation Agency, and an engineer from one of the leading aircraft manufacturers. Following each speaker, or after all speakers have completed their presentations, the audience can participate in the discussion or a panel might be used to challenge or confirm the major points raised by the speakers. The following diagram illustrates possible physical arrangements for such a program:

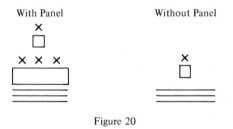

Figure 20

Dialogue. The dialogue is a free interchange involving two communicating participants. The discussion is directly conversational with one person asking questions and the other person providing answers or information on the topic being discussed. Used quite frequently in radio and television, the dialogue is generally informal and is well adapted to the informational type of discussion. In a dialogue situation, the participants can be either in front of the audience or placed in the center of the room, as illustrated.

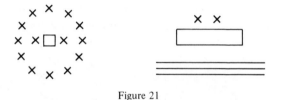

Figure 21

Forum. The forum generally applies to a meeting, or that portion of a meeting in which members of the audience may participate in the discussion. If the audience participates from the beginning of the program, it is designated as an open forum. This type of format has been used for many years in American communities for conducting town meetings. A forum following a lecture is called a lecture forum, or one might have a symposium forum, dialogue forum, community forum, or panel forum. Seating arrangements for a forum are as follows:

Figure 22

Clinic. The clinic provides an opportunity for the audience to listen to experts speak on a specific topic or problem. The members of the audience are given the opportunity to ask questions of the experts, who are generally selected because of their experience and knowledge of the subject under discussion. This type of situation places the participants in a trainee role, whereas the clinic leaders are the trainers. General sessions as well as face-to-face groups can be used as diagrammed:

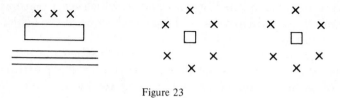

Figure 23

Seminar. A seminar involves a small number of persons who share experiences, with a high degree of participation among members of the group. Resource people and/or the discussion leader not only contribute to the subject under discussion, but encourage all group members to contribute. A seminar work group with a task orientation might use tables for convenience; however, for a more informal discussion-type seminar a small circle, without tables, is appropriate.

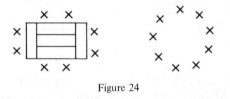

Figure 24

Institute. An institute can be characterized by its general function, that is, the training of the participants by a staff that provides most of the resources. This type of program is usually of longer duration than other short-term programs, possibly one to two weeks or longer in length. The topic is usually one of a specialized nature designed for a specific group. For example, a group of government economists or urban planners might conduct a one-week institute for municipal finance officers. Seating arrangements for such a program could be as follows:

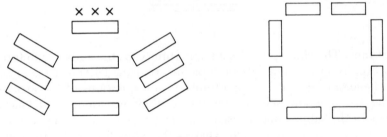

Figure 25

Workshop. A workshop can be defined as a meeting in which people work together in small groups and in which each person has an opportunity to participate in and contribute toward the achievement of the group goals.

The workshop technique is used primarily when the participants are placed in an active rather than a passive role. The participant has a responsibility to himself, as well as to the total group, to become involved in the task assigned or the learning situation. Since workshops are frequently used as an instructional method, the program planner should be aware of the responsibilities of the *discussion leader, recorder, observer,* and *resource person.*

The following suggestions are provided if such assignments are appropriate:

DISCUSSION LEADERS

1. Your primary function is to help the participants determine the problems which they wish to discuss and progress as far as possible toward solving these problems in the time available.
2. Remember, you are a member of the group with no more authority or prestige than the other members.
3. You may want to start the discussion by requesting the group members to state their problems on a priority basis, listing these on the blackboard.
4. To avoid too long a list, combine similar problems and try to reduce the number of problems to which the group is to address itself.
5. Have the group establish which problem they wish to start with and how many problems they want to deal with in the time available. This procedure calls for a realistic appraisal of the depth of the problem and the time allocated to the group.
6. Try to encourage participation from all members of the group. Prevent a few members from monopolizing the discussion. Assist the group members in clarifying statements and recognizing the strengths and weaknesses of participant contributions.
7. Attempt to keep the group "on target" unless a new track is desirable. This can be accomplished by providing a brief summarization to be sure all members know where the discussion is at a given point in time.
8. You may occasionally have to remind the group of their time limitations.
9. Assist the participants to reach some conclusions concerning the problem as a group, if conclusions are a desirable goal of the group.

RECORDERS

1. Your primary function is to listen to all that is said. Then record the main points from what you hear and organize them in such a way that they can be used by the group and, more selectively, for use by the total workshop.
2. Record issues on which members agree or on which formal action is taken.
3. Record issues on which there are differences of opinion among the members.
4. Record issues on which you are not sure how the members feel, and issues that are mentioned but not discussed.
5. Report to the group what was discussed and concluded.
6. Ask other members of the group to amend your report or suggest how it can be improved.

7. If the conclusions of each group are to be communicated to the total workshop, you will have the responsibility of summarizing your group's conclusions for that purpose.

OBSERVERS

1. Your primary responsibility is to observe the group process to see how the group is working, if it is making progress, if participation is balanced, and if any roadblocks are hindering the group.
2. Keep a record of your observations so, when called upon, you can briefly summarize your comments.
3. Phrase your comments so as not to offend group members. Ask for suggestions to overcome obvious hindrances.
4. Your report will usually be requested at the end of the meeting but may be called for during the meeting if the group becomes stalled.
5. You may be asked to pass out, tabulate, and report on reaction or evaluation sheets. Also, it is important to determine if this information is to be shared with the group or is to be used as a basis for another workshop.

RESOURCE PEOPLE

1. Your primary task is to contribute relevant facts, points of view, and experiences to the group discussion when and if they are needed.
2. Such contributions should usually be made when requested by the discussion leader.
3. You may be asked to "float" from group to group, depending on a group's need for your contributions.
4. You may also be requested to provide suggestions on further steps for the group to take in future discussions or in applying their conclusions to action.

An important consideration for the conference planner to remember is that the speakers, discussion leaders, recorders, observers, and resource persons should be adequately briefed prior to the workshop on precisely what they are expected to do.

Workshop groups generally sit at tables either in a square or facing the task leader, as shown:

Figure 26

It should be obvious to the reader that the format selected for a group meeting will be determined by the type of program one wishes to design. The important group in any meeting is the audience; to be effective, programs must be structured to utilize the most efficient means of communication and participation.

When the meeting is attended by a large number of people and full participation is not possible, the participants will tend to be passive rather than active. Also, communication tends to be conducted on a one-way basis from the platform to the audience.

Several additional methods that are useful in dealing with audience passivity and communication problems are question-and-answer periods, listening teams, buzz groups, and role playing.

Effective Question Periods. The major advantage of an effective question period is its indication of the feelings of the audience. The question period, however, should be a basic part of the program, not an afterthought.

Leland P. Bradford, in his article "How To Plan The Question-and-Answer Period," has suggested that preparing the audience for critical listening is a crucial factor in developing effective question periods.

Such preparation should do the following:

1. Help the members of the audience listen to the program in terms of specific areas of questions that should be answered.
2. Give examples of questions that will be pertinent and significant.
3. Make them feel comfortable in raising questions.
4. Set the standard that everyone asks questions.
5. Start the preparation early enough so the audience can have an opportunity for careful thinking.[8]

Questions can be directed to the platform from the floor or 3×5 cards can be passed out to the audience, collected, and read by a moderator. A useful technique which increases the number of questions asked is a screening panel to read the written questions before they are submitted to the moderator. Such screening helps to eliminate duplicate and embarrassing questions, assists in distributing the questions to cover a wide range of topics, and helps direct questions to all speakers.

Listening Teams. Another useful device to obtain greater audience participation is to divide the group into listening teams. The chairman can suggest that participants situated on one side of the room listen for certain points, those in another location listen for different items, and so on. Upon the conclusion of the speaker's presentation, the audience can be divided into listening team sub-groups to identify and clarify their findings.

Buzz Groups. The buzz group is an extremely useful technique to get the audience involved. A large audience can be divided into many small groups by a few simple directions. When seats are moveable, the audience can be asked to turn their chairs to create small groups of 6 to 8 people. In a large auditorium where theater seats are in use, a similar situation can be created by having row 1 turn and face row 2, and so on. Dividing lines established and communicated by the leader to the audience can be used to determine the size of the groups.

The participants are then told they have specific time allocated for discussion—usually five, ten, or fifteen minutes. The time period will depend on the purpose of the discussion. If opinions are to be shared, less time may be required than if the participants are to reach a decision on a particular matter. One person in each group can be designated to report the group's conclusions or questions.

Role Playing. While role playing by several selected members of the audience may not directly involve the total group, it can serve a useful purpose. Participants may identify with a person playing a specific role; consequently, such role identification may stimulate questions and involvement on the part of the audience. Problems and issues that are important can be brought out before the group to motivate the audience to take part in the question-and-answer period or general discussion.

Various types of alternative program formats have been suggested for the conference planner. Regardless of which format is used, the planner of a meeting should be concerned with the problems of communication, involvement, and participation. He may plan a series of separate evening programs conducted over a period of several weeks. Thus a lecture series using various speakers can be arranged in this manner or one or several speakers can be utilized over a weekend at a retreat-type location. A residential setting materializes giving the planners and speakers a captive and usually interested audience. Such a plan is popular with college alumni in some areas. In addition, clubs, orientation sessions, and training programs often utilize this type of an environment for their meetings. These types of programs are usually attended by small numbers of people.

Quite different in size is the large convention which thousands of people may attend. For example, the American Psychological Association may assemble to learn about new techniques and discoveries

METHOD	CHIEF CHARACTERISTIC	PATTERN OF PARTICIPATION	SPECIAL USEFULNESS	LIMITATIONS
Lecture, film, reading, recitals, etc.	Information-giving.		Systematic presentation of knowledge.	Little opportunity for audience to participate.
Forum	Information giving followed by questions for clarification.		Audience can obtain the specific information it wants on particular aspects of the subject.	Formality; lack of freedom to interchange ideas.
Symposium panel or debate	Presentation of different points of view.		Different points of view spotlight issues, approaches, angles; stimulate analysis.	Can get off the beam; personality of speakers may overshadow content; vocal speaker or questioner can monopolize program.
Discussion	High degree of group participation.		Pooling of ideas, experience, and knowledge; arriving at group decisions.	Practical with only a limited number of people.
Project, field trip, exhibits, etc.	Investigation of a problem cooperatively.	PROBLEM	Gives first-hand experience.	Requires extra time and energy for planning.
"Buzz groups"	100% participation by large audiences through small clusters of participants.		Makes individual discussion, pooling of ideas, possible in large groups. Develops leadership skill in members.	Contributions are not likely to be very deep or well organized.
Group interview	Spontaneous giving of opinions and facts by experts in response to questions.		Brings knowledge from a number of sources to bear on one problem.	Becomes disorganized without careful planning of material to be covered.

— Courtesy of ADULT LEADERSHIP

Figure 27 Handy Checklist of Instruction Methods

in psychological research. School superintendents from all over the country may gather in Atlantic City to discuss public school matters. An industrial trade society may meet in Detroit to provide its members with an opportunity to see the latest machinery and equipment. Usually, the convention format calls for multiple meetings occurring simultaneously at least part of the time. Sessions will vary depending upon the subject discussed and the method of presentation. Exhibits are often included in a convention along with tours of various locations, business meetings, banquets, social hours, and perhaps a special wives' program. Considerable socializing occurs in corridors, hotel rooms, and between meetings.

Obviously, participation and communication are more difficult in the large convention than in programs designed for fewer people. However, by using multiple sessions and other methods previously suggested, these problems can be reduced. The appropriate method selected for conducting a large program will depend upon factors peculiar to a specific conference and sponsoring organization.

The checklist (p. 183) is reproduced from *Adult Leadership* to illustrate some of the instructional methods suggested.

Specific Guidelines for Conference Planning

Up to this point the information presented has been of a general nature, describing various factors one should consider when planning a group meeting. The remainder of the chapter provides more specific information for the reader who desires a series of precise steps to follow in planning, conducting, and evaluating a program.

Except for certain types of programs such as process-oriented workshops, I believe conferences should be planned in an effective systematic manner. The following guidelines are suggested for the conference planner and include both educational and administrative functions. The sequence suggested does not necessarily follow priority ordering since a priority of functions will vary depending on circumstances and specific situations. Also, it is important to note that the guidelines presented represent only one method of planning a meeting.

1. *Select a planning committee.* The initial step in planning for an educational conference is to select a planning committee. The question of whom to invite to assist in the planning must be considered. Generally, all organizations that will be involved in the program should be represented on the planning committee. This procedure has

the advantage of broadening the base of people participating. The preferred size of a working committee is generally from five to eight persons. Consideration should also be given to the role of the persons invited to assist in the planning.

It will probably be necessary to select a person to serve as chairman of the planning committee. The person should be willing to share planning tasks and assume a leadership role. He should anticipate problems that may develop, handle the administrative and management functions for the program, and serve as an overall conference trouble shooter.

If the conference chairman is to select his own committee, he should choose persons who have not only an interest in the program, but perhaps represent different points of view. This will provide for varied inputs into the program plan. It will be helpful if the persons invited to serve on a program planning committee also have some knowledge and skills in planning and management. Their attitudes should reflect a sincere desire to assist in planning a successful program experience for all participants.

It should be helpful for the conference planner to be aware of several characteristics generally inherent in a conference planning committee. Several of these characteristics are as follows:

1. The conference planning committee is a *small group*. As it grows in size, the interaction among the members in the planning process may become more difficult.
2. The conference planning committee is a *primary group*. Interaction is accomplished by face-to-face discussion.
3. The conference planning committee is a *task-oriented group*. Planning and organizing the conference program is its primary responsibility.
4. The·conference planning committee is a *formal leader group*. Its leader is either appointed by the conference sponsor or elected by the other members of the planning committee. Although there may be, and usually are, others who exercise leadership during the meeting discussions, the appointed or elected chairman constitutes the task leader for the group.
5. The conference planning committee is a *temporary group*. It is brought into existence for the purpose of planning a specific program.
6. The conference planning committee is usually an *autonomous group*. Although a sponsor may support a program financially, the planning function is generally given as a total responsibility to the planning committee.

Once the planning committee has been selected and meets for its initial planning session, the committee should begin with the purpose for holding the program.

2. *Determine the purpose of the conference.* The purpose of the conference should be defined at the beginning of the planning and should be related to the sponsoring organization, its philosophy, and its goals. Discussion should include such questions as: Why are these people being brought together? What persons should attend? What are their needs? What are their expectations? How meaningful will the conference be for those who attend?

Six common purposes for holding conferences are (1) to provide educational emphasis on training and learning, (2) to provide information and motivation, (3) to develop policy, (4) to help problem solving and decision making, (5) to help resolve conflict, and (6) to provide for discussion and interaction. The importance of determining the purpose for conducting the program cannot be overemphasized. The purpose, in effect, gives the rationale for bringing the people together.

Once the overall purpose for the conference is established, the specific objectives to be achieved can be spelled out. This then leads to the third guideline.

3. *Establish specific objectives for the conference.* Once the specific objectives for the conference are determined, the planning committee can design the program to produce some specific achievement based on these objectives. The conference planner's choice of alternative types of program formats will be determined by his judgment of the methodological processes he thinks will be most effective in achieving the conference objectives. For example, a group of social agency administrators had as the purpose for an in-service training program a need to develop and reformulate agency policy as related to community needs and services. One of the objectives established for the program was for the group to spell out quite clearly their individual perceptions of the need for policy change. The need to obtain information of a personal nature along with other kinds of data collection suggested to the planner that a series of workshops would be the most productive method for the participants to reach this objective. In addition to the series of workshops, tapes were interspersed on a rotation basis among the participants in an attempt to bring about a better understanding of each group member's thinking on the subject.

Important! The planning committee should ask itself the question, "What objectives can realistically be accomplished during the program?" The achievement of objectives makes it possible to evaluate to what extent the participants have realized their fundamental aspirations. When objectives are clear and meaningful, the gathering of facts, the articulation of plans, the presentation of a program, and the evaluation of results are greatly facilitated. A conference evaluation becomes quite meaningful in terms of whether or not the conference has been a success.

If evaluation is defined as the process of assessing the degree to which objectives are achieved, it becomes clear that evaluation assumes that goals or objectives have first been set down.

4. *Select a conference theme.* A theme is generally used to describe or characterize the subject of the conference. Thus the theme can be useful in identifying the main thrust of the conference to the potential participants. In addition, the theme should relate to the purposes and objectives that have been established for the conference and should give the potential participant an understanding of why the conference is being held.

5. *Determine conference topics.* Once the overall purpose for holding the conference has been established, the specific objectives determined, and the theme selected, the planning committee can then turn its attention to the topics to be covered.

Ideally, the topics should be selected to cover the subject area suggested by the objectives. For example, if the committee selects as one objective for an assessors' conference that the participants learn the proper procedures for assessing depreciation on a commercial building, this subject must then be discussed in detail so that the participants will be able to achieve that objective. Using this approach to conference planning, the objectives will identify the subjects to be discussed and will tend to eliminate superfluous and nonessential information. The discussion will hold to specific information designed to help the participant achieve the objective established for the program.

6. *Determine the conference speakers.* Finally, after the committee, purposes, objectives, theme, and topics have been selected, the planning committee can turn its attention to selection of the conference speakers.

Speakers should be chosen on the basis of their knowledge of the topics, as well as of their ability to cover successfully and to communicate information on the topic to the audience.

The selection of speakers for a program is an extremely important part of the planning process. All too often the speakers are determined by reputation and not necessarily by how successfully they can perform a specific task.

However, the selection of the speakers does not end the planning committee's responsibilities. The committee must communicate to the speakers specific information pertaining to the purposes and objectives of the conference, who the potential participants are, and the probable backgrounds and expectations the participants will bring to the conference. The sophistication of the audience should also be considered and related to the speakers so they can address themselves to the level of understanding of the participants. This procedure will increase the possibility that the speakers' presentations will cover the specific areas the planning committee had intended. A useful technique, when appropriate, is to provide the potential audience with suggested reading lists, materials, films, or other advance information concerning the speakers' presentations or topic areas to be discussed. Preconference study or briefing can be quite helpful in preparing participants both for discussion and to increase their knowledge of the subjects to be covered.

It should be emphasized that other methods previously suggested might also be appropriate at this stage of the planning process. For example, it might be desirable to utilize small group discussions, panels, clinics, or some other form of interaction to reach the desired outcomes for the conference. Utilizing a telelecture when a speaker cannot be present in person is a useful technique. Closed circuit TV, video tapes, and audio tapes are used to present information for training purposes in conference situations. Long-play records, tape recorders, programmed units, games, and computers are all possible methods of instruction which the conference planner may wish to consider in structuring the program. The specific technique selected by the planner will be determined by the conference objectives and the most appropriate methodology to use in achieving those objectives.

7. *Evaluate the conference.* The preparation of an evaluation instrument and the time of its distribution are important considerations that should be determined during the planning phase. An effective evaluation is necessary to identify and measure the degree to which the objectives for the conference have been achieved, and should be designed to provide the information the planners want to know. Several questions that can be asked are: What were your expectations for this conference? What did you gain from this program? How will you be able to perform better or differently as a result of this experience? Were the methods used in presenting the materials acceptable to you?

It is important for the conference planner and his committee to concern themselves with some form of an evaluation at the time the objectives for the conference are established. I would suggest that the process of evaluation begin with a clear understanding of the educational elements or objectives of the program. Once the objectives for the program have been formulated, the conference planner can ascertain the type of evaluation procedure he wishes to follow. If behavorial change or specific learning is to occur, a pre-post test design might be in order. Individual or group interviews, questionnaires, and open discussion can also be utilized for evaluation purposes. In addition to receiving feedback from the participants, the evaluation instrument should be of benefit to them. If properly prepared and administered, the evaluation process should motivate the participants to assess the value of the program as it relates to their needs and interests. If the program is designed to provide a continuity of experiences, an evaluation will be necessary for both the planners and participants to measure their achievements in the time allocated.

The planner should be concerned with the adequacy of evaluation information to be obtained. Several questions to ask oneself when preparing an evaluation process are:

1. How well does the evaluation measure what it purports to measure? (validity)
2. Are the questions clear enough so if you ask a respondent the same questions a second time the responses would be consistent? (reliability)
3. Is the information being collected from the respondents in an efficient manner? (efficiency)
4. Will an analysis of the data collected be helpful in future program planning? (utilitarian value)

The responses to these questions will assist in preparing an effective and useful evaluation. Mann, Carter, and Larson suggest the specific purpose toward which an evaluation could be directed are:

1. To clarify and possibly redefine objectives.
2. To appraise the participant's conference experiences.
3. To improve the methods of instruction, including instructors and subject matter.
4. To identify problems and areas where adjustment is required.[9]

If a questionnaire is to be used and distributed to the program participants, Richard Beckhard provides the following suggestions for preparing the evaluation instrument:

1. Keep it short—one page is desirable.
2. Tell the respondent why you are asking his opinion.

3. Suggest that it is not necessary to sign the questionnaire.
4. Determine the categories of answers you need before you write the questions.
5. Do not be too specific. Put problems on a general basis so that participants have an opportunity to express personal feelings.
6. Include at least one open-ended question such as general comments or suggestions.[10]

Here are sample evaluations of the questionnaire type:

SAMPLE EVALUATION NO. 1

Designed for a workshop experience

1. Name of your group_____ Your responsibility in it_____

2. Please circle the A.M. session you attended: Brainstorming, Discussion Leader Techniques, Parliamentary Procedure, "Phillips 66," Problems of New Chairmen.

   Did you find the information presented:

   _____Excellent _____Good _____Average _____Fair
   _____No help?

3. Please circle the P.M. session you attended: Brainstorming, Discussion Leader Techniques, Parliamentary Procedure, "Phillips 66," Problems of New Chairmen.

   Did you find the information presented:

   _____Excellent _____Good _____Average _____Fair
   _____No help?

4. One of the purposes of the workshop was for the participant to learn by doing, rather than by listening. How would you rate its accomplishment?

   Highly Satisfactory__1__2__3__4__5__6__7__Highly Unsatisfactory

5. Were your expectations realized?

   _____Completely _____Adequately _____Partially _____Not at all

6. Considering the workshop as a whole, how would you rate its content?

   _____Excellent _____Good _____Average _____Fair
   _____Poor

7. Was the take-home material of value to you? _____Yes _____No

8. Would you be interested in another workshop on another aspect of leadership? ____Yes ____No

9. If you were planning for next year, where would you place the emphasis? What would you like to see repeated, what would you add, subtract?

10. Looking ahead, do you think your group would be interested in participating in the planning of a workshop on some aspect of leadership that is needed in the community?

_____Yes _____No _____Maybe

11. Comments:

SAMPLE EVALUATION NO. 2:

Designed for a symposium involving technical papers and panel discussions

PARTICIPANTS' EVALUATION SHEET

1. What were your objectives for attending this conference?

2. To what extent have these objectives been realized?

Not at All	Very Little	Partially Realized	Fully Realized

3. Please evaluate the sessions by responding to the following items:

A. Research Papers

	No Value	Some Value	Much Value
Paper no. 1 . . . . (System Analysis)	0	5	10
Paper no. 2 . . . . (Motivations and Attitudes)	0	5	10
Paper no. 3 . . . . (Input and Skill Development)	0	5	10

PARTICIPANTS' EVALUATION SHEET

A. Research Papers

	No Value	Some Value	Much Value
Paper no. 4 . . . . (The Role of Alcohol)	0	5	10
Paper no. 5 . . . . (Decision Making— Risk Taking)	0	5	10
Paper no. 6 . . . . (Legal Sanctions)	0	5	10
Paper no. 7 . . . . (Knowledge Utiliza- tion)	0	5	10

B. Individual Presentations

	No Value	Some Value	Much Value
	0	5	10

C. "Safety Meets the Media" Press Forum

	No Value	Some Value	Much Value
	0	5	10

D. Panel Discussion (check the panel you attended)

	No Value	Some Value	Much Value
_____ Education	0	5	10
_____ Legislation	0	5	10
_____ Licensing	0	5	10
_____ Law Enforcement	0	5	10
_____ Man-Machine-Road	0	5	10

D. Panel Discussion (check the panel you attended)

	No Value	Some Value	Much Value
———— Public Information	0	5	10

4. What part of the program was the most significant for you?

5. What part of the program was the least significant for you?

6. Suggestions for next year's symposium.

SAMPLE EVALUATION NO 3:
  Designed for one-week institute

1. What did you expect to gain from attending this institute?

2. Were your expectations realized? ———— Completely ———— Adequately
   ———— Partially ———— Not at all

3. What aspects of the institute were *most* significant for you?

4. What aspects of the institute held little significance for you?

5. Please evaluate the sessions by responding to the following items:

	Little Value	Some Value	Much Value	Sessions Liked Most (Check one)
Preparation: Miller	————	————	————	————
Economics: Carter	————	————	————	————
"Becoming": Smith	————	————	————	————
Sociology: Brown	————	————	————	————
Instruction: Ericksen	————	————	————	————
University: Platt	————	————	————	————
Faculty: Jones	————	————	————	————
Residential: Cohen	————	————	————	————
Utopia: Black	————	————	————	————

6. Do you have any changes to recommend for future institutes?

SAMPLE EVALUATION NO. 4:
Designed for a problem-solving conference

1. Considering the meeting as a whole, how satisfied are you with this conference session?

| 1 | 2 | 3 | 4 | 5 | 6 | 7 | 8 | 9 | 10 | 11 |

Highly   *Highly*
   Dissatisfied   *Satisfied*

2. How satisfied are you with the decisions or conclusions reached in this conference?

| 1 | 2 | 3 | 4 | 5 | 6 | 7 | 8 | 9 | 10 | 11 |

Highly   *Highly*
   Dissatisfied   *Satisfied*

3. How satisfied are you with the part you played in this conference?

| 1 | 2 | 3 | 4 | 5 | 6 | 7 | 8 | 9 | 10 | 11 |

Highly   *Highly*
   Dissatisfied   *Satisfied*

4. How satisfied are you with the leader in this conference?

| 1 | 2 | 3 | 4 | 5 | 6 | 7 | 8 | 9 | 10 | 11 |

Highly   *Highly*
   Dissatisfied   *Satisfied*

5. Did the leader (check)

    _____ a. talk too much
    _____ b. talk too little
    _____ c. talk about right number of times

6. Did your group reflect teamwork (We-Feeling) or was disjointedness (I-Feeling) predominant?

| 1 | 2 | 3 | 4 | 5 | 6 | 7 | 8 | 9 | 10 | 11 |

"I-Feeling"   *"We-Feeling"*

7. **Comments**

  a.

  b.

  c.

In addition to instruments used for evaluating program content and/or achievement of objectives, the program planner may wish to provide an opportunity for individuals with specific assignments to evaluate their own or the group's performance. For example, if discussion leaders and observers are used in a workshop setting, the following questionnaires could be used for individual self-appraisal and an analysis of the group process.

OBSERVING GROUPS AT WORK

1. How far did the group progress toward its goal for this meeting?

  None   A little   Halfway   Much   All the way
  Any comment?_____

2. To what extent did the members understand what they were trying to do?

  Nobody did   A few did   Half did   Most did   All did
  Any comment?_____

3. How well did they understand *how* they were trying to do this?

  Nobody did   A few did   Half did   Most did   All did
  Any comment?_____

4. To what extent was the group stymied by lack of information?

  Badly stymied   Half the time   Not much
  Any comment?_____

5. To what extent did the members seem to be interested in what the group was trying to do?

  Nobody was   A few were   Half were   Most were   All were
  Any comment?_____

6. Would you say that interest lagged or held up?

  Lagged badly at times   Held up pretty well   Held up all the time
  Any comment?_____

7. To what extent were the members able to subordinate individual interests to the common goal?

  Seldom   Half the time   All the time
  Any comment? _____

SELF- APPRAISAL WORK SHEET FOR DISCUSSION LEADERS

	Check One *Yes No*	*Remarks: Ways* *to Improve*
1. Did the meeting show careful planning?		
2. Was proper selection made of the persons who attended?		
3. Did leader do all that should have been done in advance of the meeting to prepare the group for the meeting?		
4. Were materials and equipment ready?		
5. Were the seating, ventilation, and lighting properly arranged?		
6. Did the meeting start on time?		
7. Was the group at ease?		
8. Was the problem or objective clearly defined?		
9. Was the group genuinely interested in the subject?		
10. Were facts and ideas clearly presented?		
11. Was the leader skillful in the use of questions?		
12. Did the leader keep the discussion moving progressively on the subject?		
13. Did the leader utilize the thinking of everyone in the group?		

	Check One		*Remarks: Ways*
	Yes	*No*	*to Improve*

14. Was the discussion clarified and speeded up by the effective use of the blackboard or other visual aides?

15. Was the leader open-minded?

16. Did the leader help the group weigh and analyze?

17. Did he get general agreement from the group?

18. Was the meeting effectively summarized?

19. Were logical decisions reached, action planned, or the objectives otherwise accomplished?

20. Did the meeting close on time?

Administrative Details of Conference Planning

An interesting aspect in planning, conducting, and evaluating a conference is that the conference planner will play the role at one time or another of an educator, administrator, and facilitator. Ideally, he serves as an educator, particularly during the planning stage of the program. He will function as an administrator in the coordination of the entire program and play the role of facilitator when the situation calls for that kind of activity.

When a person assumes responsibility for planning and conducting a program, he will be called upon to coordinate all kinds of details. Coordinating a conference is an administrative responsibility, and the mechanics involved in conducting the program are extremely important. The best possible program can be planned with excellent speakers and everyone can seem quite happy, but if the coffee does not arrive on time or the food is poor—someone will hear about it. Conversely, the mechanics can be handled without the slightest mishap, but if the substantive part of the program is poor the conference will not be considered a success. Clearly, the mechanics should not be separated from the program content. In my view it is a package, a total experience, and should be planned and operated as such.

The following checklist suggests administrative functions that require attention during the planning and operational phases of the conference.

1 . CLARIFY POLICY MATTERS

_____ a. Who is the sponsor in terms of financial responsibility?
_____ b. Who are the cooperating agencies?
_____ c. Who has the authority for final decisions?
_____ d. Who has what responsibility?

Several additional items can affect the administrative aspects of a conference or the policy decisions.

As a conference planner, the specific involvement for an administrator in coordinating a conference may vary in each conference situation. This may be true unless the planner initiates the program or is involved in the planning from the beginning.

If a person or a group of persons representing an organization expresses the need for a conference, the planner's involvement will begin at a specific point in a continuum of time. In other words, the conference planner may not necessarily be involved during the conception of the program, but may be brought in at a point where planning has progressed to a given stage.

Another variable is the amount or degree of involvement which for the conference administrator will vary, depending on when he is brought into the program, the role he is expected to play, and the organizational structure of the group sponsoring the program.

For example, it is possible for the planner to handle all the administrative and logistical functions or only a few. If the administrator initiates and administers all conference activity—these two possibilities will not necessarily pose a problem.

2 . SELECT DATE FOR THE CONFERENCE

_____ a. What time of the year?
_____ b. What time of the month?
_____ c. What time of the week?
_____ d. What should be the duration of the program?

That the answers to these questions will have an effect on conference attendance is obvious. The decisions will have to be based on such factors as the persons to be invited, tradition, location, other commitments, and the like. In addition, the timing for the program needs to be considered in relation to other activities which may attract the same participants. Holidays, school vacation periods, and conflicting national, state, or local conferences will influence attendance.

3. SELECT A CONFERENCE FACILITY

_____ a. Number of meeting rooms required?
_____   1. general sessions
_____   2. small group sessions
_____   3. type of seating arrangements required
      _____ conference   _____ theatre (aud.)   _____ schoolroom
      _____ "U" shape   _____ head table   _____ no. of persons
_____   4. room rental
_____   5. restroom availability
_____   6. checkroom facilities
_____ b. Convenience of location
_____ c. Transportation
_____   1. plane
_____   2. bus
_____   3. taxi and limousine
_____   4. parking
_____ d. Lodging accommodations
_____   1. no. of rooms needed?   Singles_____

                                                          Doubles_____

                                                          Suites_____

_____   2. room rates?
_____   3. clean, comfortable rooms?
_____   4. individual controls—heat and air conditioning
_____   5. written confirmation received?
_____   6. date uncommitted rooms are to be released?
_____   7. hospitality rooms needed?
_____ e. Meal service
_____   1. dates and times?
          2. breakfast_____ luncheon_____ dinner_____
             receptions_____ coffee breaks_____
_____   3. menu selections?
_____   4. price per plate (incl. gratuities and taxes)
_____   5. total number to be served

_____	6. meal guarantees required?
_____	7. head table. How many persons?
_____	8. place cards for head table?
_____	9. flowers for head table?
_____	10. reception arrangements?
_____	f. Organization of exhibits
_____	1. number of exhibits
_____	2. floor plans furnished? Yes_____ No_____
_____	3. date of set-up and dismantling
_____	4. floor assignments and rentals
_____	5. directional signs
_____	6. labor charges
_____	7. electric power
_____	8. partitions, backdrops
_____	9. storage
_____	10. guard services
_____	11. badge requirements
_____	12. union clearance

Each of these items related to the conference facility must be handled well to assure both comfort and convenience for the participants. A wise selection of the conference facility is necessary to provide the proper environment for the program. In addition, the conference location should be one that is relatively easy to reach via adequate transportation facilities. If the site selected is well known to the potential participants as a good place to hold a program, so much the better.

4. PREPARE AN ESTIMATED BUDGET

An estimated budget is necessary to determine anticipated expenditures. Once the estimated budget is prepared, a registration fee can be established to make the conference self-supporting, if necessary. Obviously, the sponsor needs to know the costs for the program and can then use the estimated budget to compare with the final financial statement prepared after the program is held. It may be appropriate and necessary to prepare a preliminary or tentative budget during the initial planning stages for the proposed program. It is helpful to estimate a final budget approximately four weeks prior to the conference. This procedure serves the purpose of providing comparative cost figures between the preliminary and final budgets. If expenses are higher than anticipated in relation to income, possible administrative and/or program changes may be possible to reduce expenditures. A sample conference budget form for estimating costs follows:

ESTIMATED CONFERENCE BUDGET

Date:

CONFERENCE TITLE AND DATE . . . .

INCOME

Registration fees_____@ $_____ $_____
Meal income. . . . .
Other . . . .

TOTAL INCOME $_____

EXPENSE

Food service
    Breakfasts. . . . . $_____
    Luncheons . . . .   _____
    Dinners . . . .   _____
    Coffee hours . . . .   _____
    Planning committee . . . . .   _____
Total food service . . . . $_____
Travel . . . .   _____
Program expense
    Stipends. . . . . $_____
    Clerical . . . .   _____
    Printing . . . .   _____
    Art work . . . .   _____
    Multilithing. . . . .   _____
    Addressing service . . . . . .   _____
    Postage . . . .   _____
    Telephone . . . .   _____
    Audio-visual
        Projection . . . .   _____
        PA system . . . .   _____
        Recording . . . .   _____
    Flowers . . . .   _____
    Delivery service . . . .   _____
    Buses . . . .   _____
    Signs . . . .   _____
    Badges . . . .   _____
    Supplies and materials . . . .   _____
                                         _____
    Total program expense . . . .   _____
Total conference costs. . . . .   _____

TOTAL EXPENSE $_____

Surplus   _____
Deficit   _____

The sample estimated conference budget form is relatively simple and does not include space for exhibits costs and other possible contingencies. The budget form can, therefore, be expanded to meet individual program needs.

5. PREPARE PLANNING DEADLINES

———— a. date flyer copy is due
———— b. date program copy is due
———— c. date stipend information is due
———— d. date travel information is due
———— e. date budget information is due
———— f. date complimentary list is due
———— g. date materials for stuffing in envelopes is due

A deadline sheet can be helpful to the conference planner as a reminder of the dates established for specific information to be received. It also aids in clarifying responsibility for specific tasks and the time schedule to be followed.

6. PROVIDE PUBLICITY

———— a. flyer to be mailed
———— b. program to be mailed
———— c. news releases prepared
———— d. photographer requested
———— e. directional signs necessary
———— f. radio and TV coverage
———— g. mailing lists required

Generally, a flyer is mailed several months prior to a conference. The purpose of the flyer is to inform potential participants of the impending program. This information should include the date, time, and location of the conference, the major speakers, and topics to be covered. The purpose and objectives for the conference should also be included. A detailed program and registration card should be sent four to six weeks in advance of the program. However, the timing will vary depending upon the group and the situation. For example, it may be more appropriate to inform the potential program participants through an individually addressed letter. Or perhaps an organizational newsletter or publication is advisable.

7. OBTAIN EQUIPMENT REQUIRED

_____ a. projection equipment

    _____ 1. 35 mm.   _____ 6. film strips

    _____ 2. 16 mm.   _____ 7. overhead

    _____ 3. 8 mm.   _____ 8. opaque

    _____ 4. slide projector _____ 9. other: chalk, erasers, pointer,

    _____ 5. carousel   extra cords, place cards

_____ b. tape recorders

_____ c. blackboards

_____ d. easels, charts

_____ e. public address system

_____ f. screens

_____ g. lectern

An audio-visual form sent to the conference speakers along with a marked copy of the program is a useful technique to obtain advance information concerning equipment required. The form suggests that the speaker make a decision in advance based on his needs; the proper equipment can then be ordered in advance.

AUDIO-VISUAL EQUIPMENT REQUEST FORM

Please check the item(s) which you will need for the conference indicated below. *This form should be returned even if equipment is not required.*

CONFERENCE:

DATE:

Projection Equipment

_____ 8-mm. movie projector   35-mm. (2 × 2) slide projector

_____ 16-mm. movie projector   _____ carousel

_____ opaque projector (paper can   _____ standard

     be no larger than 10″ × 10″)   _____ 3¼ × 4 slide projector

_____ overhead projector (paper can   _____ projectionist

     be no larger than 10″ × 10″)

Microphone Equipment Other Equipment

_____ table mike   _____ pointer   _____ bulletin board

_____ floor mike   _____ lectern   _____ table(s) and

_____ lapel mike _____ easel _____ chair(s) for panel

_____ blackboard _____ table(s) for display

Signature_____

Complete Mailing Address_____

MAIL NO LATER THAN_____**TO:**

8. ESTABLISH REGISTRATION PROCEDURES

_____ a. registration personnel available

_____ b. approximate time required

_____ c. registration tables available

_____ d. registration cards required

_____ e. name badges prepared

_____ f. briefcases to contain general conference information

_____ g. handout materials to be used

_____ h. typewriters: number and type

_____ i. paper, pencils, pens

_____ j. signs

_____ k. telephones

_____ l. bulletin boards

_____ m. cash boxes

_____ n. presence of administrator to make policy decisions

_____ o. policy for registration of members after desk is closed

_____ p. provision for checking funds at closing time

_____ q. need for removing cash overflow

Probably the most important aspect of the registration process is the registration card. The basic purpose of a registration card is to provide both preregistration and late registration information on persons attending the conference. These data enable the conference administrator to give meal guarantees and make group and room assignments. They also provide preliminary information regarding conference income and an efficient means of maintaining audit records. Name badges, meal tickets, folders, and other materials can then be prepared. In addition, acknowledgments can be sent to persons preregistered; and billings, CODs, and refunds can be processed. It is necessary to provide the registration personnel with an adequate supply of pens, pencils, typewriters, and other clerical supplies. Blankets on the registration tables are beneficial for providing protection for registration personnel against cold drafts and improving the overall appearance of the registration area. Persons used for registration should be well briefed on the program and able to provide general information about the conference facility and the local community.

9. CHECKLIST—PRIOR TO MEETING

_____ a. checkroom facilities opened
_____ b. check operation of lights
_____ c. proper seating arrangements
_____ d. enough seats
_____ e. cooling / heating system operating
_____ f. equipment set up and operating properly:
　　　　　　1. projectors_____ PA system_____
_____　　2. recording equipment
_____　　3. lectern (check light)
_____　　4. special lighting (if any)
　　　　　　5. chart stands_____ easels_____
　　　　　　6. blackboards_____ pointer_____
　　　　g. materials properly distributed:
_____　　1. water and glasses
_____　　2. ashtrays
　　　　　　3. pencils_____ note pads_____
_____　　4. flowers
_____ h. arrangements made to take telephone messages
_____ i. special decorations properly set up

As mentioned previously, many administrative tasks are necessary in preparing for a conference. Time goes by quite rapidly when the planner is trying to meet deadlines. The chart that follows provides suggested time allocations for essential conference administrative tasks. The advance time required to accomplish these tasks will vary depending on each specific situation.

CONFERENCE CHAIRMAN AND PLANNING COMMITTEE TASKS	DATE
Establish purpose of the conference, objectives, theme, dates, facilities needed, sponsoring and cooperating organizations, prospective attendees, etc.	**At least six months prior to conference date.**
Develop program.	
Identify and secure speakers and resource persons, set registration fee.	

CONFERENCE CHAIRMAN AND PLANNING COMMITTEE TASKS	DATE
Identify mailing list information (labels, availability of Addressograph plates, typed lists, etc.).	**One month prior to first mailing date.**
Flyer copy ready for printing.	**One month prior to mailing date. Mail several months prior to conference.**
Program copy ready for printing.	**At least two months prior to conference. Mail four to six weeks prior to conference.**
Complimentary list for registration and/or meals.	**One month prior to conference.**
Materials for stuffing into folders.	**Two weeks prior to conference.**
Evaluation of conference.	**Imediately upon conclusion of conference, or possibly a back-home evaluation.**

Summary

The administrative tasks suggested in this chapter should be sufficient to express a personal point of view that the key word in conference planning is organization.

The business of planning, conducting, and evaluating conferences involves many tasks and in this chapter I have attempted to express one person's opinion as to what conferences are all about. A definition of an educational conference and its components has been given, the participants that attend conferences and some of their functions have been identified, and various planning options and alternatives have been mentioned. Last, guidelines have been suggested for the administrator to follow in implementing the planning of the educational context of the program and the administrative functions necessary to support the program.

Obviously, more goes into conference planning than has been mentioned in this chapter. The approach suggested should provide the committee and the administrator charged with the planning responsibility for a conference with specific information and guidelines that are important in planning an educational conference experience. Instead of a "hit-or-miss" proposition, one can approach the conference with confidence that it has been planned to make the experience meaningful and valuable for the participants.

Notes

1. William M. Sattler and N. Edd Miller, *Discussion and Conference* (Englewood Cliffs, N.J.: Prentice Hall, 1962), p. 4.
2. Halbert E. Gulley, *Discussion, Conference and Group Process* (New York: Holt, Rinehart and Winston, 1968), p. 8.
3. Howard Y. McClusky, Unpublished mimeographed materials, University of Michigan, 1963.
4. Alfred W. Storey, "Participant Functions," *Adult Leadership*, vol. 12, no. 10 (April 1964), pp. 299, 315.
5. Harleight B. Trecker, *Group Process in Administration* (New York: Womens Press, 1950), p. 233.
6. Leroy H. Marlow, "The Camel Back of Conference Participation," *Adult Leadership*, October 1965, p. 121.
7. Sattler and Miller, *op. cit.*, p. 137.
8. Leland P. Bradford, "How To Plan The Question-and-Answer Period," *Adult Leadership*, July–August 1952.
9. Raymond E. Carter, Carl E. Larson, and David K. Mann, *Program Evaluation in Institutes and Conferences* (Lawrence: University of Kansas Press, 1963), p. 6.
10. Richard Beckhard, *How to Plan and Conduct Workshops and Conferences* (New York: Association Press, 1950).

Selected References

Concerning Conferences

Adult Leadership. Published monthly by the Adult Education Association of the U.S.A., Washington, D.C.

BECKHARD, RICHARD. *How to Plan and Conduct Conferences*. New York: Association Press, 1956.

BERGEVIN, PAUL. *A Philosophy for Adult Education*. New York: Seabury Press, 1967.

CAPES, MARY (ed.). *Communication or Conflict Conferences: Their Nature, Dynamics and Planning*. New York: Association Press, 1960.

ELLIS, WILLIAM D. and FRANK SIEDEL. *How to Win the Conference*. Englewood Cliffs, N.J.: Prentice-Hall, 1955.

ESSO TRAINING CENTER. *Conference Leadership*. Elizabeth, N.J., 1958.

FALES, ANN WOHLLEBEN. "The Pattern of Anxiety in Residential Conferences." *Continuing Education Report*, no. 11. Chicago: Studies and Training Program in Continuing Education, University of Chicago, 1966.

GESSNER, QUENTIN H. "Planning Educational Conferences." *Adult Leadership,* June 1969.

———. "Conference Planning for Administrators." *Continuing Education,* January 1970.

GULLEY, HALBERT E. *Discussion, Conference and Group Process.* New York: Holt, 1960.

HARE, P., E. F. BERGATTA, and R. F. BALES. *Small Groups: Studies in Social Interaction.* New York: Knopf, 1955.

KNOX, A. B. "Conference Objectives: Prelude to Evaluation." *Adult Leadership,* February 1962, p. 234.

KRATHWOHL, DAVID R., BENJAMIN S. BLOOM, and BERTRAM B. MASIA. *Taxonomy of Educational Objectives.* Handbook 11: Affective Domain. New York: David McKay, 1964.

LACOGNATA, A. A. *A Comparison of the Effectiveness of Adult Residential and Non-Residential Learning Situations.* Chicago: Center for the Study of Liberal Education for Adults, 1961.

———. "An Analysis of Selected Conference Programs." *Adult Education,* vol. 13 (Autumn 1962), pp. 34–41.

LEATHERS, CHESTER W. and WILLIAM S. GRIFFITH. "The Conference Coordinator: Educator or Facilitator" *Continuing Education Report,* no. 2. Chicago: Studies and Training Program in Continuing Education, University of Chicago, 1965.

LIFTON, WALTER M. *Working With Groups: Group Process and Individual Growth.* New York: Wiley, 1961.

MANN, DAVID K., RAYMOND E. CARTER, and CARL E. LARSON. *Program Evaluation in Institutes and Conferences.* Lawrence, Kans.: University of Kansas Press, 1963.

MARLOW, H. L. "The 'Camel Back' of Conference Participation." *Adult Leadership,* October 1965, p. 121.

———. "The Conference Method: Its Birth and Growth." *Adult Leadership,* May 1963, p. 8.

MILLER, HARRY L. *Teaching and Learning in Adult Education.* New York: The Macmillan Company, 1964.

NATIONAL UNIVERSITY EXTENSION ASSOCIATION. Conference and Institute Division, Conference Proceedings. New Brunswick, N.J.: Rutgers, The State University, 1965.

———. Conference and Institute Division, Conference Proceedings. Ann Arbor, Mich.: University of Michigan, 1967.

———. Conference and Institute Division, Conference Proceedings. East Lansing, Mich.: Michigan State University, 1969.

SARGENT, E. H., JR. "Ground Rules for Group Process." *Adult Leadership,* October 1966, p. 122.

SPENCE, JOHN A. *Conference Handbook.* Knoxville, Tenn.: University of Tennessee for the Division of University Extension, 1958.

STOREY, ALFRED W. "Participant Functions." *Adult Leadership,* April 1964, p. 299.

Publications Concerning Program Evaluation

BLANEY, JOHN P. and DOUGLAS McKIE. "Knowledge of Conference Objectives and Effect Upon Learning." *Adult Education,* vol. 19 (Winter 1969), pp. 98–105.

BROWNELL, WILLIAM A. "The Evaluation of Learning under Differing Systems of Instruction." *Educational Psychologist*, vol. 3, no. 1 (November 1965).

DURSTON, BERRY H. "The Evaluation Process in Adult Education." *Journal of the International Congress of University Adult Education*, vol. 7 (September 1968), pp. 14–25.

JOHNSON, RAYMOND L. et. al. "Measuring the Educational Relevance of a Short-Term Training Program for Teachers." Paper presented at the National Seminar on Adult Education Research, Toronto, February 9–11, 1969. 17 pp.

MILLER, HARRY L. and CHRISTINE H. McGUIRE. *Evaluating Liberal Adult Education*. Chicago: Center for the Study of Liberal Education for Adults, 1961. 184 pp.

CHAPTER EIGHT

The Public Relations Factor in Planning Successful Adult Education Ventures

AGNES DRUMMOND

Mrs. Agnes Drummond is Director of Adult Education and former Director of School Community Relations for the Port Washington, Long Island, Public Schools in New York.

N E V E R I N H I S T O R Y has there been so much competition for the eyes and ears of John Q. Public. The voice of the turtle has been drowned out by the voice of television and radio. Appalling statistics have been compiled concerning the number of printed words with which, for example, the average executive is confronted daily. And there you are in the midst of a jumble of sound and symbol—trying to attract the attention of the particular groups you want to reach with your message.

There are no easy solutions to your problem—no ABCs of effective communication. There are certainly many XYZs but, hopefully, the pages that follow will help to point out the pathways to your goal: the development of a sound, two-way relationship with your publics. The plural, "publics," is intentional. Your potential audience is almost always made up of several groups and subgroups, each of which responds to a different type of approach. Too often we think of segments of the public as large single-minded entities. Groups come together on the basis of race, political orientation, religion, educational achievements, geography—you name it. Your task is to find a common denominator of interest around which you can build your program.

The Public Relations Function

Historically, the public relations function was created by social change, increasing specialization in our society, and the resulting interdependence among individuals.

Normally, one starts with a definition of terms, but to attempt to define the public relations function—or PR, if you will—would be foolhardy. Each practitioner has his own pet set of phrases to explain what he does. In the first place, PR is an art rather than a science. A practical definition might be that the public relations function is a planned effort to influence opinion through acceptable methods, based on two-way communication. For example, if your object is to involve people in a particular program, it does not suffice for you to announce the program in the public press. Before the program is actually planned, there must be some dialogue with the public you wish to reach. You must listen to what your public wants to know before you will be able to devise and promote. In short, it is an aid to adjustment to change. We should also consider what PR is and does. First and foremost, PR is concerned with the evaluation of public thinking. Its policies and procedures are, ideally, identified with the public interest and lead to a planned program of action to earn public acceptance.

To some people, PR is synonymous with "creating an image." The widespread use of the terms "image" and "image-makers" has been a somewhat mixed blessing. The very phrase creating an image connotes an attempt to contrive—the production of an artificial effect, not necessarily the whole or true picture, with the intent to persuade. On the other hand, when the image is a reflection of what actually exists, you are "telling it like it is." Certainly a responsible PR practitioner prefers the latter approach.

A word about publicity, which everyone concedes "we need more of." Publicity per se is not public relations. Let us suppose, for example; that you and your advisors from the community have decided that a forum on drug abuse is needed. Someone in the group is sure to suggest press releases, posters, and flyers. The PR practitioner realizes that each of these techniques is an important factor in the promotion, but he is also aware of the efficacy of a few well-placed phone calls for help to community leaders. He knows the value of the original planning committee in getting the word around. He knows how to time the release of notices so that a climax is achieved at the right point in time. Though publicity does provide the most direct contact with the general public, through mass media, this exposure merely informs—it does not change attitudes. However, since it does play an important role in the total PR program, we will consider the essentials of publicity as well as the writing of news releases later on in this chapter.

PR is also more than simply communication. The total PR program is based on policies and procedures which are identified with the public interest. When these facts are communicated there will be understanding which, in turn, leads to public support and progress.

As in every "information loop," two-way communication comes from each level involved in the organization—board members, staff, administrators, participants, and all others affected by your program. It should flow up, down, and sideways. Every so often someone comes up with "a great idea": we should develop a Speakers Bureau that will be able to talk to community groups about the proposal for which you seek acceptance. Good, informed speakers are solicited to help. Sometimes slide presentations are prepared, and the Speakers Bureau is in business. Equally important, but rarely developed, is a Listeners Bureau. In such an arrangement, the public is invited to contribute. They know that the "Listeners" are actively seeking their ideas and the resultant dialogue can make the final program a more vital one.

The likelihood that this almost "impossible dream" can be achieved is usually in direct proportion to the effort expended. There is no easy way, no prepackaged kit, no instant PR powder to which you can add the milk of human sensitivity kindness.

Developing the Basic Program

Let us now consider the "nitty-gritty" that underlies the successful public relations program.

If you are responsible for the PR function in your organization, there are certain prerequisites to consider before you begin your task. As a PR practitioner, you must operate at the policy-making level and be a member of the policy-making team. You must be concerned with process and method. You are the change agent who "earns" for your organization the right to survive.

Figure 28 may, at first glance, seem a sort of dog-chasing-its-tail activity. Admittedly, it involves going round and round until the goals of your PR efforts are achieved.

Figure 28 The Six Basics of the PR Program

This six-step process is a must if you are to develop a sound plan of action:

Step 1 Develop organizational goals and objectives.
Step 2 Research attitudes of the community.
Step 3 Plan the program—both short- and long-term aspects.
Step 4 Implement program—the action phase.
Step 5 Evaluate the results of previous steps.
Step 6 Correct, change, modify, and start again if necessary.

Each of the above elements of a successful program involves the use of relatively tried-and-true techniques. However, each community is different. If you know your publics, you will be able to adapt the following information to your needs.

Step 1: Setting Goals

The format of this step depends upon the size and scope of your organization. It may be as simple as a small group sitting around a table and setting down objectives. On the other hand, it might entail meetings of staff, citizen groups, and so on. The important fact to remember is that your goals should be the by-product of a concerted effort to analyze the needs of the organization. Be sure to state your purposes clearly. Determine where you are going and why you want to get there.

Step 2: Research

You will need to know what people think about your organization and its past efforts. You must build a climate of belief and target your information program to reach the right audience. To proceed with your overall plan, you must determine what these publics know or do not know about the association you represent.

How you plan to obtain these opinions and attitudes also depends upon the size of the group with which you are working. The techniques you may use are many and varied and, in general, you must choose between the formal or informal approach. If the decision is the latter, you may achieve the desired result by asking the right people. For instance, you might meet with community leaders; your staff, volunteers as well as paid; and any others you might consider helpful to you in reading the pulse of the community.

If you decide to conduct a formal opinion poll, you will have to consider some questions before you begin:

1. What do you want to know?
2. Why do you want this particular information? Do you wish to adjust, amend, toss out, or improve?
3. What will you do with the results?
4. When are you going to conduct the poll and should you continue to do so at specific intervals?
5. Where and how do you intend to get the information? Will you telephone, personally interview, or send a questionnaire through the mail?

6. Who will make the survey? Will the polling team be objective?

7. How will you pay for the survey?

8. Can you use the survey for other purposes?

Another vital factor in the success of your effort is the selection and size of the right sample. The sample should be a valid representation of the community and based on an agreed percentage figure. With a 1 percent sample, accurate predictions can be made. The larger the sample, however, the greater the reliability.

Let us invent a town with a total population of thirty thousand. Suppose you wanted to survey the attitude of this town toward the building of a new high school. If you select the list of registered voters for school elections as your base—some four thousand people— you have already loaded the sample with people who are interested in schools. In that case a 1 percent sample would involve only forty people and would certainly be suspect. On the other hand, if you used the entire adult population, tabulated at nineteen thousand by the school census, a 1 percent sample would give you 190 people. A fair cross-section of the town could be obtained by just going down the list and picking out every one-hundredth name.

As for the questionnaire itself, the questions should be selected carefully and then pretested by trying out the questions on a small group to see if desired information is elicited. A warning—don't write your own questionnaire. Get help!

The method of conducting your poll is the next decision you face:

1. Mail Questionnaire. This approach is the most economical and easiest to tabulate. The drawback is that you will not get a 100 percent return—15 percent is considered good. To use our hypothetical 40-person sample, 15 percent would give us 6 returns! If we use the 190 figure, the return would be 28–29 people responding. Also, among the returned questionnaires will be some which will have to be discarded because the answers are ambiguous.

2. The In-Person Interview. Here both time and cost will be increased. The results are harder to tabulate although the data will be more reliable. The interviewers must be carefully trained and taught to adhere strictly to the questionnaire. An impersonal attitude without emphasis by the interviewer is a must. The key here is listen— listen—listen.

3. The Telephone Interview. A compromise situation! Objectivity is the key. This has been a more successful approach in the past than it is currently. The telephone has come to be considered an invasion of privacy since the instrument has been used for so much commercial or charitable solicitation. People are less apt to be cooperative as an unknown voice begins to talk at them. Who can tell—they may be asked to buy magazines, subscribe to a newspaper (only thirteen weeks for a worthy charity), donate discarded clothing, or even vote for a particular candidate.

Whatever technique is employed, the tabulation of data is an important factor. For reliability, one central source of control is essential. If the project is large enough, you might talk to a data processing firm about tabulating the results.

Step 3: the Plan

As you reach this point—planning the program—the basic considerations are your budget and staff. Planning a Madison Avenue sort of campaign when money and manpower are not available is wasteful of your time and effort. On one side, you are bound by the amount you can spend; on the other, by the number of people who will do the actual work. After you have made a realistic appraisal of these two factors, you are ready to go to work.

Your program should have two elements: the short-term plan which involves dealing with a crisis, and the long-term element which is preventative. Underlying both is the recognition of the need for policy change as well as the need to develop a sound communications program that is continuing, ongoing, and involves all media.

Each year suburban school districts participate in what is, in effect, a massive adult education project. It is known as "Passing the School Budget" and involves all the PR know-how available to the school administration. A high point in the campaign to win community acceptance is the budget hearing, at which the public is informed of the inevitable projected tax increase.

In this situation assume that the two previous steps have already been performed. The goal is to present a budget which will preserve the quality of the school system as economically as possible. Citizen groups have been involved. The overall plan is agreed upon:

1. A preliminary budget hearing at which the new tax rate is presented to the public.
2. Modification of the original budget in light of citizen reaction.
3. Dissemination of a budget brochure to the entire community.

4. Small group meetings to explain various special aspects: the state aid picture, state mandates for special groups, transportation costs, and so on.
5. A final large group meeting at which the entire budget is reviewed.
6. Vote.

Step 4: Implement Program

Various techniques can be used for that preliminary meeting at which the school tax bombshell is dropped. One of the most successful has been a speech by members of the Board of Education with an accompaning slide presentation. The following is a suggested format:

President of Board:

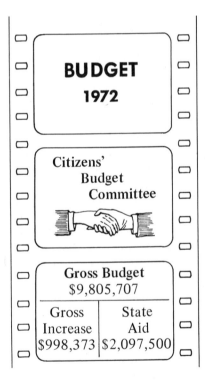

Grateful for the opportunity to discuss the budget with you.

Thanks to the Citizen Budget Committee for the hours spent in reviewing budgetary needs of the district.
(*Names members.*)
Announce gross budget requirements and increase over previous year. Mention state aid which covers ¼ budget costs.

Amount to be raised by local taxation is expected to be $7,-259,207—an increase of $915,-565 over the current year.

Let us look at specific increases. Largest is for salaries—up $545,477 over the current year.

Because salaries have gone up, there are also increases in the employer's contributions to federal Social Security, Teachers Retirement Fund, and employee benefits.

There will be an increase of $108,526 for new personnel. Included will be four new teachers, a speech therapist, a staff assistant to the Board of Education, and $15,000 for additional teacher aides to relieve teachers of non-teaching duties.

Other increases in budget include a rise in the per pupil allowance for supplies from $11 to $14. This·is the result of higher costs of material and growing emphasis on individual instruction.

Another instructional item is next year's Pre-Kindergarten Program. The total cost is $69,673, of which $10,173 must be raised by local taxes.

The general inflationary trend of the country is also reflected in higher costs of transportation, maintenance, and supplies.

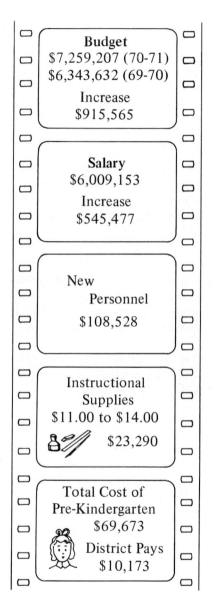

Budget
$7,259,207 (70-71)
$6,343,632 (69-70)
Increase
$915,565

Salary
$6,009,153
Increase
$545,477

New
Personnel
$108,528

Instructional
Supplies
$11.00 to $14.00
$23,290

Total Cost of
Pre-Kindergarten
$69,673
District Pays
$10,173

The sum total of all increases will cause an estimated rise of 89¢ in the tax rate. This is an estimate only and will not be firm until the assessed valuation of the district is set by the county on August 1. We estimate assessed valuation will be $93,500,000.

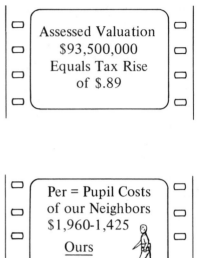

Assessed Valuation
$93,500,000
Equals Tax Rise
of $.89

Comparisons have always been a feature of our budget presentation. Usually, we use 7 neighboring districts with same general problems. Let us look at our neighbors for a per-pupil cost analysis. The range is from $1,960 to $1,423. We rank sixth with $1,446. As for pupil-teacher ratios, we rank sixth with 19.99 students per classroom teacher.

Our tax rate in 1973 was $7.61 while the median on a countywide basis was $7.75.

Per = Pupil Costs
of our Neighbors
$1,960-1,425

Ours
$1,446

Tax Rate
Median—on County
Basis—$7.61

Ours
$7.75

That's the story, neighbors. This budget represents our best efforts to provide your children with the quality of education to which we have become accustomed. Are there any questions?

V
O
T
May 4th   E

Your visual presentation may be photographs, drawings, or whatever. Just keep it simple. Do not make visuals too hard to read. Have a few run-throughs with the speaker and projectionist to be sure that the timing is smooth.

Arrange for a signal to change slides. Try to avoid the usual "click," as this is distracting to your audience. Be sure the equipment is in working order. Replace the bulb in the projector and have a spare on hand. Even if your last run-through was close to meeting time, check the equipment again before your audience arrives. Nothing is more devastating than to start a meeting and find that the audio-visual equipment is not working. A sure-fire way to lose your group.

From here on in the timetable is important. Your printed brochure should be distributed about three weeks prior to voting. Keeping enthusiasm high until election day can be helped with a well-prepared sequence of press releases. As both the preparation of a brochure and the role of publicity are very vital to the success of your efforts, a section on each has been included later in this chapter.

Another method of generating interest is to schedule a series of "coffees" around town. The speakers can be a volunteer team of local residents and a member of the school staff. This school person could be a board member, an administrator, or a teacher. In any case the team must be well informed and able to handle questions from the audience. The representative from the school should be used as a resource for the community person. These "coffees" are an effective tool since they reach women, and in suburban communities women have increasingly assumed the responsibility for family information gathering.

Special interest groups must somehow be reached. For instance, senior citizens are usually considered "no" votes. However, if an attempt is made to tell them that a defeated school budget can mean lowered property values, they may be less anxious to vote against the budget. Also, if the district supports a senior citizen center—either through its recreation or adult education programs—the possibility of losing this project under a defeated budget can be mentioned.

The final large meeting, frequently held the night before the election, provides an opportunity to review once again the entire budget with its emphasis on quality education for all children.

On the actual day of the vote, PTA ladies, the Girl Scouts, and other community service agencies can help. Transportation and baby sitting services can be utilized to get people to the polls.

Step 5: Evaluation

In this phase you attempt to answer the question, Did we accomplish what we set out to do?

The answers to the following queries will be helpful:

1. What were our basic objectives, and were they realized?
2. What evidence is there of the effectiveness of what was done?

If you have had a relatively simple goal—"to pass the budget"—you can evaluate your efforts in terms of the voters' acceptance or rejection. However, evaluation should have taken place at every step. The use of several neighborhood citizens' committees can sometimes be an effective tool. One broadly based committee from the community can evaluate goals before you even start to identify need. The results of your research can also be subjected to scrutiny by a well-informed, overall citizens' committee. These various large and small group meetings will also produce results which can be used in this evaluative phase.

While discussing the matter of evaluation, mention must be made of the necessity for analyzing the groups with which you have worked. Whenever citizens' committees are involved in a task, there are some cautions to be noted. Beware of "instant expert" and factions within the committees. Sometimes committees attempt to assume the role of a super-super school board. The membership may consist largely of a combination of eager beavers and the "big name" who lend their names but do not expect to work. To be effective, the committee must clearly be truly representative of all aspects of the community. Also, in your evaluation of the citizens' groups involved in your organization, you must consider your own role. Were you able to keep the committee's attention on its assigned task? Did you present the facts realistically, without overgeneralization or oversimplification? Was the necessary guidance provided so that the group could be realistic about the financial implications of what it wanted done?

Do not overlook the "thank-you" note. And you might also wish to plan a recognition night when all volunteers will be given a "Certificate of Appreciation."

Step 6: Correct and Change Program

On the basis of the evaluation, you may find it necessary to make some changes in your overall plan. Even though you may be successful in your effort, there were almost certainly some experiences during the campaign which resulted in changes of attitude on your part. In other words, you learned! Immediately, while the experience is fresh in your mind, set down the changes you will wish to include next year to make the program even more effective.

If you were unsuccessful, your review and change procedure may have to be implemented as soon as possible. That means a return to your starting point in the cycle and a repeat of the process, incorporating all the changes suggested by the evaluation, while deleting those elements which were deemed unproductive to the total effort.

As you look back on one of your PR efforts, ask yourself if you

1. emphasized the most important ingredient—people
2. knew the facts and were prepared to share them with the total community
3. listened as well as told. Did you encourage two-way communication?
4. involved many people in the planning
5. kept printed materials simple, factual, and inexpensive
6. communicated effectively through the local press, mass media, public meetings, speakers' bureau, informal groups, printed materials, and telephone committees

In summary, the basic PR program should

1. develop a moving equilibrium
2. operate within the *central* tendency of public opinion
3. be responsive to other groups in the community

Perhaps, however, your task is not so ambitious as selling a $9,-000,000 budget to an already tax-ridden community. You may, for example, need only to tell people about a simple adult education project in your community. The basic tenets outlined above will still be valid: you will have to determine goals, research and identify needs, plan a program, put it into action, evaluate and modify.

Let us, then, consider such a less complex project. Assume that the State Education Department informs you that money is available for a home economics program geared to the needs of the disadvantaged. You would certainly be happy to accept funds for such a program and can think of at least three or four possibilities.

Stop right there! You have set a goal—to develop a worthwhile project for the disadvantaged in the home economics field. Before you fall into the trap of deciding what *they* need, gather together a community advisory committee to research and identify the actual areas of greatest need.

If your community has a day care center, and/or a prekindergarten program, and/or a Community Action Agency which operates under Economic Opportunity Commission guidelines, you have a built-in advisory council working in the area that you wish to serve. Visit these programs and ask parents to tell you what kinds of programs they want. You will also want to include some representatives from community service organizations, as well as a sample representation from church groups. If there are Vista volunteers working in your town, invite them in. How about representatives from the local federal credit union? Do not forget the Spanish-speaking domestic who has a day off to fill each week!

In addition, you will need some expert advice. Here, the Home Extension Bureau will help, as will the home economists in the County Health and Social Services departments. If there are local experts in the community itself, be sure to involve them.

After this group has had an opportunity to study the needs, identify one or two as your prime target.

The advisory council may decide that the formal classroom approach is not for them. They may wish to try a women's center where ladies could learn particular skills in which they are interested. This could present a difficult planning problem, but it can be done if everyone is willing to work together. The advisory committee should also be consulted before determining the hours during which the center would be open. Some ladies would prefer daytime classes with babysitting facilities in the building. Others would rather come at night. Let the community representatives settle that knotty problem.

So you open the center! You have a teacher and aides waiting to teach sewing, knitting, crocheting, crafts, making of boutique items, slipcovers, or furniture refinishing. How do you get the students?

If your advisory council was truly representative, you also have built-in recruiters—at least three groups in the community— prekindergarten mothers, day care mothers, and domestics. Let each member of the planning group sell the center to her own subgroup. Certainly you will announce the opening of the center in the newspapers. Posters will be placed in food stores as well. However, the people-to-people pitch will probably prove most efficacious.

The program will build as the ladies find there is someone at the center to give them instruction in the particular field of their interest. On any given day you may have a group of four working on children's clothes; another small group learning to sew knits; and still another crocheting ponchos. The desire to learn is the overriding motivation, but most of the ladies will enjoy the informal setting with the opportunity to socialize and share ideas.

As the weeks go by, you should be evaluating the effort. If you had not considered supplying transportation in the original project, you may find that some willing prospective participants are unable to attend because they cannot get to the center. Here is a case of the evaluate-modify-change pattern in operation. The need for transportation kicks off the whole process all over again. You will have to set a new goal to provide transportation to all who wish to attend the center. Your research element would involve investigation of the number of ladies who would come if transportation were available. Also included in the research would be a look at both public and private transportation resources in the community.

Next you must do the planning. If a minibus is used, you will have to schedule pickups. An education component will have to be included to teach the recipients of the service to be on time, to notify the driver if they are not going to be at the scheduled stop, and so on. Should you decide on a corps of volunteer drivers, they will also have to be educated about the duties of volunteers. After you put the program into action, you will find some kinks that will necessitate a change in the operation. And away we go!

Child care is another element which can make or break your program. If this area is identified as a need, you may have to repeat the whole process in order to provide this service.

Flexibility is the key word in planning adult education projects of any kind. In this case it is doubly important. From casual conversation among the women, you may uncover a desire for some consumer information. Everyone wants to get the most for his money in today's economy. This is the point at which you may want to bring in the county and state experts in the consumer service field. Arrange for field trips to the supermarket, a testing institute, a food packaging plant, or whatever.

These "specials" will give you an opportunity to get additional publicity for the project. Do not forget the human interest pictures!

Just as the steps in the basic program apply to this project, they can also be followed in planning community meetings on drug abuse, environmental problems, town master plans, housing needs—you name it.

Throughout the previous pages there have been many references to utilization of publicity and the printed brochure means of telling your story to the community. These facets of the overall program are so important that each will be considered in separate sections.

Publicity

Since so much of your work involves telling your story, publicity must of necessity play a large part in your effort. Successful publicity must be achieved through good works and obviously honest motivation. Events can shape opinion much more effectively than words. Therefore, it becomes essential to explain an action of an organization carefully because of the impact on the general public. It follows that the publicist must have the full confidence of his organization and of the press. In the latter case it has to be earned; it can easily be lost.

Accuracy, integrity, and performance are essentials in sound publicity as are the five Ws (Who? What? Where? When? Why?) in the preparation of a news story or press release. Publicity serves as a spotlight to attract attention to the good works of activities of an institution, corporation, government agency, association. But it cannot be a convenient substitute for good, sound performance of any organization. Publicity is an all-or-nothing proposition, the objective of which is to make somebody or something known. It can be a forceful instrument for good if used wisely and well.

The two-way communications effort between an educational organization and the community is of paramount importance in today's dynamically changing world. An informed community will enable a school or institution to blunt a variety of charges from many sources and to receive support for new programs. Knowledgeable public relations and education experts state that the objectives of educational publicity should be to build good will for the organization; add to its reputation through full and complete reporting of accomplishments; gain community support for budgets, building expansions, bond referendums, and other financial requirements; acquaint the community with new programs and education trends and build and maintain good working relationships with the news media. The education information program should use its own newspapers and newsletters, community newspapers, local radio and television, public meetings, and personal contacts to bring its many messages to the audiences it wishes to reach. Personal contact is most essential between the sponsoring group and the community it serves.

It should be borne in mind that mass media—particularly newspapers—are interested in one thing from the publicity person: news. They are not interested in simply providing free space or time for publicity. Hence the news release must contain news. And the one person who decides what is news is the editor of the newspaper—or the news director of a television and radio station. Statistics show that the vast majority of publicity releases wind up in the wastebasket. Why? Generally, the reasons given by the editors are, in order of frequency:

1. limited local interest
2. no reader interest at all
3. story poorly written
4. reasons of policy
5. disguised advertising
6. material obviously faked
7. apparent inaccuracy in story
8. duplication of release
9. material stretched too thin

The publicist who is conscientious about providing newspapers with news, photographs, and worthwhile timely features is building up a reservoir of good will with media and improving the press relations image not only of himself but also of the organization he represents. A further suggestion is to learn as quickly as possible the importance of dealing with the specialist in the newspaper city room: education editor, women's editor, society editor, and so on. At the same time, the publicist should give serious consideration to the Sunday edition of the local daily newspaper and its supplements for special features and pictures which are not deadline items but have readership appeal. The Sunday newspaper is usually read in greater depth than any issue during the week. Radio and television can be handled in the same general way except news items for both must be brief yet cover all essential facts of the story. The news editor has no time to edit and rewrite the press release. Do it for him. In the area of public service for nonprofit organizations, publicity messages can be sent over the airwaves, either by interview programs or spot announcements. As the newspapers have only one commodity to sell—space—so, too, do radio and television stations—time. Press releases must use the special format acceptable to radio and television news directors.

To obtain local television station time, the following suggestions may be helpful:

1. Approach the right person at the television station.
2. Bring a definite plan for discussion containing ideas with audience appeal.
3. The program must be within the station's capabilities.

Good mass media relations must be earned and rightfully develop from the premise that the public has a right to public information. The press conference is one sure-fire way of putting this principle into practice. There is no better way for all news media to get the story at the same time and from the original source. However, a simple rule to follow in calling a press conference is never to do so unless the subject matter contains important news. Otherwise, do not call a press conference.

In evaluating the publicity effort, it is essential to remember the two-step mass communications process. The message in the publicity release flows from the source to the listener and reader. Hence these precautions should be followed:

1. Too much publicity can be worse than none at all and, in fact, can be poor public relations.
2. The ratio of response depends on what is said in the message and its acceptance by the public it is reaching.
3. Publicity merely mirrors the organization it seeks to promote; publicity it receives is not always something it can control.
4. Not all public relations activities will generate publicity and sometimes it is better to avoid publicity.

According to Scott M. Cutlip and Allen H. Center, noted authors on public relations, good publicity can generally be obtained by applying some basic principles:

1. Shoot Squarely.
2. Give Service.
3. Don't Beg or Carp.
4. Don't Ask for "Kills."

The essential feature of publicity is the press release. In the preparation of the press release certain steps should be followed. They are:

1. Outline the individual project.
2. Have the outline checked by the project supervisor.
3. Prepare press release copy.
4. Submit copy for approval to project supervisor and others directly concerned.
5. If security is involved, get government approval.
6. Decide on release date, media to be serviced and how.
7. Recheck copy before actual servicing.
8. Make sure release is dated with person to be contacted for additional information if media sources deem it necessary.
9. Keep copy of release in publicity file.

In preparing the press release, it is important to consider its content. Will the information be complete so as to answer every question the news media might want to ask? Are facts, names, and dates correct and technical terms properly explained? Is the information of sufficient interest to the media editors and the public it is intended to reach and influence? Can it withstand the stiff competition of other news items for space in newspapers or magazines and time on radio or television stations? Will it further the objectives and image of your group or organization reflecting accurately its character and nature?

In style and structure the copy should be readable, factual, and without recourse to puffery and superlatives. Remember the 3 Cs of news writing—curt, clear, concise. The lead must be sharp, terse, and to the point so that a good headline can be written. The release must have news value, not exaggerated or an exercise in obtaining free space.

In typing copy, leave the top third of the first page blank so the editor can pencil in a headline. Double space the copy, making sure that each page is correctly numbered and insert the word "More" at the bottom of each page to indicate continuation. Use "30" or "End" to indicate that the story is ended. Show your name or another contact and the release date plainly on the first page.

Are there other publications not on your regular circulation list that might be interested in the news release? The release should be serviced promptly while the news or information is still fresh and timely.

Producing Publications

Equally as important as publicity in the overall PR program is the production of effective publications, each of which projects the image of the organization. Like publicity, a publication is only one facet of the total PR effort. But, because it is a convenient way to reach your public, a more detailed study seems indicated.

The glaring fault of most publications is the lack of a publication goal. Do you have a specific list of objectives for your publication? What are you going to do? Is the publication needed? To whom will it be sent?

After you have decided on the purpose of the piece, there are some simple guidelines to be observed:

1. Do not settle for the shoddy.
2. Budget adequately.

3. Avoid the danger of assuming that the printed word will necessarily communicate.
4. Keep it simple—no gobbledegook—and factual, including only the necessary information.
5. Make it short—most publications are too long.
6. Put yourself in the readers' place.

Your publication should look good. The design is important only insofar as it encourages people to read the work and get the message. Be sure that you do not overdo this element. The same might be said for the artwork which is not essential per se. If you decide on an elaborate graphic approach, try to get some professional help.

Do

- Put aside your personal likes for a sensible format.
- Have material well organized and factually correct.
- Use type that can be easily read.
- Keep to a short line for scanning and readability—26 picas wide is the most desirable.
- Provide for generous borders and white space.
- Illustrate with good drawings or photos. If you decide on the latter, use candids.
- Keep a file of publications that you like. Analyze each piece— "Why do I find this one attractive?"

Don't

- Expect to attract the attention of the reading public unless you like the piece yourself.
- Print anything unless you can do so neatly and with readability.
- Use artwork unless the purpose of publication is served by it.
- Print copy over seals and photographs. Neither purpose is served since you can neither read the copy nor see the seal.
- Put letters one under the other to spell out words. We read across.
- Use too much bold type—it makes for spottiness.
- Lose continuity by using too many different type faces.

The single most helpful person is likely to be your printer. He will assist you to decide on the type and color of paper. Inks, too, can be utilized to produce a colorful publication. A single press run on colored stock with a contrasting ink can be most effective. As soon as a third color is introduced on any given page, you have involved another run and increased the cost considerably. If you are concerned with the price you should investigate, with your printer, the most economical number of pages that will tell your story. A six-page publication can be more costly than an eight-page piece, depending on the size of the press.

Preparing a publication is a tedious task. Once again, there are no instant or easy routes. A successful one can be accomplished if you

- know the public toward which the content is beamed
- insist on a quality production (not necessarily the most expensive)
- concentrate on information the reader will want to know
- yell for expert help when you need it

After the brochure, newsletter, or whatever has been completed, but before it is printed, evaluate your effort as objectively as possible. Look at the layout. What is the tone? Does it accomplish the planned objective? Ask around—get some reader reaction. And then, if you decide to print, get help in proofing from someone who has not seen the copy before.

In conclusion, there is just one other qualification for the person who is charged with producing a public relations program—a thick skin. Everyone in the community is convinced that he or she could have planned a better campaign, written a better news release, or produced a better brochure. And what is more—they could have done it more economically. Ned Hubbell, president of Ned S. Hubbell Associates, a public relations firm in Port Huron, Michigan, has this to say about the public relations practitioner: "PR people should make like a duck—remain cool and calm on the surface and paddle like hell underneath."

Selected References

CARROLL, HANSON. *A Climate of Faith*. Communication Research Seminar, Temple University, April 1965.

INSTITUTE OF CERTIFIED PUBLIC ACCOUNTANTS. *Public School Costs*. New York, 1963.

McCLOSKY, GORDON. *Education and Public Understanding*. New York: Harper & Row, 1959, pp. 52–55, 235–242.

MEHLING, HAROLD. "How to Win the Fight for a New School." *Redbook Magazine*, January 1964.

NATIONAL SCHOOL PUBLIC RELATIONS ASSOCIATION. A list can be obtained from the office at 1201 16th Street, N.W., Washington, D.C. 20036. All are excellent.

PARSONS, CYNTHIA. "Education: What It Costs." *Christian Science Monitor*, 1965.

PRESS, CARL. "How to Sell a School Bond Issue to the Public." *Public Relations Journal*, July 1963.

Index

Index